Belfast Studies in Language, Culture and Politics
General Editors: John M. Kirk and Dónall P. Ó Baoill

1: *Language and Politics: Northern Ireland, the Republic of Ireland, and Scotland* published 2000 ISBN 0 85389 791 3

2: *Language Links: the Languages of Scotland and Ireland* published 2001 ISBN 0 85389 795 6

3: *Linguistic Politics: Language Policies for Northern Ireland, the Republic of Ireland, and Scotland* published 2001 ISBN 0 85389 815 4

4: *Travellers and their Language* published 2002 ISBN 0 85389 832 4

5: Simone Zwickl, *Language Attitudes, Ethnic Identity and Dialect Use across the Northern Ireland Border: Armagh and Monaghan* published 2002 ISBN 0 85389 834 0

6: *Language Planning and Education: Linguistic Issues in Northern Ireland, the Republic of Ireland, and Scotland* published 2002 ISBN 0 85389 835 9

7: Edna Longley, Eamonn Hughes and Des O'Rawe (eds.) *Ireland (Ulster) Scotland: Concepts, Contexts, Comparisons* published 2003 ISBN 0 85389 844 8

8: Maolcholaim Scott and Roíse Ní Bhaoill (eds.) *Gaelic-Medium Education Provision: Northern Ireland, the Republic of Ireland, Scotland and the Isle of Man* published 2003 ISBN 0 85389 847 2

9: Dónall Ó Riagáin (ed.) *Language and Law in Northern Ireland* published 2003 ISBN 0 85389 848 0

10: *Towards our Goals in Broadcasting, the Press, the Performing Arts and the Economy: Minority Languages in Northern Ireland, the Republic of Ireland, and Scotland* published 2003 ISBN 0 85389 856 1

11: J. Derrick McClure (ed.) *Doonsin' Emerauds: New Scrieves anent Scots an Gaelic / New Studies on Scots and Gaelic* published 2004 ISBN 0 85389 860 X

12: Neal Alexander, Shane Murphy and Anne Oakman (eds.) *To the Other Shore: Cross-Currents in Irish and Scottish Studies* published 2004 ISBN 0 85389 863 4

13: *Legislation, Literature and Sociolinguistics: Northern Ireland, the Republic of Ireland, and Scotland* published 2005 ISBN 0 85389 874 X

14: Shane Alcobia-Murphy, Johanna Archbold, John Gibney and Carole Jones (eds.) *Beyond the Anchoring Grounds: More Cross-currents in Irish and Scottish Studies* published 2005 ISBN 0 85389 885 5

15: Dónall Ó Riagáin (ed.) *Voces Diversae: Lesser-Used Language Education in Europe* published 2006 ISBN 0 85389 886 3

Voces Diversae: Lesser-Used Language Education in Europe

Edited by

Dónall Ó Riagáin

Cló Ollscoil na Banríona
Belfast 2006

First published in 2006
Cló Ollscoil na Banríona
Queen's University Belfast
Belfast, BT7 1NN

Belfast Studies in Language, Culture and Politics
www.bslcp.com

© Cló Ollscoil na Banríona and Contributors

The publication of this volume has been made possible through the generous support of Foras na Gaeilge.

British Library Cataloguing-in-Publication Data
A catalogue record for this book is available from the British Library.

ISBN 0 85389 886 3

Typeset by Nigel Craig and John Kirk in Granjon
Cover and map design by Colin Young
Printing by W. & G. Baird, Antrim

Contents	v
List of Maps and Tables	viii
Nótaí Beathaisnéise / Contributors	ix
Focal Buíochais / Acknowledgements	xv
Brollach / Preface	xvi
Éagsúlacht Teanga san Oideachas / Linguistic Diversity in Education *Éamon Ó Cuív*	xviii
Introduction: Voces Diversae: Lesser-Used Language Education in Europe *Dónall Ó Riagáin*	1

OVERALL CONSIDERATIONS

The Common European Framework of Reference for Languages: Learning, Teaching and Assessment *Joe Sheils*	9
Education and the Development of Early Childhood Bilingualism *Viv Edwards*	16
Children with Learning Difficulties: Second Language Acquisition *Sue Davies*	25

CASE STUDIES

The Lesser-Used Language as a Medium of Instruction or as a Subject: the Basque Experience *Joana Abrisketa*	32
Accommodating Linguistic Diversity in Hungary's Education System *Judit Solymosi*	40
The Sámi Languages in Education *Nils Ø. Helander*	47
Friulan and other Lesser-Used Languages in Education in Friuli Venezia Giulia *Silvana Schiavi Fachin*	52
First Encounters with Ulster-Scots Language, History and Culture *Hilary Avery and Andrea Gilbert*	64
Developing Language Teaching Strategies: the Kalmyk Experience *Bosya Kornusova*	69
The Role of Education in Reversing Language Shift: the Estonian Experience *Mart Rannut*	78

Bilingual Malta: Language Teaching and the Future
Joe Zammit-Ciantar   89

A Slavic Island in a Germanic Sea: Sorbian in Education
Leoš Šatava   97

A Decade of Kashubian in Education
Tomasz Wicherkiewicz   103

Minority Languages in Education in Slovenia
Sonja Novak-Lukanovič   113

Khakas in Education and Ethnic Identity
Tamara Borgoyakova   126

Language Reforms in Tatarstan's Education System and the Ethnolinguistic Orientation of Young People
Yagfar Garipov and Marina Solnyshkina   131

TEACHER TRAINING IN LESSER-USED LANGUAGES

Un Aperçu de la Récuperation de la Langue Catalane pour l'Enseignement et la Formation du Professorat
Joaquim Arenas i Sampera   138

Coláiste Ollscoile Naomh Muire agus Túsoideachas do Mhúinteoirí Lán-Ghaeilge / St Mary's University College and Irish-Medium Teacher Training
Gabrielle Nig Uidhir   145/151

Issues in Minority Language Teacher Education: A Scottish Gaelic Perspective
A.G. Boyd Robertson   157

COMMON ISSUES AND COMMON SOLUTIONS

Mercator-Education: A Support Service
Cor van der Meer   163

Le Défi qui Consiste à Fournir des Livres Scolaires et autre Matériel Pédagogique
Eliane Kerjoant   170

Linguistic Diversity in University Education: Are Traditional University Structures Sufficient?
Wallace Ewart   177

Na Féidearthachtaí atá ann do Líonráil agus do Roinnt Eolais / The Possibilities of Networking and Information-Sharing
Liam Ó Dochartaigh   182/188

The European Network of Language Planning Boards
Meirion Prys Jones   194

The papers in this volume were first presented at **Voces Diversae Conference on Minority Language Education in Europe** held at the Alexander Hotel, Dublin, from 22-24 April 2004, organised by Dónall Ó Riagáin on behalf of Foras na Gaeilge.

Editorial Disclaimer
The views expressed in each paper are those of the author. Publication in this volume does not signify either editorial agreement or disagreement or editorial responsibility for these views.

Publisher Disclaimer
The publisher has used its best endeavours to ensure that the URLs for external websites referred to in this book are correct at the time of going to press. However, the publisher has no responsibility for the websites and can make no guarantee that a site will remain live or that the content is or will remain appropriate.

viii *Contributors*

List of Maps

Map of Welsh-speaking area	26
Map of Basque- and Catalan-speaking areas	33
Map of Hungary and the surrounding countries	41
Map of the Sámi Languages	47
Map of the Friulian-speaking area	54
Map of the Traditional Ulster and Lowland Scots speaking areas	65
Mapof Kalmykia	70
Map of Estonia	79
Map of the Maltese Islands	89
Map of the Sorbian-speaking area	97
Mapof the Kashubian-speaking areas	103
Map of Slovenia	114
Map of Khakassia	127
Map of Tatarstan	131
Léarscáil de Ghaelscoileanna i dTuaisceart Éireann 2002-03	149
Map of Irish-medium Schools in Northern Ireland, 2002-03	155
Map of traditional Gaelic-speaking areas in Scotland	157
Carte de la Bretagne	170

List of Tables

Welsh: Speaker Percentages by Age Group	17
Hungary: Results of 2001 Census for Minority Populations	42
Hungary: Minority Polulation by County (2001 Census)	43
Minority Languages in Friuli	53
Friuli: *Il Frut: E Il So Mont*	59
Slovenia: Language Acquisition at School	120
Slovenia: Bilingual Education in Lendava	122
Slovenia: Bilingual Education in the Coastal Region	123
Khakassia: The Khakas Language in Abakan Municipal Schools	128
Khakassia: Levels of Competence of Schoolchildren and Students	129
Khakassia: Language Use with Parents, Grandparents, Friends	129
Tatarstan: Language of Communication in the Home	133
Tatarstan: Native Language versus Language Spoken in the Home	133
Tatarstan: What does the native language mean to you?	134
Tatarstan: What language do you speak at home?	135
Tatarstan: What state languages must the following groups use?	136
Catalan: Écoles Primaires	141
Catalan: Écoles Secondaires	141
Gaeilge: Codanna den chúrsa a dhéantar trí mheán na Gaeilge	148
Irish: Sections of the course carried out through the medium of Irish	154
Scottish Gaelic: Provision for Minority LanguageTeacher Training	161

Nótaí Beathaisnéise / Contributors

Dr. Joana Abrisketa is a professor in Public International Law and European Law at the University of Deusto, Bilbao, where she teaches in Basque. She graduated with a PhD in Human Rights and Humanitarian Action and is currently translating fundamental international treaties into Basque with the help of the Academy for the Basque Language (Euskaltzaindia).

Joaquim Arenas i Sampera is a pedagogue, writer and sociolinguist. He laid the foundations of the language policy in the educational system of Catalonia and has made substantial contributions to its implementation during the last 25 years. He set up the language immersion programmes and has played an important role in the revitalisation of the language and culture of the Catalan countries since the period of resistance during Franco's dictatorship. He has a BA in Pedagogy and a diploma in Catalan Language and Social Sciences. He is the author of various works on language and education.

Hilary Avery is Director of the Ulster-Scots Curriculum Development Unit at Stranmillis University College, Belfast, which is producing materials to introduce Ulster-Scots language, history and culture into primary and secondary schools. She was born in Dublin. She graduated in Geography and did her postgraduate research at Queen's University Belfast. She taught in a Belfast grammar school before joining the staff of Stranmillis University College. She was Head of Geography before setting up the Ulster-Scots Curriculum Development Unit.

Dr. Tamara Borgoyakova is a professor of Linguistics and Director of the Institute of Sayan-Altay Turkology, Khakas State University, Abakan, Republic of Khakasia. She was born and grew up in the Republic of Tyva, Russia. She is a graduate in English from the Irkutsk State Pedagogical Institute of Foreign Languages and received her doctorate in Sociolinguistics at the Institute of Linguistics, Academy of Science of Russia, Moscow. She has served as Deputy Director of the Research Institute of Humanities and Provost at the Khakas State University, and also as Deputy Prime Minister of the Republic of Khakasia. Her main publications are *Sociolinguistic Situation and Language Law in the Republic of Khakasia* (Moscow: Russian Friendship University Press, 2003), *Sociolinguistic Situation in the Republics of Southern Siberia* (Abakan: Khakas State University Press, 2002), *Minority Languages: Problems of Preserving and Development* (Abakan: Khakas State University Press, 2001), and *Khakas-Russian Idiomatic Dictionary* (Abakan: Khakas State University Press, 1996). In 1999, she was awarded the state-honored title of a "Professional in Higher Education of Russia". In 2003, she was awarded a grant for studying and helping with the preservation and protection of Native American languages at the University of Arizona through the Fellowship Program administered by the International Research and Exchanges Board (IREX). She also worked as a visiting researcher at the Center for Applied Linguistics in Washington, DC during the summer of 2003. Her commitment to native peoples and the preservation of their languages extends into the private sector, where she also serves as a vice-president at the Aias Foundation, a non-governmental organization dedicated to this mission.

Sue Davies is Head of the School of Education Studies and Social Inclusion at Trinity College, Carmarthen. She was born and grew up in Wales and studied at Trinity College as a student. She has a first degree in Social Science, and a Master's Degree in Special Education from the

Open University. She is currently undertaking doctoral study in the field of Inclusive Education. A former teacher and deputy headteacher, she has worked in the field of Special Educational Needs (SEN) in local education authority (LEA) administration and as a project manager investigating provision for pupils with low incidence disabilities. As Development Officer for SEN at the Welsh Assembly Government, she was part of a team leading forward the Inclusion agenda, and played a major role in the preparation of guidance documents focusing on SEN.

Dr. Viv Edwards is Professor of Language and Education at the University of Reading, where she is also Director of the National Centre for Language and Literacy. She is editor of the journal *Language and Education* and has published widely on linguistic diversity. Her most recent book: *Pedigree of Nations: The Other Languages of the English-speaking World* (Blackwell, 2004) makes important links between 'lesser-used languages' and 'new minority' languages in the family, in school and in the wider community.

Professor Wallace Ewart is a former pro-vice-chancellor of the University of Ulster and, before that, Dean of Business and Management and Director of Informatics. He was born and grew up in Northern Ireland. He is a graduate in Mathematics from Queen's University Belfast. In 1997, he was awarded the OBE for services to Higher Education in Northern Ireland. His key interests include Communications and Information Technology. He has contributed to the development of wide area networks in the education, training and library sectors in Northern Ireland. Another major interest is the impact of Further and Higher Education on the educational, social and economic regeneration of local communities. He worked on the Springvale Project which proposed the development of a new campus, to be jointly managed by two autonomous institutions and strategically located across the peaceline in West Belfast. He now provides consultancy support to universities and other educational bodies in Ireland, UK and overseas.

Dr. Yagfar Garipov is currently a senior lecturer at Institute of Sociology, Academy of Sciences, Kazan, Russian Federation. Previously he held the positions of Vice-Rector in the Institute of Economics, Management & Law, Kazan. He obtained his PhD in Applied Sociology at Sociology Institute, Academy of Sciences of the USSR, Moscow, in 1978. His research concerns various aspects of majority-minority relations in the Russian Federation. He is especially interested in language policies as a means of conflict settlement.

Andrea Gilbert is a primary school teacher from the integrated sector in Northern Ireland. She graduated from the School of English at Queen's University Belfast and then studied for a Master's Degree in Medieval Studies at Bristol University. She was seconded to Stranmillis University College in 2002 to design Ulster-Scots curriculum materials for the primary school and guidance materials for teachers. She is currently trialling the Primary School materials in schools across the province.

Nils Ø. Helander is an associate professor in Sámi language at Sámi University College in Guovdageaidnu, Norway. He is doing work on Sámi Linguistics and has also been member of the Sámi Language Council for several years.

Eliane Kerjoant has been a teacher in Diwan primary schools since 1983. Since 1995. she has been a member of the Educational Council of Diwan and, since 2000, she has been the educational director, responsible for the coordination of all Diwan primary schools. She is also a member of the editorial board of the Ti Embann ar Skolioù, which publishes educational material for Breton-French bilingual schools. She is responsible for courses at KELENN, Diwan Teacher Training Institute, and for courses for learning Breton (bilingual education distinction) at the University of Rennes 2.

Dr. Bosya Kornusova is an associate professor of English in the Department of Philology at Kalmyk State University. She was born and grew up in the Republic of Kalmykia, Russian Federation. She is a graduate in English and German and in the methodology of foreign language teaching from the Moscow State Pedagogical University. She took her PhD in Pedagogy at the Institute of National Problems of Education, part of the Ministry of Education of the Russian Federation. She has been involved with the Kalmyk language revival since 1990 when she started to work at the Kalmyk Centre for Intensive Languages Teaching. She has been actively participating in developing an up-to-date methodology for Kalmyk language teaching. She is a co-author of a native-language teaching set for the elementary school and the author of *Communicative Approach to Kalmyk Language Teaching: Concept of Teaching Materials* (Elista, 2005). She has been awarded the title of "Honorary Teacher of Secondary Education of the Russian Federation". She is a member of the International Advisory Committee of the Linguapax Institute and a director of the Eurasian Delegation (based at Kalmyk State University) and of the international Linguapax Network [UNESCO], which has its headquarters in Barcelona.

Dr. Sonja Novak-Lukanovič is a researcher at the Institute for Ethnic Studies at the University of Ljubljana, Slovenia, from which she graduated with the degrees of MA and PhD. Her research work is focused on the minority language and education in a pluralistic society, as well as on language accommodation. She is involved in many research projects within the institute's programme and has participated in different international projects including OECD, UNESCO, and the Council of Europe. She has published several articles and attended several international conferences. She is Vice-President of the Slovene Association for Applied Lingusitics, a member of Slovene National Commission for UNESCO, and is a representative for Slovenia in the Working Community of Alps-Adriatic.

Dr. Gabrielle Nig Uidhir is a lecturer in Irish-medium Education at St. Mary's University College, Belfast. She is author of *Our Own Language* (Multilingual Matters, 1991). She based her Queen's University of Belfast PhD thesis on a sociolinguistic and linguistic study of the emerging Irish-speaking community in Belfast. She has taught in Irish-medium primary and secondary schools and in further education. She is currently chairperson of Gaelscolaíochta.

Éamon Ó Cuív is a Teachta Dála (Member of the Irish Parliament) for Galway West. He is Aire Gnóthaí Pobail, Tuaithe agus Gaeltachta (Minister for Community, Rural and Gaeltacht Affairs) in the present Irish Government.

Liam Ó Dochartaigh has been the Director of International Education since 2001 at the University of Limerick, Ireland, where he is responsible for the implementation of the EU Socrates/Erasmus programme. He was born in Galway and graduated from the National University of Ireland at Galway with degrees in Celtic Studies. He held academic positions in the Irish language in the University of Ulster (1969-76), Thomond College of Education (1978-91), and the University of Limerick (1991-2001). He was also a development officer for Irish in education with Foras na Gaeilge (1976-78). He has published numerous academic papers in the areas of Irish literature and folklore, and on Irish in education and society. At the University of Limerick which, in 2004-05, operated 192 bilateral agreements with third level institutions in 22 European countries, he designed and taught *ab initio* Irish language courses for international students, first introduced in 1991.

Dónall Ó Riagáin works as an independent consultant on language planning. A founding member of the European Bureau for Lesser Used Languages, he was subsequently the organisation's first President and Secretary General. He was involved in preparing a number of reports for the European Parliament, the European Commission, the Organization for Security and Co-operation in Europe's High Commissioner on National Minorities, and the Council of Europe, for which he was an author of the *European Charter for Regional or Minority Languages*. An Honorary Fellow of Trinity College, Carmarthen, he is a member of the International Advisory Board of Linguapax [UNESCO], Barcelona and the Stakeholder Consultation Group on Languages, which will assist the European Commission in preparing the implementation of its Integrated Lifelong Learning Programme.

Meirion Prys Jones is originally from Bridgend, and was educated in schools in Carmarthen and Wrexham and later at the University of Wales, Bangor, where he graduated in Welsh Language and Literature. He then went on to complete a PGCE course at the University of Wales, Aberystwyth, gaining a distinction in teaching parctice, his specialist subject being Welsh as a first and second language. He was Head of Welsh at Castell Alun and Glan Clwyd schools before moving to work for West Glamorgan County Council as a senior advisor for Welsh. He has also been a registered inspector of Schools for Her Majesty's Chief Inspector of Education and Training in Wales (ESTYN). He was appointed Chief Officer of the Education and Training Deptartment at the Board in 1994, Leader of the Language Planning Team in 2001, Deputy Chief Executive of the Welsh Language Board in March 2003, and in April 2004 he became the Board's Chief Executive.

Dr. Mart Rannut is an associate professor at Tallinn University, Estonia, where he was born and grew up. He graduated with an MA in mathematical and computational linguistics from the Saint-Petersburg State University and received his Ph.D from the University of Tartu. His previous positions have included Director-General of the Estonian Language Board, Presidential Adviser on human rights issues, and Research Fellow at the Institute of the Estonian Language. He has also been a diplomat in the office of the Human Rights Commissioner of the Council of the Baltic Sea States. He has written three books and scores of articles on language policy and planning issues especially relating to Estonia.

A.G. Boyd Robertson is a senior lecturer in Gaelic at the University of Strathclyde in Glasgow. He was born and brought up on the island of North Uist in the Outer Hebrides. He is a graduate in Celtic Studies from the University of Aberdeen. He was formerly Principal Teacher of Gaelic at Oban High School. He has written extensively on Gaelic education, is co-author of the *Teach Yourself Gaelic* course (Hodder & Stoughton, 1993, 2002) and co-compiler of the *TY Gaelic Dictionary* (Hodder & Stoughton 2004). He chairs the Scottish Qualifications Authority Gaelic Assessment Panel and the Board of An Lòchran, the Glasgow Gaelic Arts Agency. He was a member of Bòrd na Gàidhlig, the first Government appointed Gaelic development agency, Vice-Chair of the language promotion body, Comunn na Gàidhlig, and Chair of Comhairle nan Leabhraichean, the Gaelic Books Council.

Dr. Leoš Šatava is a professor at the Institute of Ethnology, Charles University, Prague. Previously he worked as a 1996–2001 researcher at the Sorbian Institute, Bautzen/Budysin,

Lusatia. He has participated in a number of research projects and study visits among ethnic minorities in Europe (e.g. the Sorbs, the Faroese, the peoples of Daghestan, the Sámi, the Gagauz, the Kalmyks) and overseas (the Maoris, the Czechs in the USA). He has published several books and articles on language and ethnic identity. His fields of interest are ethnicity, ethnic/linguistic minorities, sociolinguistics, and migrations.

Silvana Schiavi Fachin is a senior lecturer in Modern Language Teaching at the University of Udine, Italy. She graduated in Foreign Languages at the University 'L. Bocconi' in Milan and for several years she was a teacher of English in secondary schools. She specialized in the teaching of English to speakers of other languages in multilingual and multiracial classes thanks to a Fulbright scholarship in the United States and a British Council grant in the U.K. As a member of the Italian Parliament (Lower Chamber), she was successful in getting the general policy law in favour of the Italian linguistic minorities. She was member of the Committee for the Standardization of Friulian and is a member of the Scientific Committee of the Regional Agency for the Friulian Language (ARLeF). She has produced several multimedial materials for the learning and teaching of many native, second and foreign languages.

Joe Sheils is Head of the Language Policy Division at the Council of Europe in Strasbourg. The Division is responsible for programmes to develop language education policies and standards for the languages of school education, minorities, migrants, as well as for foreign languages. Before joining the Council of Europe in 1992, he was Head of the Modern Languages Department at the Linguistics Insititute of Ireland (ITÉ).

Dr. Marina I. Solnyshkina is a senior lecturer in Linguistic Typology at Tatar State Humanitarian and Pedagogical University, Kazan, Russian Federation. Previously, she held position at Saratov State University, where she graduated with her PhD on Professional Sublanguages in 1994 from Kazan State University. She edited a number of the series *International Communication* at Kazan State Pedagogical University in 1997–2004. She is an active member of National Association of Applied Linguistics (NAAL).

Judit Solymosi is the Head of the International Department of the Office for National and Ethnic Minorities in Hungary. She was born and grew up in Budapest. She is a graduate in French and Russian Linguistics and Literature from the Eötvös Loránd University of Budapest. Her previous position was as an international advisor at the Hungarian Institute of Adult Education and Socio-Cultural Animation, where she was also engaged in community development and in international partnership building activities. Her publications include *Associative Cultural Centres in France* and *Identity, Philosophy, Strategy: Thoughts for the Organisations of Civil Society* (both published by the Association for Community Development, Budapest, in 1993) as well as numerous articles on community development and minority issues in international periodicals. She is the editor of *Minority News*, an electronically distributed quarterly selection of news on Hungarian minority policy.

Cor van der Meer has been a project co-ordinator of Mercator-Education since 2004. He was born and grew up in Fryslân in the Netherlands. He is a graduate in Sociology from the University of Groningen. His previous positions have been as a scientific staff member and a senior data specialist employed at the national digital data archive in the Netherlands. He served on several working groups and committees to develop international standards and agreements. In addition, he has experience on projects on metadata, digitisation and digital preservation. He is active in a number of international organisations such as the International

Association of Social Science Information Service & Technology (IASSIST) and has published a number of articles in this field. Cor van der Meer is also responsible for the project "digibyb", a pilot project to build a digital library for regional and minority languages in the European Union.

Dr. Tomasz Wicherkiewicz is an adjunct professor in Linguistics, Ethnolinguistics and Minority Studies at the Institute of Oriental Studies and Head of the Department of Language Policy and Minority Studies, Adam Mickiewicz University, Poznań, where he graduated with his PhD in Comparative Linguistics (*Germanic Ethnolinguistic Enclaves in Southern Poland*) in 1998. He is founder and President of the Polish Bureau for Lesser Used Languages and a member of the Kashubian Institute in Gdansk.

Dr. Joe Zammit-Ciantar is a graduate of the University of Malta and is now a lecturer in Maltese at the University of Malta Junior College and also at the Università degli Studi 'L'Orientale' of Naples. As a representative of the Maltese Government, he was one of the authors of the *European Charter for Regional or Minority Languages*. His most recent books are *A Benedictine's Notes on Seventeenth Century MALTA* (1997) and *The Place-names of the Coast of Gozo* (2000). In 2004, as editor, he launched two new journals: *Symposia elitensia* and *Fora Melitensia*.

Focal Buíochais / Acknowledgements

Go raibh maith agaibh! The various sessions of the conference were conducted in a relaxed, yet efficient, manner, thanks to the work of a series of chairpersons from both Ireland and further afield. The opening session was chaired by Maighréad Uí Mháirtín, Chairperson, Foras na Gaeilge. Subsequent sessions were chaired by Helen Ó Murchú, former President of EBLUL, Caoimhe Ní Mháirtín, Coláiste Mhuire, Marino, Muireann Ní Mhóráin, An Chomhairle um Oideachas Gaeltachta agus Gaelscolaíochta, Vera Capkova, University College Dublin, Pól Ó Muirí, Irish language editor of the *Irish Times*, Cathal Mac Coille from RTÉ, Máire Ní Annracháin from NUI Maynooth, Stefal Moal from Brittany and Thomas Stolz from the University of Bremen. The final session was chaired by Seosamh Mac Donncha, Chief Executive of Foras na Gaeilge.

A committed and highly motivated staff, working for weeks and months before the conference ensured its success. They included Breandán Mac Craith and Niall Ó Muilleoir, who handled press relations, Ger Fitzgerald who designed the **Voces Diversae** logo, Irene Ní Mhuireagáin of Cumarsáid Creative who designed the programme, Gillian Roufail of Resóstán who handled hotel bookings, Anne-Marie Nolan who prepared the many translations in the lead-up to the conference, and the excellent team of interpreters, assembled and led by Eoghan Ó Loingsigh, who ensured top-quality Irish-English-French interpretation throughout. Dónal Ó Cearúil worked long and hard hours on the administrative work and his unassuming manner and cheerful demeanour belied a commendable dedication to the success of the event. Many members of the Foras na Gaeilge staff made significant contributions to the success of the conference – through their hard work and dedication, the **Voces Diversae** conference was the success it turned out to be. Three people deserve special mention: Seosamh Mac Donncha, the organisation's Chief Executive, whose idea it was to mark the Irish Presidency of the EU with such an event, Ferdie Mac an Fhailigh, the Deputy Chief Executive, whose expertise in the field of education was invaluable, and Deirdre Davitt. Deirdre's vision and creative approach to every issue made working with her a real delight.

This is no ordinary publication. It contains material in three languages from no fewer than 27 contributors. And most of the contributors wrote in a language which was not their mothertongue. As one can easily imagine, this led the editorial process into some exciting but uncharted waters. I am deeply indebted to our publishers, Cló Ollscoil na Banríona, and especially Dr. John Kirk, for their thorough, yet sensitive, approach to editorial matters, in particular those of a literary or stylistic nature. John's professionalism and insistence on striving for perfection have been a guiding light for me.

If this book is one part of the **Voces Diversae** legacy, the web-site, still under construction, is the other part. My heartfelt gratitude to our Celtic cousins in Trinity College, Carmarthen, for their willingness to bring the web-site into being. The College Principal, Dr. Medwin Hughes, unhesitatingly offered his full support and delegated the practical work to Tim Burton and Gwilym Dyfri Jones, both of whom undertook the task with enthusiasm. The initial meeting of the web-site action group in Belfast was made possible with the financial and moral support of the British Council, Foras na Gaeilge and Tha Boord o Ulstèr-Scotch. My personal thanks to Lynda Wilson and Isabelle Martin of the British Council, to the Ulster-Scots Agency's Chief Executive, George Patton, and its newly appointed Chairman, Mark Thompson, who kindly undertook the design work, and to my good friends in Foras na Gaeilge, Seosamh Mac Donncha, Ferdie Mac an Fhailigh and Deirdre Davitt.

Gura fada buan gach duine díobh!
Dónall Ó Riagáin
Fómhair 2005

Brollach

Dónall Ó Riagáin

Agus Uachtaránacht na hÉireann ar an Aontas Eorpach sa chéad leath de 2004 ag teannadh linn, thug Príomhfheidhmeannach Fhoras na Gaeilge, Seosamh Mac Donncha, cuireadh dom moltaí a chur os a chomhair faoi bhealaí ina bhféadfadh an Foras a rian a fhágáil ar an ócáid stairiúil úd. Ó mo thaithí ar chur chun cinn teangacha ar leibhéal Eorpach thuig mé nach raibh dream ba dhíograisí ná nó ba dhúthrachtaí ann ná iadsan a raibh teangacha neamhfhorleathana ár mór-roinne á múineadh acu nó a bhí ag úsáid na dteangacha úd mar mheáin teagaisc. B'fhada ó bhí deis acu teacht le chéile agus a gcuid eolais is a saintaithí a roinnt ar a chéile. Níorbh fhearr rud a dhéanfadh an Foras, dar liom, ná comhdháil Eorpach dá leithéidí a thionól le linn na hUachtaránachta Éireannaí. Glacadh le mo mholadh agus tugadh cuireadh dom bheith mar chomhordaitheoir ar an ócáid. Is mar sin a thángthas ar an gcoincheap a dtugaimid **Voces Diversae** anois air.

Eagraíodh comhdháil ar ar fhreastail breis is 120 duine i mBaile Átha Cliath ó 22 go 24 Aibreán 2004. Bhí lucht rannpháirtíochta i láthair ó Árann go Poblacht na Cacáise sa tSibéir agus ó chríocha Artacha na Sámi go hoileán grianmhar Mhálta – a scéal is a thaithí féin ag gach duine le roinnt ar an gcuid eile againn. Bhí ionadaithe ann ag an gCoimisiún Eorpach agus ag Comhairle na hEorpa. Bhí saineolaithe ann a labhair ar oiliúint mhúinteoirí, ar mhúineadh teangacha do pháistí le deacrachtaí foghlama, ar mhalairt struchtúir chun oideachas ollscoile a sholáthar, ar bhunú líonraí oideachais idirnáisiúnta, ar acraí teagaisc a chur ar fáil ar chostas réasúnta agus ar sheirbhísí tacaíochta. Cá hionadh gur thug Ambasadóir Mhálta 'seoid i gcoróin Uachtaránacht na hÉireann' ar an imeacht ag dinnéar na comhdhála!

Tháinig teachtaireacht láidir chugainn ón lucht rannpháirtíochta ag deireadh na comhdhála gur theastaigh uathu go leanfaí den obair ar cuireadh tús léi. Thug Foras na Gaeilge faoin dúshlán. I gcomhar le Cló Ollscoil na Banríona, tá páipéir na comhdhála á gcur ar fáil anois i dtreo is go mbeidh teacht ag pobal léitheoireachta sách leathan ar an saibhreas ar bhlaiseamar de i mBaile Átha Cliath. Le tacaíocht fhial ó Chomhairle na Breataine, ón Boord o Ulstèr-Scotch agus ó Coleg y Drinod i Caerfyrddin na Breataine Bige ní fada anois go mbeidh suíomh gréasáin ag **Voces Diversae** a chuirfidh ar chumas lucht múinte ár dteangacha ar fud na hEorpa eolas, scileanna agus tuairimí a mhalartú ar a chéile ar bhonn leanúnach. Tuar dóchais breise é go bhfuil beospéis á léiriú ag an gCoimisiún Eorpach sa tionscadal.

Ach cur le chéile cloisfear go hard ár nguthanna éagsúla ar fud na hEorpa.

An Nás, Fómhair 2005

Foreword

Dónall Ó Riagáin

When the Irish Presidency of the European Union in the first half of 2004 was in the offing, Seosamh Mac Donnchadha, the Chief Executive of Foras na Gaeilge, invited me to make suggestions to him as to how the Foras might mark that historical event. From my experience in the field of lesser-used language promotion at European level, I knew that no group was more enthusiastic or more committed than those who were involved in teaching our languages or in using them as media of instruction. It had been a considerable time since they had been afforded an opportunity to meet and share their knowledge and expertise. In my opinion, Foras na Gaeilge could do nothing more appropriate to mark the Irish Presidency than host a conference which would afford such an opportunity. My suggestion was accepted and I was invited to act as coordinator of the event. It was thus that the project, which we now know as **Voces Diversae**, came into being.

A conference was organised and was attended by more than 120 people from Árann on the Irish west coast to the Siberian Republic of Khakassia, and from the Artic homeland of the Sámi to the sunny island of Malta – each person with his/her own case story and experiences. The European Commission and the Council of Europe were represented. Experts spoke on teacher training, on teaching language to children with learning difficulties, on various structures to provide for university education, on the establishment of international educational networks, on the provision of teaching materials at a reasonable cost and on backup services. Small wonder that the Maltese Ambassador, speaking at the conference dinner, should describe **Voces Diversae** as 'a jewel in the crown of the Irish Presidency'!

A strong message came from the participants towards the end of the conference that they wished the work that had been started should be allowed to continue. Foras na Gaeilge rose to the challenge. In cooperation with Cló Ollscoil na Banríona, the papers delivered at the conference are now being published so that a wider public might have access to the wealth of knowledge that we experienced in Dublin. Thanks to the generous support of the British Council, the Ulster-Scots Agency and Trinity College, Carmarthen in Wales, a website is now being developed that will enable lesser-used language teachers throughout Europe to exchange information, skills, and opinions with each other on an ongoing basis. We are furthermore greatly encouraged by the interest shown by the European Commission in the project.

By combining our efforts we can ensure that our diverse voices will be clearly heard throughout Europe.

Naas October 2005

Voces Diversae: Éagsúlacht Teanga san Oideachas

Éamon Ó Cuív

Tá áthas orm an chomhdháil seo a oscailt, **Voces Diversae**, a bhfuil mar aidhm aici díriú ar na bealaí is fearr le héagsúlacht teanga a chur chun cinn san oideachas. Comhdháil oideachais idirnáisiúnta atá inti don 300 teanga neamhfhorleathan a úsáidtear san Eoraip. Tátrí mhóraidhm leis an gcomhdháil seo:

- Eolas a scaipeadh i measc na ndaoine atá ag múineadh na dteangacha/trí na teangacha seo faoin méid atá tarlaithe le déanaí ag leibhéal Eorpach faoi mhúineadh na dteangacha i gcoitinne agus faoin tacaíocht atá le fáil ón Aontas Eorpach agus ó Chomhairle na hEorpa ina leith seo.
- Malartú eolais agus taithí i measc an lucht rannpháirtíochta a éascú.
- Iadsan atá ag plé le teangacha neamhfhorleathana san oideachas a spreagadh le líonra Eorpach a bhunú – a mbeidh mar aidhm aige leas iomlán a bhaint as gníomhphlean an Aontais Eorpaigh ar mhúineadh agus éagsúlacht teangacha agus as aon bheartas eile a bheadh úsáideach.

Sa tír seo inniu feictear saibhreas cultúir ó gach cearn den Eoraip, agus den domhan. Tugann sé sin misneach dúinne a bhfuil sé mar chúram orainn na teangacha mionlaigh agus réigiúnach a chosaint, a chothú agus a bhuanú. Tá éagsúlacht le feiceáil go soiléir i measc ionadaithe na comhdhála, le 25 teanga éagsúil á labhairt ina measc.

Tá an chomhdháil seo á reachtáil ag Foras na Gaeilge ag am tráthúil. Is cúis áthais don Fhoras é go bhfuil sí á reachtáil le linn Uachtaránachta na hÉireann ar an Aontas Eorpach, le naoi dteanga oibre eile ag teacht isteach san AE. Seo an chéad uair ar reachtáladh comhdháil den chineál seo aon áit san AE.

Caithfimid ar fad leanúint ag saothrú linn chun na teangacha tábhachtacha seo a chosaint agus a chaomhnú. Tá Acht teanga anois i bhfeidhm in Éirinn chun cearta teanga a chosaint do lucht na Gaeilge. Is é príomhaidhm an Achta ná seirbhísí poiblí a bheith ar fáil i nGaeilge chun freastal ar éileamh. Beidh an cur i bhfeidhm ag tarlú ar bhonn céimiúil, thar thréimhse trí bliana.

Cloistear caint faoi dhrochstaid na dteangacha mionlaigh ach ní aontaím leis sin. Táimid ar fad mar phobail theanga mionlaigh. Is cuid dhílis d'oidhreacht chultúrtha na hEorpa iad uile na teangacha neamhfhorleathana agus ní mór iad a cheiliúradh agus a fhorbairt agus ceart lucht a labhartha a chosaint. Is cóir dúinn a bheith muiníneach agus dóchasach ag dul amach as seo agus fios againn go bhfuil neart againn le chéile.

Gur fada buan na teangacha agus an éagsúlacht. Ós rud é gurh iad sin a léiríonn ár bhféiniúlacht. Tá moladh tuillte ag Foras na Gaeilge as ucht an chomhdhálail seo a reáchtáil agus go bhfaighimid ar fad dóchas, eolas agus misneach mar thoradh uirthi.

Voces Diversae: Linguistic Diversity in Education

Éamon Ó Cuív

I am pleased to open this conference, **Voces Diversae**, which is intended to examine the best ways in which to promote linguistic diversity in education. It is an international education conference for the 300 lesser-used languages of Europe. This conference has three principal aims:

- To disseminate information among those who are teaching, or teaching in, these languages about what has happened recently at European level regarding language-teaching in general and the support that is available to them from the European Union and the Council of Europe.
- To facilitate the exchange of information and experience among participants.
- To inspire those who are dealing with lesser-used languages in education to form a European network, with the aim of taking full benefit from the European Union action plan on teaching and linguistic variety, as well as from any other policy which would be useful.

In this country today we see cultural richness from every area of Europe, and the world, and that encourages those of us whose responsibility it is to protect, to nurture and to preserve the minority and regional languages. Diversity can be seen clearly among the conference representatives, with 25 different languages being spoken.

This conference is being run by Foras na Gaeilge at a timely moment. The Foras is proud that it is taking place during the Irish Presidency of the European Union, with nine different working languages coming into the Union. This is the first time that a conference of this sort has been organised anywhere in the European Union.

We must all continue working to protect and preserve these important languages. A language Act is now operating in Ireland to protect the language rights of Irish-speakers. The primary aim of the Act is to satisfy demand for the provision of public services in Irish. Implementation is by degrees, over a three-year period.

There is talk about the poor state of the minority languages, but I do not agree with that; we are all minority language peoples. The lesser-used languages are all a cherished part of the cultural heritage of Europe and it is essential to celebrate and develop them and to protect the rights of their speakers. We have reason to be confident and hopeful as we move on from here, knowing that together we are strong.

Long live the languages and the diversity. They demonstrate our self-identity. Foras na Gaeilge deserves praise for organising this conference and may we all take hope, knowledge and courage from it.

Voces Diversae: Lesser-Used Language Education in Europe

Dónall Ó Riagáin

Language acquisition normally comes about by either one of two key processes – intergenerational transmission and schooling. The manner in which almost all of us acquire our L1 is in our family circle; our L2 may be acquired by contact with users of that language in formal or informal situations but for most of us it is at school that we learn for the first time languages that are not our mother tongue – Irish is an extreme example. Over 90% of people who can speak Irish today learned the language not in their family circle but at school – indeed, had it not been for the work of the schools the language might well be extinct by now.

Of course, it is at school that most children acquire certain skills associated with even their mother tongue, for example, reading and writing. Where the mother tongue is not the dominant language of the community, and the family language is not in receipt of the normal linguistic support from the immediate neighbourhood, the role of the school in developing the child's linguistic proficiency becomes even more important. Recent studies, for example, *Euromosaic: Brussels and Luxembourg*, 1996, suggest that schools are playing an ever increasing role, not only in the development of competent bilinguals, but, critically, in supporting the intergenerational transmission of lesser-used languages. It is therefore imperative that the teaching of lesser-used languages be carried out in as effective a manner as practicable, and that their role as media of instruction be enhanced as much as possible.

Societal changes, for example, the urbanisation of society, the people's dependence on networks rather than on physically close neighbourhood relationships, the dramatic increase in one-parent families, and the all-pervading mass media, especially television, thrust a greater role on the formal education system for the development of children's linguistic competence.

Teachers of Europe's lesser-used languages are often leaders in the field of language teaching – often bereft of proper state support, depending on scant resources and inadequate pedagogical materials, their dedication and imaginative approach have time and again overcome seemingly insurmountable difficulties.

Major and Minor: Europe's Changing Linguistic Face

When the European Coal and Steel Community was established in 1951, it (rather reluctantly)[1] accepted four official and working languages – French, German, Italian and Dutch. Its successor, the European Union, now has 21 official and working languages. With the latest enlargement, it has become clear that, while all official and working languages are legally equal, some have much greater *de facto* importance and power than others. Languages such as English, Spanish and French are used for international communication, whereas languages such as Maltese, Slovene and the three Baltic languages are rarely used outside their home territories. Some, for

---

[1] It was originally intended that the European Coal and Steel Community would have only one working language – French. However, the Flemings recognised that such an arrangement could impinge on the delicate linguistic balance in Belgium and refused to accept it.

example, Estonian, Latvian and Lithuanian, have only recently emerged from situations where they were pressurised by dominant "imperialist" languages and are still undergoing what on the Iberian peninsula is called a process of "normalisation". The situation of those languages is not all that different from that of some stateless languages, known generally as "regional" or "minority" languages – indeed, proponents of certain small national languages might look enviously at the numerical strength and administrative support enjoyed by some of those so-called regional or minority languages, for example, Catalan.

The organisers of **Voces Diversae** sought to address the users of all lesser-used European languages, be they the official languages of EU member states or with recognition only in the regions where they are used. Furthermore, they decided to focus on "unique" language communities, for example, Friulans, Bretons, Occitans and Sámi as distinct from cross-frontier linguistic minorities, for example, Swedish-speakers in Finland, German-speakers in Italy, Danish-speakers in Germany. It was also decided to be inclusive, rather than exclusive, and speakers from Kalmykia and Khakassia in the Russian Federation made fascinating and useful contributions.

The conference organisers and the participants focused their attention on questions such as, "How best do we address common challenges?", "What are European organisations doing that can be of use to us?", "What are our experiences of problem solving and best practice?", "What support structures are available?" and "How can we go forward together?"

European Institutions

Both major European organisations – the European Union and the Council of Europe – have been and continue to be active in the field of language teaching.

The European Union has had a direct and official involvement in supporting language teaching since the introduction of an article on education into the Treaty establishing the European Communities at Maastricht in 1992. **Teresa Condeço**[2] of the European Commission's Directorate-General for Education and Culture explained that, while the EU's educational programmes had originally focused on the official and working languages of the member states, it had now taken a new orientation and its current policy was to support *linguistic diversity*. That would henceforth entail supporting the learning of all languages, including regional or minority languages, and immigrant languages. The Commission pursued its policy mainly through two programmes: *Leonardo da Vinci* and *Socrates*. Its current action plan contained a list of 45 actions in three main areas: lifelong language learning, better language teaching, and building a language-friendly environment.

At the time of writing, the Commission's current language teaching programmes are entering their final year but will be revamped and continued from 2007 onwards as part of an exciting new venture – the integrated lifelong learning programme.

Joe Sheils, Head of the Council of Europe's Language Policy Division, explained that the Council of Europe was concerned with the teaching of *all* languages and aimed at producing tools which could be used by language professionals everywhere, irrespective of what language they were teaching. The *Common European Framework of Reference for Languages* was adopted in 2001. It offered a common basis for the elaboration of curricula and syllabuses, teaching or learning materials and

---

[2] It is regretted that **Teresa Condeço** did not submit her paper for publication in this volume.

examinations. That, in turn, led to common standards, with six reference levels. The *European Language Portfolio* was based on it. The Council or Europe distinguished between *multilingualism,* which was societal, and *plurilingualism,* which was individual. As well as its Language Policy Division, based in its Strasbourg headquarters, the Council of Europe has the European Centre for Modern Languages in Graz.

Common Issues

As already observed, the education system has had thrust upon it a crucial role in conserving and redeveloping lesser-used languages. Over-reliance on schools is not good, according to **Viv Edwards**. In her paper on "Education and the Development of Early Childhood Bilingualism", she points to the crucial role that the family must play if the work of the school is to be successful. The benefits of bringing up children bilingually must be explained to parents – to illustrate that, she describes the *Twf* programme, initiated by the Welsh Language Board.

How and when to introduce the second language to children with learning difficulties is a recurring theme with teachers of lesser-used languages. **Sue Davies** of Trinity College, Carmarthen, dealt comprehensively with that issue in her paper on "Children with Learning Difficulties: Second Language Acquisition". Her approach was pragmatic and compassionate while based on the results of research and experience.

Case Studies

Participants at the **Voces Diversae** conference had the benefit of learning from no fewer than twelve case studies. Those covered the situations of Kashubian in Poland, the Sámi languages, Hungarian and Italian in Slovenia, the Khakas language in Southern Siberia, a plethora of languages in Hungary (i.e. German, Slovene, Slovak, Croatian, Romanian, Bulgarian, Ruthenian, Greek, and the languages of the Gypsy people – Romani and Beash), Basque, Occitan, Sorbian, Maltese, Estonian, Kalmyk, and Ulster-Scots. Two further papers were submitted after the conference – one regarding Friulian, German, and Slovene in Friuli Venezia Giulia, and the other on the situation of the Tatar language. All the papers, with the exception of the Occitan paper, are included in this publication.[3] It is a particular delight to learn of three different situations in the Russian Federation: Kalmyk, Khakas and Tatar. For too long, the approximately 150 languages of the Russian Federation have been almost totally disregarded in Western Europe.

Every language finds itself in a unique situation, and there would appear to be no uniformity in teaching approaches either. **Bosya Kornusova** argues that what she calls the efficient teaching of a language was more important than the number of hours spent on it. She said that the Kalmyks lacked suitable textbooks, and that shortcomings in teaching had led to a lack of communicative competence. Using the lesser-used language as a medium of instruction was a key factor in achieving such competence. Nowhere is that clearer than in the case of Basque, where four different models are in use. **Joana Abrisketa** assures that only in model D, the all-Basque one, is bilingualism (Basque and Spanish) guaranteed.

---

[3] It is regretted that the paper on Occitan by **Patricia Rosenthal** was not submitted for publication in this volume.

Some languages are under very severe pressure, and their very life may depend on the success of their being taught effectively. **Leoš Šatava** tells us that Sorbian is one such case. Although theoretically supportive, 40 years of Communist rule has left it very much weakened. Only in the western part of Upper Lusatia is the language still found in its full vigour. Although the approach to the challenge of language preservation has improved and is now on a more conceptual, planned and targeted basis, only time will tell if it is enough. Another language under severe pressure is Khakassian. **Tamara Borgoyakova** tells us that the use of the Khakas language as a language of instruction is decreasing. That decline can be ascribed to a policy of ethnolinguistic assimilation practised during the final decades of the Soviet era. A shift in the ethnic composition of the population of the Republic of Khakassia is another factor. Nevertheless, an overwhelming majority of young people have a positive emotional attitude to the mother tongue as a part of their ethnocultural identity and express readiness to take part in language-preserving and -developing activities.

In contrast, there were also accounts of courageous and seemingly successful revivalist policies. **Yagfar Garipov** and **Marina Solnyshkina** depict an encouraging situation in Tatarstan. As they report:

> For the last 10–12 years, the Republic of Tatarstan has achieved significant success in the functional development and revitalisation of the language of its eponymous people.[3] Some 51% of Tatar children are nowadays being schooled in their native language, while 12 years ago such children accounted for only 12%. At that time only 10.6% of Tatar children were being taught through their native language in pre-school educational institutions, but that figure has now increased to about 65%.

Estonia offers us an example of unapologetic revivalism. The Estonian people and their language suffered terribly under Soviet rule. As **Mart Rannut** writes:

> The thus enforced totalitarian regime entailed disastrous changes to the population, including its ethnic composition, as a result of extra-judicial killings, mass deportations to Siberia and the far north, and the imprisonment (in GULAGs) of autochthonous inhabitants, with the simultaneous immigration of populations from the occupying country. For the non-Russian minorities in Estonia, no possibilities remained to promote or maintain their ethnic culture and language. All their institutions were abolished, including media, schools, societies, clubs, and so on.

Article 37(4) of the *Estonian Constitution* now states that "All persons have the right to instruction in Estonian" and provision is made to ensure that this happens. Estonian is now the sole official language, and even non-Estonian citizens are acquiring it.

Joe Zammit-Ciantar gave us a fascinating overview of the Maltese situation. The majority of the population are fluent in both Maltese and English, and everyone seemingly wants to keep it that way. Regarding the teaching of languages in primary education, the *Education Act* of 1989 states that children should learn the Maltese and English languages, in the spoken, read, and written forms. The *Education Act* provides for the further teaching of the Maltese and English languages in secondary education too.

New policies and new visions were evident in other instances. **Silvana Schiavi Fachin** explains that it has been only since the 1980s that the three regional languages spoken in Friuli-Venezia Giulia, Friulian, Slovene and German, have been formally granted a foothold in the education system. Thanks to the professionalism and dedication of a small number of people, the situation continues to improve.

Different problems confront what **Tomasz Wicherkiewicz** calls "eclipsed languages" – those structurally close to the official language of the state and consequently often perceived as dialects or some kind of sub-standard variety. Kashubian, a West Slavic language spoken in the north of Poland, is one such language. Since the 2002-03 school year, the teaching of Kashubian has been permitted and funded in primary schools if seven written applications from the parents of children in the class are received. The corresponding figure for secondary schools is 14 – a modest, yet encouraging start. A similar case in some respects is that of Ulster-Scots. Scots is a West Germanic language, and Ulster-Scots is the form used in Ireland's northern province of Ulster. Language and ethnic identity are closely linked in Ulster and, although an estimated 25% of Ulster's Scots-speakers are from the Catholic community, it is generally associated with the descendants of the seventeenth-century Protestant planters. It has always been marginalised and used only in domains such as family and farming. **Hilary Avery** and **Andrea Gilbert** describe the teaching materials which they have designed for use in schools and the methods which they deploy to instruct teachers to use those materials. The emphasis is on the broad agenda of cultural identity and not solely on linguistic matters.

The Sámi languages started to gain some reasonable degree of support only from the 1960s. Like many other lesser-used languages, they have experienced policies of attempted linguicide. To make matters even more complicated, Sámis inhabit four sovereign states – Norway, Sweden, Finland and Russia. **Nils Ø. Helander** makes an observation with which few people involved in lesser-used language would disagree:

> The Norwegian experience corresponded with that of Finland and Sweden in that it was not found possible to achieve a functionally bilingual level of proficiency in Sámi when it was taught only as a school subject to children who were not full mother-tongue speakers when they started school.

Different policies in the same sovereign state can work well. **Sonja Novak Lukanovič** describes two models in Slovenia:

1. a model in which the educational process takes place through the mother tongue and in which the other or second language is compulsory. This model is practised in the Slovene Italian region in Slovene Istria.
2. a model in which the two languages – the mother tongue and the second language – are languages of instruction and school subjects. This model is practised in the Slovene Hungarian region in Prekmurje.

As **Judit Solymosi** shows, Hungary is faced with a real challenge in catering for the needs and aspirations of its 13 minorities. Those can be divided into three broad groups – the stronger minorities, the semi-nomadic ones (i.e. the Roma), and the tiny minorities. Hungary would appear to be making a sincere and imaginative effort to address the challenge. A high degree of school autonomy is granted to minorities where practicable. In the case of the very small minorities, the state pays for the teaching of the minority language at Sunday school. Some 85% of the Roma have lost their ancestral language. While promoting integrated education to combat social exclusion, the Roma and Beash languages are taught in several schools.

Everyone can draw his or her own lessons from the case studies and see how they can be applied to their own situation. One or two common threads ran through all cases. A language teaching policy could not be successfully implemented *in vacuo*. To make language teaching meaningful, it has to be part of a policy to facilitate the use of the language outside the school. Another common thread is the determination of 'small' peoples all over Europe to conserve their linguistic heritage and transmit it to the next generation.

Teacher Training

It is impossible to teach languages effectively without dedicated and properly trained teachers. Three experts in this field shared their knowledge with us. **Joachim Arenas i Sampera**, describes the Catalan approach to the normalisation of their language in the education system. Besides a structured series of courses for the professional formation of young teachers, the Catalan authorities have also embarked on a programme of "recycling" teachers who are trained to teach only in Castilian. The upsurge of interest in – and support for – Irish in Northern Ireland in the past two decades is a striking phenomenon, and with it has come an ever-increasing demand for Irish-medium education. Responsibility for the professional training of teachers for *Gaelscoileanna* (Irish-medium schools) fell almost entirely on St. Mary's University College in Belfast. **Gabrielle Nig Uidhir**, a lecturer in that college, gives an exciting and encouraging presentation on the work being carried out there. The third presentation on teacher training came from **Boyd Robertson**, a senior lecturer in Gaelic at the University of Strathclyde in Glasgow. Teachers in Scotland receive their professional training in seven teacher education institutions (TEIs), all of which are now affiliated to universities. Training in (Scottish) Gaelic is available in three colleges. The Gaelic language is under severe pressure in Scotland and one of the challenges facing those involved in the professional preparation of teachers is the varying levels of competence in Gaelic of enrolling students.

Support Services

The final day of the conference focused on resources which could be drawn upon by teachers and teacher trainers – those presentations are reproduced in the final section of the present volume. **Cor van der Meer** explains how Mercator-Education is one of three Mercator centres, the others dealing with the media, and with law and legislation. Mercator-Education, based in Fryslân, in the premises of the Fryske Akademy, specialises in the field of minority language education – it serves as a documentation and information centre, and its databank can be accessed online.

Liam Ó Dochartaigh gives a fascinating description of his involvement in the mid-1990s in a network of nine third level educational institutions, funded by the Erasmus programme, whose aim was to support lesser-used languages. He describes not only the benefits reaped by the participants but also the difficulties which they had to overcome and some perceived weaknesses in the current structure of EU education programmes as regards linguistic diversity. He makes a practical proposal to the EU Commission aimed at encouraging the teaching and learning of non-dominant languages in future Erasmus student mobility programmes (2007 and beyond).

The dearth of teaching materials in lesser-used languages is one of the perennial problems with which educationalists must contend. **Eliane Kerjoant** tells us how the Diwan (Breton-medium) school movement has always attached great importance to having proper materials available for its teachers and pupils. Starved of adequate funding by the French authorities, they are making creative use of modern technology – for example, desk-top publishing – to address the challenge.

"Are traditional university structures sufficient?" asks **Wallace Ewart** in his challenging paper on linguistic diversity in the provision of tertiary education. His answer could be said to be a resounding "no!" Inspired by efforts to establish a new university in strife-ridden west Belfast, he advances some challenging ideas on how a new college could operate with a minimal administrative structure and draw on the academic resources of existing institutions.

Several official language boards have, with the support of the European Commission, established the European Network of European Language Boards. Bwrdd yr Iaith Gymraeg (the Welsh Language Board), Foras na Gaeilge (the cross-border Irish-Language Board) and Euskal Autonomia Erkidegoa / Comunidad Autónoma del País Vasco (the Government of the Basque Autonomous Community) were the main movers. The idea is to promote cooperation between official agencies working for lesser-used languages throughout Europe. The European Network of European Language Boards website (www.languageplanning.com) contains a section on education policies and is already proving to be a valuable resource.

The Future

As the amount of shared information grew with each new presentation, the answers to the common questions became clearer. Furthermore, EU programmes promise to be more accessible in future in the light of the policy of supporting linguistic diversity. While there was no 'one size fits all' approach to the teaching of lesser-used languages and the situation of each language required its own set of policies, one could learn from other communities' experiences and apply some of their strategies to one's own situation. It was clear that EU and Council of Europe actions in the field of language teaching could be very useful. The EU is pan-European, however, and it would be much more effective if small linguistic communities could make joint approaches rather than having each make its own proposals. The need for ongoing dialogue and experience-sharing became more and more evident. One group's success in overcoming a certain problem could be the key to a solution for another group.

As the conference progressed, participants started to say, "We needed this badly: don't let what we started slip away." **Medwin Hughes**, Principal of Trinity College, Carmarthen, went to the rostrum towards the end of the conference and offered the services of his college to set up a **Voces Diversae** website so that the exchange of information and expertise could be set up on an ongoing basis. **Ann Malamah Thomas**, then director of the British Council's Belfast office, offered her organisation's support. In June 2005, a meeting was held in the British Council office in Belfast, with the support of Foras na Gaeilge and the Ulster-Scots Agency, and the necessary arrangements to set up such a website were put in place. At the time of writing, the website is under construction, under the dedicated and expert direction of **Tim Burton**, a member of the Trinity College Carmarthen staff.

Purely by coincidence, a public demonstration took place in Dublin on the final day of the conference. Thousands of people, most of them young, took to the streets to demand official and working status for Irish in the EU. Three months later, a hesitant and, one suspected, somewhat uneasy Irish Government bowed to public opinion and formally made the request. Early in 2005, the EU Council of Ministers gave its approval, and Irish is now taking its place alongside the 20 other official and working languages of the Union.

On that final day of the conference, in April 2004, one sensed a wind of change blowing through Dublin – a wind which, one hopes, will in time herald a new Europe, where tolerance and understanding will guide decision-makers, and where linguistic diversity is no longer feared and resisted but rather embraced as a source of cultural wealth. Europe can then speak with a united voice in its many and rich *voces diversae*.

The Common European Framework of Reference for Languages: Learning, Teaching and Assessment

Joe Sheils[1]

Introduction

Siúd is go bhfuil hata Chomhairle na hEorpa buailte ar mo cheann agam, is Éireannach mé, agus tugann sé sásamh ar leith dom, mar sin, bheith anseo i mBaile Átha Cliath ag an gcomhdháil seo. Tá 46 ballstát ar an gcomhairle, agus tá na céadta teanga á labhairt iontu idir mhór is bheag, idir theangacha oifigiúla stáit agus theangacha atá ar bheagán aitheantais.

Tá polasaithe agus scéimeanna na rannóige a bhfuil mise mar cheann uirthi dírithe ar mhúineadh is ar shealbhú teangacha i gcoitinne agus ní ar theangacha áirithe seachas a chéile a chur chun cinn. Ní heol domsa go cinnte cé chomh tairbheach daoibhse is atá an obair atá ar lámha againn, ach tá sé tábhachtach go mbeadh sibh lán-eolach fúithi. Fúibhse atá sé an t-eolas a scagadh agus cibé leas is féidir a bhaint as.

I shall begin by very briefly situating the Common European Framework of Reference for Languages, or CEF, in the broader context of the goals of Council of Europe language education policy.

I shall then examine how that policy translates into what we define as plurilingualism – the development of the plurilingual repertoire of individuals.

In the third and main part I shall recall the main characteristics of the CEF and how it might help support greater diversification and plurilingualism in language-learning. I shall also refer to the potential of the CEF – which is a generic, non-language-specific instrument – for the promotion of individual languages.

In the fourth and final part I shall briefly link the CEF – which is an instrument for policy-makers and language education-providers – with the European language portfolio, which is a tool for learners, and which is designed to support them in developing their plurilingual repertoires throughout life.

In my conclusion I shall recall that the CEF is designed for use in foreign- or second-language rather than mother-tongue education and seek views on the value of a similar instrument for the mother-tongue sector.

Council of Europe Policy

Our work on language education is carried out under the terms of the European Cultural Convention, which provides a framework for intergovernmental co-operation among our member states. Under Article 2, governments commit themselves to taking the necessary measures to promote the teaching of one another's languages in the other states party to the convention. The convention celebrates its fiftieth anniversary this December, and work in language education has been going on for just over 40 years.

Such work has been guided by broad policy goals which include the maintenance and promotion of linguistic and cultural diversity, the protection of language rights,

---

[1] The views expressed in this paper are those of the author and do not commit the Council of Europe.

the promotion of deeper mutual understanding for living together in multicultural Europe, language skills for participation in democratic citizenship processes in national and European contexts, and language-learning for social cohesion. Our programmes aim to promote LANGUAGES FOR ALL – there can be no plurilingual elite – and developing plurilingual skills is both a necessity and right for all our citizens.

Our activities have always been directed towards lifelong language-learning – the school is only the beginning and can achieve a good start. However, plurilingual skills must be built up throughout life as work needs and interests change. Schools must provide the skills and confidence for further language-learning.

A series of recent medium-term programmes has focused on policies and tools to support the development of plurilingualism in citizens and linguistic diversity in our multilingual societies.

Plurilingualism

I now come to the concept of plurilingualism, central to the function of the CEF, and its relation to multilingualism. We distinguish between multilingualism and plurilingualism. By "multilingualism" we refer to the presence in a geographical area of more than one language or "variety of language"; individuals in an area may be monolingual, speaking only their own language (variety), or they may be plurilingual, with several languages. "Plurilingualism" refers to the repertoire of languages (or varieties of language) which many individuals use, and is therefore the opposite of monolingualism. It includes all languages: mother tongue or first language and any number of other languages. Accordingly, in some multilingual areas some individuals are monolingual and some are plurilingual. Plurilingualism is not seen as the superposition or juxtaposition of distinct language competences but rather as the existence of a complex and composite competence on which the language-user may draw.

As an illustration of the meaning of plurilingualism, an adult European with at least a secondary education might be expected to have in his or her repertoire at a given point in time: a "national" language spoken and written to the standard norms of the country; a variety of the first language spoken according to the norms of the region and/or generation to which he or she belongs; a regional or minority language that he or she speaks and writes where appropriate; one or more foreign languages understood, but not necessarily spoken, to a basic or intermediate level; or another foreign language with a higher level of proficiency in speaking and writing. At a later or earlier point in time, the languages or the levels of proficiency might be different, depending on further education, work experience and leisure activities. Plurilingualism varies throughout life, and the choice of languages and levels attained may depend on one's needs, interests and geographical location.

A plurilingual repertoire is not a uniform concept. While it is seen as a global, inter-related concept, it is made up of different levels of proficiency in each language, and also of varying levels of competence in each skill. "Partial" competences such as reading or listening skills may be an important part of an individual's repertoire, and higher levels may be attained in those than in productive skills.

The CEF allows for the definition of distinct competences at different levels, and that can be particularly valuable in planning a more diversified approach to language teaching and assessment to help learners develop their plurilingual potential.

The Common European Framework of Reference for Languages

The Common European Framework of Reference for Languages (CEF), published in 2001 after a period of development and piloting, aims to provide coherence and transparency in language education by offering a common basis for the elaboration of curricula and syllabi, teaching and learning materials, and examinations. It is above all a tool for reflection and communication among language professionals across different languages and education sectors, as well as across national boundaries, and is descriptive rather than prescriptive in nature.

It offers common reference points to facilitate national and international co-ordination in planning language-teaching and in relating examination results to common European standards or benchmarks.

The CEF sets out in some detail what a competent language-user has to do to communicate effectively with other users of the language. It then identifies the various kinds of knowledge and skill that a learner requires to do so. Wherever possible, it gives a brief, easily understood characterisation of those language activities and competences at six levels of proficiency, from the most basic (A1) to the highest to which an educational system can reasonably expect to bring a student (C2) The six ascending levels of proficiency describe what the learner CAN DO (in positive terms), and HOW WELL the learner performs (qualitative aspects of communicative ability).

Figure 1 shows the approach to scaling language proficiency at different levels.

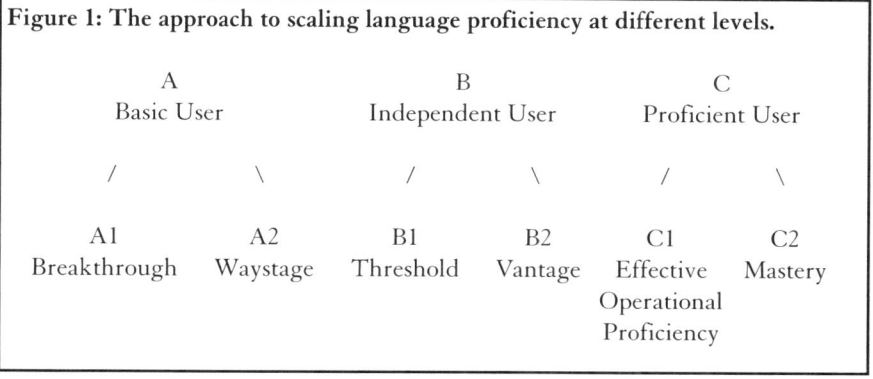

Figure 1: The approach to scaling language proficiency at different levels.

A Basic User		B Independent User		C Proficient User	
/	\	/	\	/	\
A1 Breakthrough	A2 Waystage	B1 Threshold	B2 Vantage	C1 Effective Operational Proficiency	C2 Mastery

There are three broad bands, described as "basic user", "independent user" and "proficient user". Each is divided into two levels, making a six-level scheme that corresponds closely to the kinds of "natural" levels that have developed over the last ten years. Sets of descriptors expressed as what users "can do" are then provided for each language skill or competence. That replaces the classical four-skill approach (listening, reading, speaking, writing) by distinguishing between reception, interaction, production and mediation (missing on the slide), each of which in turn is divided into spoken and written. Subcategories are offered for each of the eight "skills", with illustrative scales for most. Those scales describe what someone can typically do in this type of activity at each of the six CEF levels. A similar approach is taken with linguistic, pragmatic and sociolinguistic competence, and for strategies with regard to reception, interaction and production. The CEF thus contains over 40 sub-scales which have been empirically validated and which define, at six common levels, categories that relate to models of language use and language competence. That makes it possible to talk about language levels in a more sophisticated and detailed manner than before. It is possible to profile an individual's proficiency or plurilingual repertoire. It makes it easier also to define clearly the objectives of a syllabus or the demands of an examination in as much detail as is required. The CEF also supplies "plus levels" between A2 and B1, between B1 and B2, and between B2 and C1. Those can be used to profile at a finer degree of precision and show progress over shorter stages. Each level can be further sub-divided in a branching system to meet specific local needs. For example, level A2 could be divided into three or four smaller steps of graded objectives to plan learning and show progress at each step.

The descriptors in the levels can be used for a variety of purposes – syllabus design, self-assessment, teacher assessment, examinations, and for relating test results to common reference points.

The fact that small steps can be created and built up to be placed in an internationally transparent system, and the fact that different skills or competences can be defined and assessed separately, might be helpful in promoting the learning of a greater range of languages by individuals, including less widely learnt languages. That can, for example, facilitate the inclusion of more languages in a school timetable if there is a policy of valuing and recognising all levels of achievement in a language, including partial competences. That, of course, is one of the aims of the European language portfolio.

The common reference levels are being used for policy-planning at national level in most of our member states. Figure 2 shows one example from Switzerland – where the scales were originally developed – in planning teaching and in assessing proficiency at the end of compulsory school for the national languages as second languages in the various cantons or regions and for the first foreign language.

Figure 2: Switzerland	
Local language as L2:	B2
2nd National language:	B1 + /B1
1st Foreign language:	A2 + /A2
3rd National language:	A2 + /A1

The CEF is also influential at European level. It has been adopted by the Association of Language Testers in Europe, or ALTE, which included the body in each country responsible for teaching and testing the national language. The EC DIALANG project for diagnostic language tests delivered via the Internet is based on the CEF.

Europass, the forthcoming EU scheme for transparency in vocational qualifications, will be based on a standard European CV that includes a summary of one's language competence. In effect that will be the six-level summary self-assessment grid from the CEF. We have it in 35 languages, and it would be good to have it in all the languages of our member states, and also those of our migrant communities.

The framework itself has been translated into over 20 languages – a considerable achievement – and I understand that it is an undertaking which can stimulate corpus development in its specific domain.

The CEF is a generic, non-language-specific instrument. That has considerable advantages for coherence and transparency across languages and for international co-operation. At the same time, it must be applied in specific contexts for the teaching of individual national or regional languages. That means that it will be helpful for planning teaching and testing competence in those languages to add concrete language content and tasks in the language concerned to correspond with each of the six levels of the CEF.

That process resembles what was done for threshold level and the lower "Waystage" and higher "Vantage" specifications, but now the model used corresponds with the parameters and categories for language use in the six CEF levels.

The work has been completed for German at levels A1–B2, in the first instance by an international team of experts from Germany (Goethe-Institut), Switzerland and Austria. Work is beginning on C levels, and we have held a co-ordination meeting on those levels with developers for other languages, as they pose a special challenge. Level B2 has just been completed for French by an international team, and I understand that projects are in preparation for Italian, Portuguese and Greek, and possibly Friulian.

The Council of Europe would welcome expressions of interest from those responsible for other languages, and we shall try to help with networking and sharing experience and expertise.

Before concluding this section, I should like to draw readers' attention to a pilot scheme that we have just launched to help examination bodies relate their exams in a reliable manner to the CEF. It is one thing to claim that an exam is at level B1, but how can we be sure? To put it another way: How do I know that my B1 is the same as yours? We have produced a manual to offer concrete technical guidance on the question. It takes users through three related stages of verification, beginning with a simple self-audit of the examination content, before moving on to comparing the judgment made with exemplars which have already been standardised with the CEF levels using videos of oral performance and reading and writing test tasks. Finally, for those who can manage it, procedures for empirical validation based on test data are proposed. We are in the process of drawing together illustrative videos or DVDs of oral performances and a CD with test items and writing tasks. We wish to do so for each of the six levels and for as wide a range of languages as possible, and of course we hope to use illustrations from different educational contexts across Europe. That is particularly important in high-stakes contexts such as qualifications for study or employment, and, of course, in deciding the appropriate level of competence in the official language for granting citizenship. Readers are welcome to join the project, and the manual and further information can be found on the website.

The European Language Portfolio

In this final section, I should like briefly to turn to the portfolio, which was launched in 2001 European year of languages and has made good progress in a short time, particularly in the formal education sector. It is a concrete tool for relating the framework levels to language-learners according to their age and stage of development.

This personal document for learners is designed to assist them in recording their competences in an internationally transparent manner and in gradually taking responsibility for their language-learning in the perspective of lifelong learning. It therefore has a reporting function and a pedagogic function, both of which are fundamental to all portfolios.

The reporting function is of particular interest for the proposed EU Europass scheme, based on a database of selected documents in electronic form, and the Council of Europe is currently co-ordinating the development of electronic portfolios, which it is expected may also contribute to the goals of that scheme.

The pedagogic function of the ELP is being enriched by the development of a database of descriptors from existing validated portfolios clearly derived from the framework. We hope that it can continue to be expanded in a range of languages.

There is no single uniform ELP. It is used in many different contexts and has different forms of presentation, but all conform to a set of basic principles and include three parts: language passport, which provides an overview at a specific point in time of one's proficiency in various languages according to the CEF levels (see the generic model available at the conference – the only standard part recommended for adult users throughout Europe); language biography, which allows learners to plan, monitor and self-assess their progress over time; and dossier, which can contain evidence of claims made (project results, etc.) or certificates from courses followed. Models exist for younger learners, adolescents and adults. Readers are invited to visit the website and to contact us if they need more guidance.

Conclusion

In conclusion, I shall recall why the Council of Europe has developed the framework (and also portfolio). The instruments are intended to promote and support the development of plurilingualism – the lifelong development of the individual's plurilingual repertoire. We wish to encourage the learning of a range of languages – an individual repertoire made up of different languages – learnt to different levels and including different types of competences, depending on the purposes for which an individual may require them. Clearly, the development of a plurilingual competence includes an awareness of why and how one learns the languages chosen – motivation and a degree of learner autonomy are essential for lifelong language-learning. Of course there is no single model of a plurilingual repertoire, which will vary depending on an individual's needs and interests and be influenced by where he or she lives or moves to. Plurilingualism is a dynamic concept – evolving and changing according to one's needs throughout life. It also takes into account the fact that different languages are not learnt in isolation, and that they can influence one another, both in the learning process and in communicative use – hence, a coherent, transversal, integrated approach can be useful in formal education contexts.

The question is increasingly asked: should we not be more concerned with decompartmentalising language-learning, breaking down barriers between languages learnt or acquired – between the different foreign languages on the one hand, and on the other hand between foreign languages and mother tongues or languages of instruction? The OECD has carried out comparative surveys of educational performance which have had a major impact on the countries concerned, and the recent PISA study, which included a survey of reading skills in the mother tongue – or, more accurately, the language of instruction – has given rise to considerable debate in certain countries whose results were disappointing.

Do we not need a similar kind of common reference framework, setting standards for mother tongues or languages of instruction, at least for the communicative aspects? Our current framework was not designed with mother tongues in mind. In the Council of Europe we wish to address the policy implications of standard-setting instruments for both foreign and other languages at a policy forum in Strasbourg on 28 and 29 June 2004 on 'Global approaches to education for plurilingualism'. Among other topics, the increasing convergences between the mother tongue or language of instruction and foreign languages will be explored.

The *Guide for the Development of Language Education Policies in Europe* addresses policy issues in such a global context and offers concrete suggestions for coherent approaches to the language curriculum. Our activities to assist national or local authorities in their self-evaluation of policy also address the issue by looking at ALL languages in education – official language, mother tongue, minority languages, sign languages as well as foreign languages. That activity, known as language education policy profile – is under way for six countries, and our first local profile is about to begin on the Lombardy region.

The forum will also address the policy issues at national level which arise in the use of a common European standard-setting instrument such as the CEF. The Council of Europe intends to play its part in providing the guidance and co-ordination needed to ensure that the best use is made of that instrument, where necessary enriching it in the spirit of possible further development in specific areas.

Our priority is to contribute to the *qualitative* use of the framework, and to promote added coherence and transparency for all the partners involved, especially learners.

Reference

Beacco, J.-C. and Byram, M. 2003. *Guide for the Development of Language Education Policies in Europe*. Draft 1 (revised). Language Policy Division, Council of Europe.

Education and the Development of Early Childhood Bilingualism

Viv Edwards

Introduction

Analogies with the natural world are now commonplace in discussions on lesser-used languages. We talk, for instance, about the "health of languages"; and while previously we made reference to "the survival of the fittest", more recently we have talked of "the preservation of the species" (Skutnabb-Kangas 2000). We also use the metaphors of "language death", "language murder" and "language suicide", depending on one's personal perspective (Dennison 1977; Edwards 1985). There is certainly a growing sense of urgency regarding the vulnerability of many lesser-used languages. Leanne Hinton captures that quality in graphic terms when she describes the task of preserving the indigenous languages of California as "like trying to stitch together the fragile threads of a special cloth that is coming apart in your hands" (McBroom 1995).

Of course, not all lesser-used languages are confronted with a crisis on that scale. Catalan, for instance, with its 7 million speakers, could be described as very healthy. Many "medium-sized" lesser-used languages, such as Welsh and Basque – each with over half a million speakers – are showing signs of slowing or even halting language shift. Perhaps the most important point to note is that public awareness of the vulnerability of even the stronger of the lesser-used languages is far greater today than at any point in the recent past. The growth of interest in the subject – both political and academic – has certainly helped create a much better understanding of the conditions necessary for survival.

The Role of Education

As the number of speakers of lesser-used languages has diminished, education has increasingly played a vital role in helping to slow, halt or even reverse language shift. The following are some instances of notable achievements in the UK and Ireland.

The first Welsh-medium school was opened in 1947. The demand for Welsh-medium education has been gaining momentum ever since, but especially since the 1970s. In 2002, one in five primary school children was being taught in classes where Welsh was used either as the main medium of education or for teaching part of the curriculum (Statistical Directorate 2003). The number of mainly Welsh-medium primary schools had risen to 440, and a further 80 schools were using Welsh as a teaching medium to some extent. At secondary level, 53 of the 229 secondary schools maintained by LEAs taught Welsh as a first language, and a further 20 taught Welsh as a first and second language. The Education Reform Act 1988 further strengthened the position of the language by stipulating that all children in English-medium schools between the ages of 5 and 16 must study Welsh, with a compulsory public exam in the language at 16.

Much of the increase in both the numbers and proportion of Welsh-speakers reported in the 2001 census can be attributed to bilingual education. In 2002, three quarters of the primary school children who were fluent in the language came from English-speaking homes (Statistical Directorate, 2003). While the percentage of primary schoolchildren speaking Welsh at home fell from 7.1% in 1988 to 6.2% in 2002, the percentage of fluent speakers who had acquired the language in school rose from 6.0% to 10.5%. The cumulative impact of Welsh-medium education is clear to see in a comparison of Welsh-speakers by age for the decades 1951–2001 in Table 1.

Table 1: Welsh-speakers: Percentage by Age Group

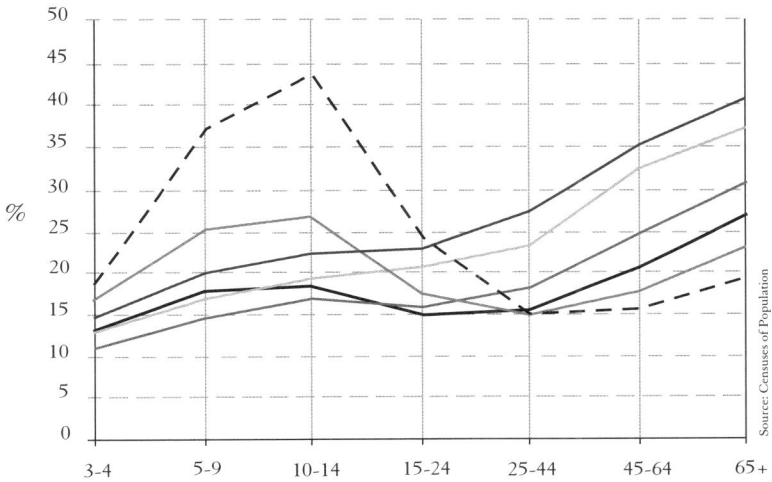

The situation in Scotland, where the number of Gaelic-speakers is currently around 55,000, is less favourable. All the same, there have been important gains. Gaelic-medium primary education was first introduced to the traditional heartlands of the language in Scotland the mid 1970s and soon followed in the wake of Gaels who had migrated to urban and Lowland areas. There is a clear mandate from parents for Gaelic-medium education: most believe that children can become bilingual without any disadvantage to their achievement in English, and about half would be prepared to enrol their children in Gaelic-medium units if they were available (Baker 1997). The Parents' Charter introduced by the Conservative Government in 1994 made it increasingly difficult to resist consumer pressure, and by 1999–2000 there were 59 Gaelic units – schools or special classes attached to English-medium schools – throughout Scotland, with Gaelic-medium classes increasingly continuing through to secondary education.

In Ireland, the situation is, of course, different. Irish has co-official status in the Republic and received a great deal more state support much earlier than other lesser-used European languages. From the start, formal schooling was seen as the most important tool in reversing language shift. Unfortunately, however, the early gains in establishing Irish as a language of education proved ephemeral, and by 1980 only 3% of secondary students were receiving Irish-medium education. Arguably, the Government placed too much confidence in the ability of schools to Gaelicise the country and overlooked the importance of creating opportunities to use the language in daily life. Yet Irish remains a badge of national identity in spite of its decline.

The Republican attachment to the language has certainly reaped benefits for the Irish-speaking community in Northern Ireland. Here Irish was taught as a subject in only a small number of Catholic schools, and parents organised the sole Irish-medium school in Northern Ireland in Belfast. Ironically, the main instance of informal learning of the language took place in the H-blocks of the Maze Prison, where Republicans protested at their classification as criminal rather than political prisoners (Dana and McMonagle 1994). Future hunger-striker Bobby Sands taught others Irish by shouting the lessons up and down the wing: "students" wrote on toilet paper and walls, or tried to commit the lesson to memory. Since most officials spoke only English, the study of Irish became a vital part of resistance to the prison regime. Such was the success of their efforts that, when the protests ended, prisoners set up a formal education programme, which they organised themselves.

The main breakthrough for Irish in the wider Northern Ireland community, however, came with the *Belfast / Good Friday Agreement* of 1998 between the Governments of the UK and Ireland. Legislation which followed now places a duty on the Department for Education and Skills to promote Irish-medium education; and the UK Government recognises both "the importance of the Irish language to many people in Northern Ireland" and its contribution to "the cultural identity and heritage of Northern Ireland's children"(DENI 1998). In the academic year 2004-05, 3713 children were enrolled in Irish-medium education in 44 nurseries, 32 primary schools, 2 secondary schools and a post-primary unit. At the tertiary level, two universities offer courses in Irish language and literature, and one teacher training college provides for the teaching of Irish.

When the numbers of speakers of lesser-used languages reach crisis point, pre-school provision becomes a particularly important player. In settings where responsibility for language transmission falls heavily on schools, pre-school education fulfils a vital role in preparing children for an immersion experience in the lesser-used language. In Wales, such provision takes two main forms: the nursery education movement supports the language-learning of children aged from two to five; and there are currently almost 600 playgroups with places for about 14,000 children between those ages. The playgroups are fed, in turn, by a growing network of parents, carers and children who meet in *Cylchoedd Ti a Fi* ('You and Me Circles') to socialise in an informal Welsh atmosphere. Nursery education is, of course, an important focus for language activists in many of the lesser-used language communities of Europe. The Irish experience, for instance, has been well documented by Hickey (1997).

Not all language-shift theorists, however, are convinced that education is the panacea that it might seem at first sight. Fishman (1991), in particular, stresses the dangers of over-reliance on efforts in the area, pointing instead to the critical role played by the family, which he describes as an "unexpendable bulwark" in attempts to reverse language shift. In that view, other developments can contribute to but not substitute for what he terms "home-family-neighborhood-community processes", in the same way that "inflating a flat tire cannot substitute for making sure that the tire has no leaks from which the air will then escape" (p. 95). Without the active involvement of the family, schools will inevitably find themselves in a frustrating struggle against the tide, with each new generation starting at the same point as the previous one. In short, while education plays an important role, it cannot assume sole responsibility for reversing language shift.

There is growing awareness of the problems associated with over-reliance on education. The Irish experience is a case in point. With the emergence of the Free State in 1921, Irish was made the national language and, outside the Gaeltacht, or traditional heartland of the language, education was seen as the main tool in language revival. Given the level of official support, the gains were disappointing. According to the 2002 census, 42.8% of the population of the Republic speak Irish, but two thirds of those reported never using the language or using it less than once a week (Central Statistics Office Ireland 2003). According to some critics (see, for instance, Ó hIfearnáin 2001), Government policy has failed to produce opportunities for speaking Irish in everyday life, leaving many people to conclude that effort expended in learning the language in school was, to some extent, a waste of time. Fishman (1996), for instance, recounts a story from the childhood of Irish psychologist John MacNamara, who studied Irish all his childhood in school.

> He was scolded one day by the lady who ran a candy store. He had just bought the candy from her and began talking English to his sister. "You have learned Irish all your life. How come you're speaking English? You should be talking Irish to your little sister." Later, out on the street, the sister asked him, "Is Irish really for talking?" That really did happen. It had not occurred to them that Irish was for talking. It was a school subject like geography and arithmetic.

Although the situation in Wales is to all intents and purposes very different, similar forces may be at work. There are strong indications that Welsh-speaking teenagers use the language less frequently as they get older (Baker 2003: 100), and that many of the students who have acquired Welsh in school use English as the only language of the home when they become parents (Aitchison and Carter 1988; Gruffudd 2000). Only four in every ten children who complete their primary school education through the medium of Welsh go on to Welsh-medium secondary education. The same proportion of Welsh-speaking adults report that they lack confidence in speaking the language.

But is Education Enough?

Most readers will be able to recount stories of the ways in which school was an important weapon in suppressing lesser-used languages at some time in the past. In Scotland the maidhe crochaidh, or hanging stick, was placed around the neck of any child caught speaking Gaelic, and, at the end of the day, all children who had worn the stick were beaten by the teacher. In Ireland, children were forced to wear tally sticks and slates on cords around their necks. Each time they used an Irish word, the teacher would make a notch on the stick or write the word on the slate. The number of notches or words was counted and punishment administered accordingly. In Wales, the Welsh Not – a wooden block – was hung round the neck of any child heard speaking Welsh in class. It was passed from one child to the next, and whoever was wearing it at the end of the day was beaten.

It is a superb irony that the same education systems that were once used as important weapons in suppressing lesser-used languages are currently playing a vital role in their preservation. The achievements of the education sector are impressive. The question remains, however, whether that contribution is enough to ensure the long-term future of the language. To answer that question, I shall turn once again to the evidence from Wales, the setting I know best.

The rapid increase in the numbers of young people who speak English is certainly testimony to the efficacy of the education system in language transmission. It would appear, however, that many of the children who have received a bilingual education make a clear division between their school and social lives and switch to English when they leave school (see, for instance, Aitchison and Carter 1988; Gruffudd 2000; Williams 2000). In attempts to address the dangers of over-reliance on education, attention has begun to shift from school to home in attempts to influence the intergenerational transmission of language (Fishman 1991; 2001).

The *Twf* Project[1]

The promotion of language transmission in the family is currently a priority for the Welsh Language Board. The Welsh are not the first to target families. In Finland, for instance, parents are required to register their children as Swedish-speaking or Finnish-speaking so that they can gain access to services, including education, in the appropriate language; parents are routinely provided with publications setting out the benefits of bilingualism. However, a new initiative in Wales is even more proactive and is currently attracting considerable attention.[2]

The logic of targeting the family in language planning is inescapable; the means by which that can be achieved are less clear. As Fishman (1991: 95) points out:

> Families are not captive audiences, as pupils are in school, as workers are in the workplace, or as soldiers in the armed forces. There is no particular, parsimonious point of assembly where one goes to find families.

Mechanisms for reaching parents vary from one country to the next. In the UK, the most efficient way of reaching not only all parents but all prospective parents is through the health care system: the antenatal services offered by midwives and the ongoing support offered by health visitors to families with children under the age of five. The starting point for the efforts of the Welsh Language Board was a partnership with Welsh hospitals. An information pack on *Bringing up bilingual children* was included in "Bounty" packs, which consist of free samples and advertising literature and are distributed to all mothers giving birth in hospital. Following a successful pilot project involving midwives and health visitors in 1998–99, the National Assembly approved a three-year project (2001–02 to 2003–04) to encourage parents to transmit the Welsh language to their children. The project was launched under the name of *Twf* ('Growth') in March 2002, with three strategic aims:
1. To bring the message of the advantages of bilingualism into the mainstream work of midwives and health visitors;
2. To raise awareness amongst parents, prospective parents and the public at large of the advantages of bilingualism;
3. To change the language patterns of the target group, namely mixed-language families, to increase the number of children speaking Welsh in the home.

Building strong alliances

The *Twf* project has worked strategically and to great effect with the health sector. With the support of directors of midwifery services, two key questions – *Which language/s do you intend introducing to your baby?* and *Have you received information about bilingualism from your midwife?* – are now routinely placed in the records of pregnancy which women carry with them, and serve as a reminder to midwives to discuss language use at an early stage. Project officers are also often invited to contribute to antenatal classes. At the same time, *Twf* is working with Health

---
[1] For details of current *Twf* activities, visit www.twfcymru.com
[2] The discussion which follows is based on an evaluation of the *Twf* project prepared by Viv Edwards and Lynda Pritchard Newcombe for the Welsh Language Board in December 2003.

Professions Wales, the body that accredits courses for midwives and health visitors, and the colleges that provide the courses, to ensure that information on bilingualism becomes an integral part of training.

Health visitors take over from midwives soon after birth. Their work is even more relevant to the project, since child development is central to their interests, and language development is a topic which parents are often keen to discuss. Language issues are routinely raised at the eight-month assessment.

There are arguments both for and against the heavy reliance on health workers for the transmission of the *Twf* message. Health professionals are respected and enjoy a relationship of trust with parents; their involvement in the promotion of bilingualism helps the project to be taken seriously. It is important to remember, however, that establishing good working relationships with health professionals is often a time-consuming process; that there are many competing, higher-priority demands on health workers' time; and that midwives and health visitors transmit the *Twf* message with varying degrees of enthusiasm and commitment, depending on their own personal agendas.

Other partners

Although collaboration with health professionals continues to form the core work of *Twf*, strong links have also been forged with a range of other partners, including Welsh-language organisations such as *Mudiad Ysgolion Meithrin* (the nursery school movement) and Mentrau Iaith ('language initiatives');[3] traditionally English-language "early years" organisations, such as the Pre-school Playgroups Association (PPA); and signposting services such as the Children's Information Bureaux and children's libraries. By working in partnership with a wide range of organisations, project officers are able to spread the net and move from an exclusive reliance on the health sector. It is clearly important that parents and prospective parents are exposed to a consistent message about the advantages of bilingualism for their children. The involvement of other partners thus has the effect of reinforcing that message.

Marketing the language

The decision to use the minority language in the home requires particular commitment, particularly when in competition with English, which has now achieved the status of a global language. English is, after all, the language of power and glitter – Coca-Cola, Bill Gates, MTV and the mass media. In comparison, minority languages can seem old-fashioned and unglamorous. One of the major challenges for *Twf* is therefore to help counteract that image. It has achieved its end by broadening the audience for its message to parents from all language backgrounds and all sections of society, and by developing a marketing strategy appropriate to the needs and interests of the target audience.

Language of families

The original targets for *Twf* were families where only one parent spoke Welsh. It became apparent at an early stage, however, that it was difficult, if not impossible, to

---

[3] A national network of *mentrau iaith* offers support for local communities to increase and develop their use of the Welsh language by offering advice and assistance to individuals, organisations and businesses; they also organise activities to raise the profile of the Welsh language. For further discussion, see, for instance, Campbell (2000).

target mixed-language families specifically. In simple terms, they do not exist as a separate group or entity. It rapidly became apparent that the *Twf* message is of potential value to *all* families, irrespective of language background. Families where both parents speak English need to be made aware not only of the potential social, cultural and economic benefits for their children of being able to speak Welsh, but also of the support which is available. And in the case of families where Welsh is being transmitted to the children, information on bilingualism reinforces the decision to use the language and potentially empowers parents to share that knowledge with incomers, friends and neighbours who do not speak Welsh.

Social inclusion

Efforts to promote bilingualism have traditionally appealed mainly to middle-class parents. That bias can be seen, for instance, in resources such as the video produced by the Welsh Language Board, which featured only middle-class, two-parent families. It is also evident in access to Welsh-medium education. In many areas, the location of schools means that bilingual education is not a realistic option for low-income families with no independent means of transport.

In contrast, *Twf* has deliberately set out to be socially inclusive. One indicator of that commitment is the attempt to establish links with organisations such as SureStart which target low-income families; another is the *Twf* presence at a wide range of national and local events. In addition to organising stalls at national gatherings, such as the *Urdd Eisteddfod*,[4] which have a clear association with the Welsh language, the project has been responsible for a range of local events which reach wide audiences. Those have included: fun evenings for the whole family, where parents were given the opportunity to learn some Welsh; visits to children's libraries to stimulate interest in books in Welsh; and colouring competitions promoting the project, sponsored by the local branches of McDonald's.

Promotional materials

Twf has a strong brand image: its logo, strap line *(Magu plant yn dwyieithog/Raising children bilingually)* and distinctive characters are instantly recognisable on a wide range of materials, as shown in Figure 1. *6 good reasons for making sure your children can speak Welsh*, a brightly coloured leaflet with a distinctive square shape and minimal text, is the centrepiece of *Twf* marketing. It was developed in response to questions that parents frequently asked about bilingualism. It reaches very large numbers of women through inclusion in records of pregnancy and "Bounty" packs; it is also widely distributed at events, through libraries and children's information bureaux and in response to initial enquiries. The *6 good reasons* leaflet is also available in poster form to be displayed in health centres, libraries and other public places. The fact that the *Twf* poster was observed in the doctor's surgery on the Welsh-language TV soap *Pobol y Cwm* is an indication of the extent of market penetration.

6 good questions was designed as a follow-up to the *6 good reasons* leaflet for parents and others requesting further information. It is to be particularly commended for its sensitivity to the different needs of Welsh- and English-speaking parents. The two language versions of the text are not a simple translation of each other; rather they address the specific concerns of the two language communities.

---

[4] The Eisteddfod is a competitive festival of the arts. Local gatherings feed into a series of regional and national events.

Figure 1: *Twf* logo

Another important marketing tool is the *Twf* newsletter, which features stories of families – including celebrities – who have successfully brought up their children to be bilingual. Project officers identify suitable families; an outside company arranges interviews and writes up the case studies. The idea is to provide role models who can offer practical advice and reassurance that it is possible to transmit the language, even in situations that are far from ideal. Project workers are responsible for distribution to parent and toddler groups, libraries, health centres, hospitals and maternity wards.

The newsletter has proved extremely popular and is another example of how *Twf* workers have been able to transform the abstract notion of family bilingualism into a concrete message with which the target audience can identify.

Lessons to be Learnt

So what lessons have been learnt in the first three years of *Twf*? The audience for the project has already widened significantly from the largely middle-class base of other Welsh-language organisations and from the mixed-language families envisaged at the outset. There are indications that it will need to adapt in other ways, too. The notion of the family, for instance, will need to be extended to include grandparents, childminders and other carers with whom many children spend a substantial proportion of their time; new ways of targeting those groups will need to be explored. The experience of a project which has developed within the space of two years from a concept to something approaching a national institution will certainly be of interest to other indigenous and lesser-used language communities. While the detailed mechanisms for reaching parents may differ from one location to the next, the strength of the initiative lies in the fact that it has successfully challenged assumptions that families are too difficult a group to target as part of language planning efforts.

References

Aitchison, J. and Carter, H. 1988. *The Welsh Language in the Cardiff Region*. Aberystwyth: Department of Geography, Aberystwyth University.

Baker, C. 1997. "Bilingual education in Ireland, Scotland and Wales". In J. Cummins and D. Corson eds. *Encyclopedia of Language and Education: Bilingual Education*. Dordrecht: Kluwer. 127–42.

Baker, C. 2003. "Language Planning: A Grounded Approach". In JM Dewaele, A. Housen and Li Wei eds. *Bilingualism: beyond basic principles*. Clevedon, UK: Multilingual Matters. 88–111.

Campbell, C. 2000. "Menter Cwm Gwendraeth: A Case Study in Community Language Planning". In C. Williams ed. *Language Revitalization: Policy and Planning in Wales*. Cardiff: University of Wales Press. 247–91.

Central Statistics Office Ireland 2003. *Census 2000: Principle Demographic Results*. Retrieved from: http://www.cso.ie/census/pdr_comment.htm#irish

Dana, J. and McMonagle, S. 1994. "Deconstructing 'Criminalisation': The Politics of Collective Education in the H-Blocks". *Irish Political Prisoner Information*. Retrieved from http://larkspirit.com/history/ira_ed.html

Denison, N. 1977. "Language Death or Language Suicide?" *International Journal of the Sociology of Language* 12: 13–22.

Edwards, J. 1985. *Language, Society, and Identity*. Oxford: Basil Blackwell.

Fishman J. 1991. *Reversing Language Shift*. Clevedon, UK: Multilingual Matters.

Fishman J. 1996. "What Do You Lose When You Lose Your Language?" In G. Catoni ed. *Stabilizing Indigenous Languages*. Flagstaff: Center for Excellence in Education, Northern Arizona University. Retrieved from: http://www.ncela.gwu.edu/miscpubs/stabilize/iii-families/lose.htm

Fishman, J. ed. 2001. *Can Threatened Languages be Saved?* Clevedon, UK: Multilingual Matters Ltd.

Gruffudd, H. 2000. "Planning for the Use of Welsh by Young People". In C. Williams ed. *Language Revitalisation*. Cardiff: University of Wales Press. 173–207.

Hickey, T. 1997. *Early Immersion Education in Ireland: na Naíonraí*. Dublin: Institiúid Teangeolaíochta Éireann.

McBroom, P. 1995. "California's Native Americans are in a Race against Time." *Berkeleyan*. Retrieved from: www.berkeley.edu/news/berkeleyan/1995/

Ó hIfearnáin, T. 2001. "Irish Language Broadcast Media: The Interaction of State Language Policy, Broadcasters and their Audiences". In H. Kelly-Holmes ed. *Minority Language Broadcasting: Breton and Irish*. Clevedon, UK: Multilingual Matters. 6–30.

Skutnabb-Kangas, T. 2000. *Linguistic Genocide in Education – Or Worldwide Diversity and Human Rights?* Mahwah, NJ and London, UK: Lawrence Erlbaum Associates.

Statistical Directorate 2003. *Welsh in Schools*. Cardiff: National Assembly for Wales.

Williams, C. ed. 2000. *Language Revitalisation*. Cardiff: University of Wales Press.

Welsh Language Board (undated) *Raising Bilingual Children: Advice for Parents*. Cardiff: Welsh Language Board.

Children with Learning Difficulties: Second Language Acquisition

Sue Davies

This paper does not set out to offer a comprehensive overview of how children with learning difficulties acquire a second language; nor does it intend to answer the question of whether children with learning difficulties *can* effectively acquire a second language. Rather, it suggests ways in which children who experience difficulties in learning may present challenges in educational settings, and how those challenges can be addressed.

What exactly do we mean by "language acquisition" in such a context – is it talking, discussion, verbal communication? Or would it be necessary to include *written competence* when discussing the effective acquisition of a second language? The latter may pose a challenge for a child already struggling to acquire the skills necessary to access a broad and balanced curriculum in its first language. What is it that a child has to develop to become an effective communicator in its second language? We often forget that although spoken language has been around in some form for over 200,000 years, the written form of communication has been in existence only for around 5,000 years – indeed, some languages remain in verbal form only, with no written format. With that in mind, is it true that language can exist in a verbal form and that acquiring a second language in verbal or conversational form only could be deemed acceptable?

How does such second language acquisition affect the child who has learning difficulties? It would be prudent to consider issues of bilingualism and the critical or sensitive age periods regarding second language acquisition. If there is a recognised critical age for first language acquisition, how can we ignore that theory when considering second language acquisition (Scovel 1988)?

The field of "learning difficulties" is vast. However, we are urged to categorise children according to their difficulties – to enable us to meet their needs effectively and to identify areas of difficulty by assessing if a child is making what may be considered "adequate progress"[1].

> Children have special educational needs if they have a learning difficulty which calls for special educational provision to be made for them. (Section 312, *Education Act 1996 (United Kingdom)*)

As laid down in the SEN Code of Practice for Wales (2002), the categories of need on which we draw are: cognition and learning difficulties; emotional, behavioural and social difficulties; sensory and physical difficulties; and communication and interaction difficulties.

Cognition and Learning Difficulties

Those may be moderate learning difficulties (MLD), severe learning difficulties (SLD), profound and multiple learning difficulties (PMLD), or specific learning difficulties (SpLD). The boundaries between MLD, SLD and PMLD are not clear.

---

[1] "Adequate progress" is a term used in the SEN code of practice for Wales 2002 (see Appendix A)

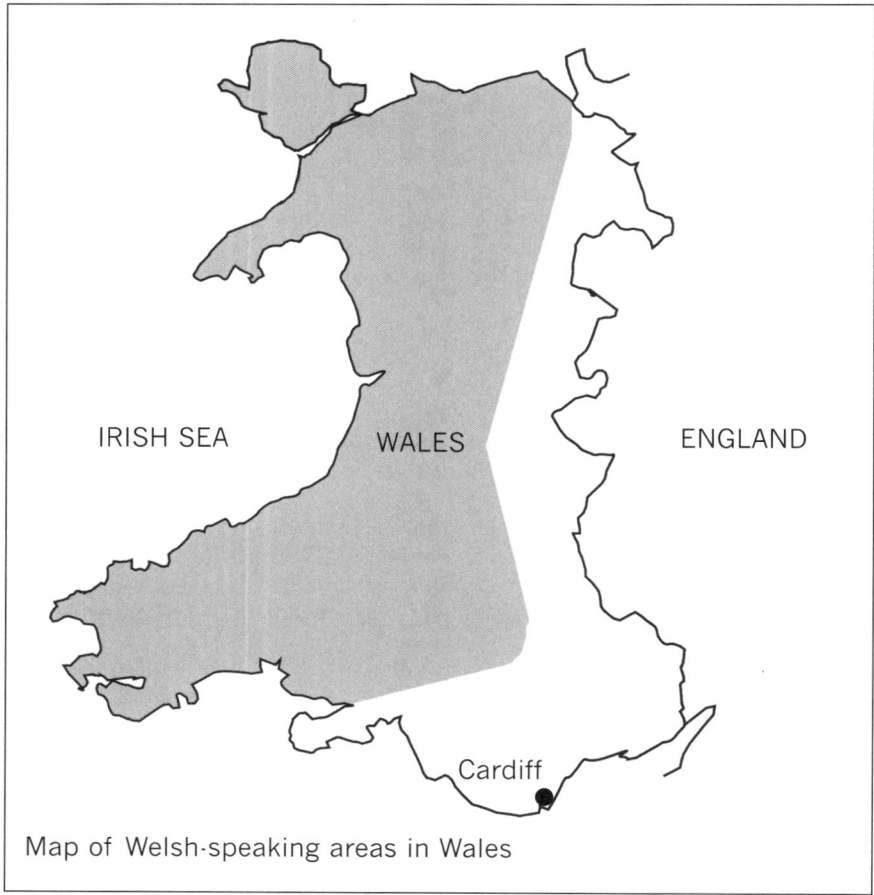

Map of Welsh-speaking areas in Wales

Emotional, Behavioural and Social Difficulties

Children affected exhibit age-inappropriate behaviour or that which seems socially inappropriate or strange. Their behaviour can interfere with the pupils themselves or the learning of peers. There are often signs of emotional turbulence, and the child may have difficulties in forming and maintaining positive relationships.

Sensory and Physical Difficulties

There is a wide spectrum of sensory, multi-sensory and physical difficulties, which may include hearing impairment, visual impairment, physical difficulties, or various combinations of those difficulties.

Communication and Interaction

Most children with learning difficulties have strengths and limitations in one, some or all areas of speech, language and communication. Their communication needs may be both diverse and complex.

> ... children and young people with speech and language delay, impairments or disorders, specific learning difficulties, such a dyslexia and dyspraxia, hearing impairment and those who demonstrate features within the autistic spectrum; ... also ... some children and young people within the autistic spectrum; ... also those with moderate, severe or profound learning difficulties. (The National Assembly for Wales 2002: 85)

When identifying learning difficulties, it is necessary to consider the child within the context of his or her home, culture, community and home language. *(In Cardiff alone, 57 community languages are used – most of the children in question are attempting to acquire English as a second language.)* However, the SEN Code of Practice for Wales urges us not to assume that a child's language status is the only reason for slow progress, and to consider that the child may have learning difficulties.

Children may also have additional difficulties that compound their learning difficulty (e.g. medical). Other conditions that may lead to learning difficulties are autism, asperger's syndrome, down's syndrome, asthma, cerebral palsy, cystic fibrosis, diabetes, ME, deaf-blindness/rubella, heart defects, epilepsy, fragile X syndrome, muscular dystrophy, spina bifida, speech and/or language impairment. There are many others.

We are all aware that the acquisition of language is probably the most amazing feat that we accomplish in our lives. Trask (1995) tells us that we manage it at an age when our skills in other areas are extremely basic. Learning languages never stops – we continue to "absorb" the latest jargon, techno-terms and fashionable phrases. Second language acquisition is yet another feat, and presents particular challenges for the child with learning difficulties. First- and second-language learning are very different experiences. We know that differences between first- and second-language learning are dependent on the age of the learner and also his or her cognitive ability. We may acknowledge that all language acquisition generally involves four distinct parts: the target language, an appropriate environment, a learning strategy, and success criteria (Gold, 1967). How, then, does the child with learning difficulties acquire a second language? Case studies may give an indication of the challenges and triumphs of some children with learning difficulties.

Schools in Wales vary in size – some primary schools house only a very small number of pupils and two teaching staff. Clearly, resources, and often opportunities, are greater in larger schools. In some counties, up to 95% of the schools are predominantly Welsh-medium. English-speaking families living in rural Wales find that their children must learn to speak Welsh if they are to attend the local school. Schools are designated categories. There are those that teach totally through the medium of Welsh; schools where the curriculum is taught predominantly through the medium of English and where Welsh is taught as a second language; some larger schools have two distinct streams, one Welsh- and one English-medium. Many schools admit pupils from a home background where at least one of the parents is a first-language English-speaker. Those children often "learn" Welsh in the school environment with limited consolidation at home. That does not appear to hinder their progress. However, the child with learning difficulties may find it challenging to encounter a second language in the learning environment without support being available at home.

Tomos

Tomos is a year 2 pupil (seven years old) and experiences moderate learning difficulties. His father speaks Welsh, and his mother is attempting to learn the language. Tomos attends a large school with over 200 pupils. The school has both a Welsh and an English stream, and when he commenced school in the nursery setting, he was unable to understand or communicate through the medium of Welsh. His parents chose for him to learn Welsh by requesting that he be placed in the Welsh stream. Tomos showed a variety of difficulties including:

- *low levels of attainment across the board in all forms of assessment;*
- *difficulty in acquiring skills (notably literacy and numeracy) on which much of his learning depends;*
- *difficulty with abstract ideas and generalising;*
- *difficulty in acquiring Welsh as a second language;*
- *difficulty in socialising with peers (many of whom were from homes where Welsh was the 'home' language).*

An educational psychology assessment indicated that Tomos has moderate learning difficulties, and it was suggested that those difficulties would be compounded should he remain in the Welsh stream. Consultation with Tomos's parents led to his being transferred into the English stream, where he is now progressing at an adequate pace and responding positively to the intervention specified in his individual education plan.

Tomos continues to be offered opportunities to learn and use Welsh as a second language, although he is instructed in English, and all his written and recording work is through the medium of English. He continues to experience difficulties when attempting to learn Welsh as a second language.

Tomos is fortunate in that the school he attends is large enough to be able to accommodate both Welsh and English streams, and consequently he is able to maintain social links with his friends. The head teacher has no qualms about having this "safety net" for the small number of children who cannot cope with the introduction of a second language.

The way learning disabilities impact on the learning of language is consistent – a pupil with dyslexia in one language will usually, but, it should be stressed, not always, experience similar difficulties in another.

Gareth

Gareth is a year 3 pupil who attends a school where Welsh is the main medium of delivery for the curriculum in the infant phase (up to and including year 2). Neither of Gareth's parents speaks Welsh, and both are attempting to learn the language, so they are not yet able to support him at home effectively. When Gareth showed initial signs of experiencing difficulties, the school staff were quick to intervene with an individual education plan tailored to meet his needs. A review of that plan showed that Gareth continued to experience difficulties and that his progress was limited in all areas of the curriculum. It became apparent that Gareth had specific learning difficulties in the form of dyslexia. His parents were consulted, and although they had attempted to consolidate schoolwork with similar programmes at home, language proved to be a barrier for them.

Gareth was supported through a multi-sensory programme of work and encouraged to develop his second-language skills through games, rhymes, story-telling and (endless) repetition. He was also part of a whole-school approach adopted to promote effective acquisition of Welsh as a second language. He is encouraged to use Welsh verbally as much as possible, and to progress to written Welsh at a slow but steady pace.

Schools benefit from adopting a whole-school approach to learning by acting on the following principles:

- the development of whole-school practices – this will include ALL staff (teaching, non-teaching, voluntary, catering, domestic)
- focusing on the National Curriculum/Cwricwlwm Cymraeg
- effective teaching (multi-sensory delivery, positive reinforcement)
- effective planning (including in this process: ALL staff, parents, pupils)
- early identification
- early and appropriate intervention
- adopting process monitoring and review
- ensuring sufficient Welsh-speaking professionals to meet the needs of pupils with SEN
- establishing balance between demand and supply for Welsh-medium provision

Learning styles must also be taken into account. We all favour one learning style over others, although we may not be aware of it. For instance, visual, auditory and kinaesthetic learners each have their preferred route for receiving information. If that information is delivered to them through an alternative route, the child will feel uncomfortable. Those learning styles must be taken into account when teaching second-language skills.

Sarah

Sarah has emotional, behavioural and social difficulties (EBSD), and becomes very frustrated when she believes herself incapable of successfully undertaking a task. She lives with her mother; her maternal grandfather is the only Welsh-speaker in the family. Sarah is reported to be unresponsive to Welsh spoken at home. She becomes extremely disruptive in Welsh activities in her year 3 class at a predominantly English-medium school. She has a statement of special educational needs. Her statement identifies that, along with her EBSD, her concentration span is less than three minutes. The statement also identifies that Sarah is a visual learner. She has in-class support for 15 hours a week to help keep her on task. A bilingual classroom assistant sensitively provides such support.

Sarah is reluctant to be part of an interactive oral language programme, often becoming frustrated and disruptive. Sarah's teacher has adopted a flexible approach to teaching Welsh as a second language – noting that "what works for a pupil with SEN will work for all pupils". Consequently, the pupils use a range of activities to gain experience in using Welsh for play, basic conversation, making simple requests, giving instructions. Sarah is encouraged to participate at her own level, tasks are changed often, and she is given many opportunities to experience success. She is given visual cues and prompts to support the verbal element of her language programme. That builds her self-esteem and increases her motivation in the task.

Staff working with her use only standard, commonly used vocabulary and shorter, less complex phrases and sentences. It is anticipated that frequent exposure to Welsh in this way will enable Sarah to acquire basic second-language skills. Sarah currently has a bank of around 100 individual words and is able to use them in very basic sentences when she allows herself to rise to the challenge.

All learners vary in their strengths, limitations, needs, interests, motivation and learning styles. The child with autism will have limitations in the areas of communication, imagination and social relationships. They often have different motivational triggers, and sometimes obsessions with specific objects.

Rhodri

Rhodri is a ten-year-old boy who was identified as being autistic when he was five. His characteristics are those of classic (Kanner's) autism, and include poor communication and interaction, limited eye contact, echolalia, no comprehension of the subtleties of language, and no imaginative play. Rhodri is obsessed with machinery and tractors.

At infant phase, attending his local mainstream school, Rhodri began communicating slowly with his parents, teachers, carers and a small number of his peer group through gestures and verbal sounds. His main method of communication was Makaton (a sign language developed particularly for those with additional needs). Rhodri's family are first-language Welsh-speakers, and he attends a rural Welsh-medium school. Rhodri was introduced to English at a very young age, and he has effectively been brought up in a bilingual environment. Because of his limited communication skills, Rhodri does not "speak".

Work has been undertaken mainly by his learning support assistant, or LSA, who is trained to have educational input. It has been a long process, starting with comprehensible input and exposure to English – always slower and clearer than what would be regarded as "normal" speech. Wherever possible, visual cues are used to trigger positive responses from Rhodri – usually those will involve machinery and tractors. That motivates Rhodri to learn. The school uses PECS, the picture exchange communication system, with Rhodri. He uses pictures to communicate, and individual words are given in Welsh and English in parallel. However, the Welsh language is always used at home, and he appears to have a better understanding of it.

Attending a mainstream primary school has allowed Rhodri to learn alongside his peers, and at his own pace, in a small, secure environment. However, now in year 6, his friends are due to transfer to comprehensive school in the autumn. Following extensive consultation with his parents, it has been decided that Rhodri will transfer to a special school where his severe needs can be met by specialist staff and individual programmes. It is anticipated that he will continue to be encouraged to "communicate" bilingually, and allowed to progress at his own pace.

Can we, after reading about Rhodri, argue that he could be classed as bilingual? He can comprehend the two languages to roughly the same level, even though he uses pictorial prompts to do so.

Nia

Nia is a five-year-old girl with severe learning difficulties. She has hypertonic cerebral palsy, exhibiting involuntary movement, poor head control and limited trunk control. Nia's vision is severely impaired, although her sense of hearing is acute. She responds positively to all sounds, but her verbal communication skills are limited to utterance in the form of a soft "coo", grunting, crying and laughter. She indicates her preferences in that way.

Nia's parents are first-language Welsh-speakers, and she attends a special school that is able to offer her a varied programme with interdisciplinary collaboration. The school attempts to ensure that all professionals working with Nia can communicate through the medium of Welsh, her "home" language.

However, a lack of Welsh-speaking specialists such as speech and language therapists means that the school has had to introduce English into Nia's learning programme. Nia's programme relies heavily on her relative strength in auditory skills. Story tapes in both Welsh and English are played to her at school and at home. Individual words and objects are described in both languages, although she responds more favourably to Welsh.

The children described above are at different levels of ability and differing levels of second language acquisition. However, those working closest with them point out that each of those special children is working at a level which allows the achievement of his or her full potential. In relative terms, one might say that their second-language skills are developing in parallel with other cognitive skills.

There are no definitive answers on *how* to teach a second language to a child with learning difficulties. It is clear that effective second-language learning will take place only when the appropriate conditions prevail. Those conditions must be planned effectively, the delivery must be sensitive to the needs and abilities of the learner, and the programme of intervention must build on the child's strengths rather than highlight its limitations. It is clear that children must have a reason to communicate before they can take that action. To reflect on the question – *can* children with learning difficulties effectively acquire a second language? – it must be weighed against the ability, difficulties and potential of that child.

References

Brown, H. D. and Gonzo, S. T. eds. 1994. *Readings on Second Language Acquisition*, Upper Saddle River, NJ: Prentice-Hall.

Cynulliad Cenedlaethol Cymru/The National Assembly for Wales. 2002. *Cod Ymarfer Anghenion Addysgol Arbennig Cymru* (2002), *Special Educational Needs Code of Practice for Wales*.

Scovel, T. 1988. *A Time to Speak: A Psycholinguistic Inquiry into a Critical Period for Human Speech*. New York: Newbury House.

The Lesser-Used Language as a Medium of Instruction or as a Subject: the Basque Experience

Joana Abrisketa

This paper aims to provide a useful analysis of the current position of Basque in education. The ultimate goal of this descriptive analysis is to identify elements of potential general use. The most useful element that we have in the Basque Country is the system of linguistic models in education, which will form the subject of this article.

The Basque Country

Before proceeding to an analysis of the current situation of the Basque language in education, it may be useful to provide some data on the political and institutional reality of the country. The troubled nature of relations between the Basque Country and the Spanish state must first be understood for a better idea of the linguistic aspects of education.

The Basque Country is located in south-western Europe, at the western corner of the Pyrenees. Its area is approximately 20,000 sq. km., 18,000 of them taken up by the Southern Basque Country, within the Kingdom of Spain, with the remaining 2,000 forming the French Basque Country, within the French Republic.

The Southern Basque Country is divided into four historical territories or provinces: *Biscay* (with its capital in *Bilbao*), *Alava* (with its capital in *Vitoria*), *Gipuscoa* (with its capital in *San Sebastián*) and *Navarra* ('Navarre', with its capital in *Pamplona*). The concept of the Basque Country referred initially to Basque-speaking populations and, subsequently, to lands occupied by them.

Nowadays, the Basque Autonomous Community, Navarre and the French Basque Country are the three territories where Basque is spoken. However it is necessary to clarify that there is a strongly held political viewpoint whereby Navarre is not a Basque territory. In Navarre, Basque identity is not shared by a large part of the population.

The current total population of the Basque Country, including Navarre, is around 2.8 million, with 90% of residents living in the part of the Basque Country within the Spanish state, and the rest France.

Institutional Organisation and Political Conflict

As far as Spain is concerned, under the 1978 constitution, the kingdom retains the structure of a single, united state, although it is characterised by a high degree of political decentralisation affecting the entire country.

The 1978 constitution strongly asserts the principle of national unity and does not recognise differences among the peoples within the state. At the same time, however, the constitution acknowledges the existence of 'nationalities' and regions within the state and envisages the possibility of territorial self-government for them, without defining a map or a definitive model. Constitutional development has given rise to the division of Spanish territory into 17 autonomous communities, each of which is endowed with broad legislative and executive powers.

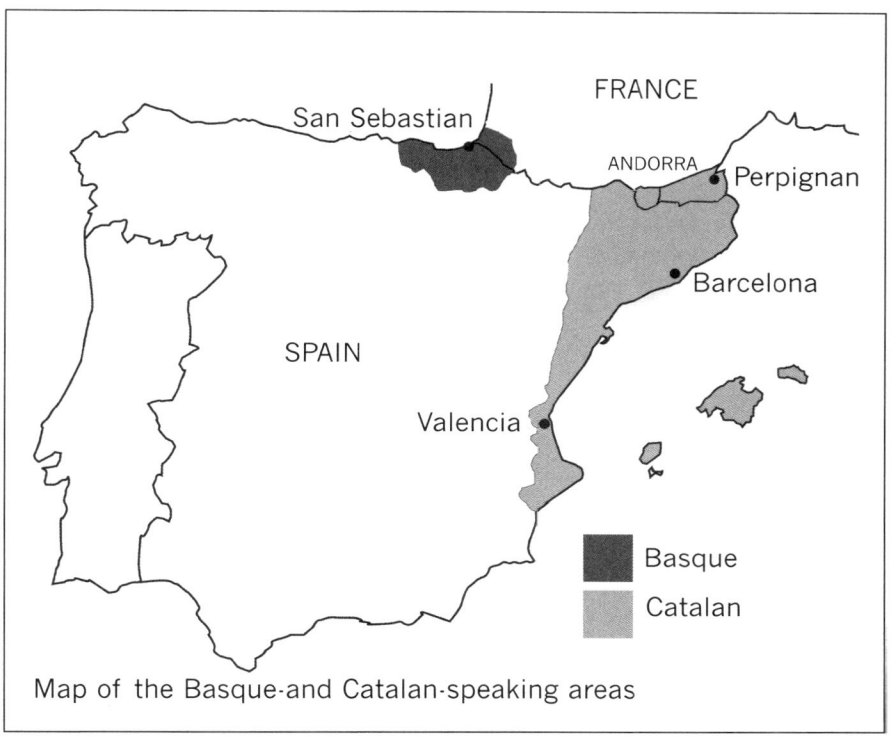

Map of the Basque-and Catalan-speaking areas

The Basque territories on the Iberian peninsula included in the Spanish state are divided into two autonomous or self-governing administrative regions: the Community of Navarre, and the Autonomous Community of the Basque Country. Both communities have their own parliament, elected by universal suffrage, and their respective Governments, with legislative and executive powers in fields such as internal security, public health, primary and secondary education, public works and taxes.

The current Basque conflict is not directly connected with the use of violence but with the political dispute surrounding sovereignty and the right to self-determination. In that sense, we can distinguish between the Basque-orientated political parties, in favour of the right to self-determination of the Basque population, and the Spanish-orientated parties, defending the contrary position.

This environment also affects the question of protecting the minority language. There is a clear correlation between Basque-speakers and support for Basque nationalist parties, whereas it is generally still very difficult for representatives of the 'Spanish' parties to communicate in the language.

The Northern Basque Country is located politically in one of the French *départements*, the Atlantic Pyrenees (in French, *Pyrénnées Atlantiques*). The population of the Basque area is only 40% of the total population of the *département*, whose capital, Pau, is located outside the Basque area. The *département* forms part of the French region of *Aquitaine*, whose capital is the city of Bordeaux. The regions in France enjoy some administrative powers, but no system of political autonomy has been developed in the French Republic. In the last few years there has been a significant movement within the Northern Basque Country, with the support of the majority of the municipalities, demanding the creation of a new Basque *département*. However, successive French governments have failed to take into account such demands.

The Basque Language: Taxonomy and Sociolinguistic Reality

The Basque language has been shown to be the last remaining European language from before the introduction of Indo-European tongues to the European mainland. It has no obvious relationship with any other language, and its origins are uncertain. Basque is not an Indo-European language, although the vocabulary shows strong influence from Latin, Spanish and French. On the other hand, Basque has some characteristics which make it completely different from Spanish. For that reason, unlike Catalonia or Galicia, where people speak Catalan or Galego as well as Spanish, almost 50% of those in the Basque Country cannot express themselves in Basque. The structure of sentences, the use of verbs, declination and so on have nothing to do with the dominant language of Spanish.

Nowadays we normally distinguish eight dialects in Basque. In 1964, the Academy for the Basque Language (*Euskaltzaindia*) codified the unified Basque (*Euskera Batua*), with a common standard for writing, the variety used in the mass media and public administration. That so-called "unified Basque" is also the Basque used in education. Thanks to the standardisation of Basque, it is now a medium of instruction.

Today, there are approximately 652,000 Basque-speakers in the three territories. The actual number of Basque-speakers and their percentage of the total population vary greatly depending on the territory in question. Such differences are shown not only in the absolute and relative figures, but also in the different age groups which compose the Basque population. Nowadays, more than 90% of Basque-speakers are bilingual, knowing Spanish or French as well as Basque.

Social use of the language on the street is even less, especially in those areas in which bilingual and monolingual Spanish-speakers live together, as happens in all urban areas over 10,000 inhabitants. Only two thirds of Basque-speakers use *Euskara* within their families.

As for Basque in education, until recently Basque was not a means of transmitting scientific knowledge but rather a familiar and colloquial language. Today, therefore, we are working on a process of modernising the language. That means finding and coining new words and terminology to take account of contemporary realities as well as the translation of texts.

Finally, we must accept that Basque authors, books, and readers are in the minority. One need only visit a bookshop to compare the number of books written in Basque and Spanish. At the same time, even if efforts are being undertaken to introduce webpages in Basque, use of the Basque language on the Internet is still limited.

Legal Framework for the Basque Language

We shall refer to the legal framework for the Basque language only in the Autonomous Community of the Basque Country, since that is the most developed.

The Spanish constitution makes common provision for the legal status of languages within the Spanish state. Article 3 of the *Spanish Constitution* of 1978 states that:

1. Castilian is the official Spanish language of the State. All Spaniards have the duty to know it and the right to use it.
2. The other Spanish languages shall also be official in the respective Autonomous Communities in accordance with their Statutes.
3. The wealth of different language varieties in Spain is cultural heritage which shall be the object of special respect and protection.

The actual Spanish constitution establishes official status for the Spanish language over the entire territory of the state, including also monolingual Catalan-, Galician- or Basque-speaking rural areas. That means that constitutional provisions consolidate the presence of Spanish everywhere, including an obligation on citizens (although not foreign residents) to know the language.

The Basque Autonomous Community

The *Autonomy Statute of the Basque Country* was passed by the Spanish Parliament and approved by the Basque people by referendum in October 1979. Article 6 refers to the Basque language as follows:

1. Euskera, the Basque People's own language, shall, like Spanish, have the status of an official language in Euskadi. All its inhabitants have the right to know and use both languages.
2. The common institutions of the Autonomous Community, taking into account the sociolinguistic diversity of the Basque Country, shall guarantee the use of both languages, controlling their official status, and shall effect and regulate whatever measures and means are necessary to ensure knowledge of them.
3. No one may suffer discrimination for reasons of language.
4. The Royal Academy of the Basque Language is the official advisory institution in matters regarding Euskera.
5. Given that Euskera is the heritage of other Basque territories and communities, the Autonomous Community of the Basque Country may request the Spanish Government, in addition to whatever ties and correspondence are maintained with academic and cultural institutions, to conclude and, where necessary, to submit to the Spanish State Parliament for authorisation, those treaties or agreements that will make it possible to establish cultural relations with the States where such territories lie and communities reside, with a view to safeguarding and promoting Euskera.

The Basque language is proclaimed as an official language all over the territory of the BAC. Therefore, every person, Basque or otherwise, can deal with any arm of public administration located inside the BAC using Basque as the normal language of communication.

In 1982, the *Act for the Normalisation of the Use of Basque* was passed by the Basque parliament with the approval of all political parties, including the "national" Spanish ones.

The Act develops the provision of the Autonomy Statute proclaiming the official status of the language over the entire territory of the BAC.

The 1982 Act also sets up a relevant body: the Institute for Literacy and the Teaching of Adults (HABE), which holds funded courses both for adult learners of the language and for illiterate Basque-speakers.

Since the approval of the *Language Act* in 1982, a raft of detailed legislation on linguistic matters has been enacted by the Basque government. Among those regulations we can highlight the programmes to fund the learning of Euskara by teachers and other civil servants and the planning of Basque administrative jobs according to the linguistic requirements of the population. Some 7% of teachers in the public sector are bilingual.

The Basque Language in Education

The education system in Spain, as well as in the Basque Country, is divided into **five stages**: nursery and infant education (birth to six years old), primary education (six to 12), Secondary education (12 to 16) and post-compulsory education (16 to 18 years old). At 16, one may leave one's studies to work. The purpose of the final period is preparation for university.

Four Linguistic Models

The implementation of the *Language Act* of 1982 included for the education system the establishment of **four linguistic models** in Basque schools.

In nursery and infant education, there are no subjects as such. The education system is one of immersion in another language, in this case, Basque. Owing to the immersion system, if children begin school when they are two or three years old, they can understand and communicate in Basque almost as well as in Spanish.

Given that the dominant language is Spanish, immersion activity must be focused on the reinforcement of Basque. The degree of difficulty with Basque is bigger than with Spanish, and children, like everyone else, tend to take the path of least resistance.

Linguistic models are applied for 6–16 year-old students, in primary and secondary school.

In **Model A**, also called the 'Spanish model', children learn everything through Spanish and have Basque only as a subject *(Euskara como materia)*, known as 'Basque Language and Literature'. Basque as a subject is taught for four hours per week. Schools cannot determine the number of hours. Every year at the beginning of the course the Basque Government issues a circular, agreed by central government, laying down the number of hours.

The medium of instruction is Spanish, so Model A does not ensure a good knowledge of the Basque language for children at the end of their compulsory education period. That is why the current tendency is to introduce art and physical education through Basque to reinforce communication in the language. The aim of the Basque government is to guarantee that students can speak and write correctly in both Spanish and Basque when they finish their compulsory education, but bilingualism is not achieved with model A. For next year, 7% of students have chosen model A (totally Spanish), compared with 8.1% last year.

Model B divides the teaching of the different subjects between Basque and Spanish, but not equally. Maths and Spanish are taught through Spanish, and students learn to read and write in the language. Most of the subjects are taught in Basque, and the language used by the teacher is Basque. The rest of the subjects are taught in Basque. This year, 29.8% have chosen model B, fewer than last year, when 30.5% did so.

Finally, **Model D** covers full-blown Basque-medium education, except for Spanish language and literature, taught as a subject for four hours per week. In this model, compared with the others, reading and writing are learnt in Basque. For next year, 63.2% of parents have chosen model D for their children, compared with the 61.4 % last year. Only in model D is bilingualism guaranteed.

The so-called **Model X** (exclusively through Spanish) is applied only in private schools with special teaching systems, the American School and the French School, for example. Also, some students, for exceptional reasons (for example, a short period of residence within the BAC) can be exempted from learning the Basque language.

The provision of the models by the Basque schools is conditioned. on the one hand, by demand and, on the other, by the capacity of teachers to use *Euskara*. The evolution during the last 20 years has been extremely positive both in the number of teachers with the ability to express themselves in Basque and in the number of children whose language of learning is *Euskara*. In the BAC, most of the private educational centres (normally founded by Catholic church institutions) receive funds from the Basque government. In that sense, there is not very much difference in the implementation of the linguistic models between public and private centres although, in general, Basque is used slightly more widely in the public sector.

Advantages and Disadvantages of the Four Models

Model A: Non-Basque-speaking parents say that with this model they will be able to help their children, something that gives them security. However, from a linguistic perspective, bilingualism is not achieved. That is why the Basque government is now trying to improve model A with the introduction of Basque as a medium of instruction for art and physical education, i.e. as a vehicular language and not simply as a subject. As most families tend to choose models B and especially D, model A is now becoming the preserve of immigrant families.

Model B: Students must learn and write in their mother tongue, and that will help them. The disadvantage is that with this model we do not achieve bilingualism, since the dominant language is Spanish. It is now being assimilated into model D.

Model D: Advantages: we get completely bilingual people, even if the dominant language in a social context is Spanish. Another advantage is that, for bilingual people, the process of learning a third language becomes very easy. It seems that our brain develops a special capacity for languages. The disadvantage is that students in model D deal with two very different languages, one which is used in school, and the other which is used on the street and with their families. Often, as the dominant language is Spanish, school becomes a sort of ghetto where they learn abstract concepts, and they do not apply what they have learnt there to their social reality. In that sense, I have studied in model D and am now an international public law teacher through the medium of Basque. From my experience, I would say that we must be more flexible with contact languages. For a teacher, as well as for students, the objective is the communication of real rather than abstract facts. To achieve a truly bilingual society we must involve ourselves in two simultaneous processes, communication and the modernisation of Basque. If we modernise Basque but students do not understand what we are saying, we are not achieving communication. If we communicate with students but we do not try to give them a good command of the language, we are not doing anything to promote it.

Higher Education

As regards higher education, in the BAC there are three universities. The University of the Basque Country is the public one, boasting around 60,000 students at its three campuses of Bilbao, Vitoria and San Sebastian. The University of Deusto, located mainly in Bilbao, is an old Catholic university, with 14,000 students of law and humanities. Finally, the University of Mondragon is a small centre offering technical studies relating to the industrial sector. The three, especially the public one, offer part of the curriculum in *Euskara*. Several degrees can be completed entirely through Basque.

In recent years, efforts have been concentrated on standardising and modernising Basque, creating bilingual education and bilingual texts. Often, at university, lessons are given through Basque but the textbooks used are in Spanish, since we do not have Basque textbooks. Now we are dealing with the translation work, which implies a process of 'linguistic creation'. As Basque is an archaic language, we often find that we have no terminology for modern concepts and have to create the words. Then the problem is that one uses those new words in class, and students do not know or 'like' them. Their argument is that if we explain everything in Basque, they will not understand reality, which is mostly experienced through Spanish. For that reason, we often teach lessons using both Basque and Spanish words.

References

Cobreros Mendazona, E. ed. 1990. *Jornadas Sobre el Régimen Jurídico del Euskera*. Oñati: Basque Institute for Public Administration.

Cobreros Mendazona, E. ed. 1989. *El Régimen Jurídico de la Oficialidad del Euskera*. Oñati: Basque Institute for Public Administration.

Fossas, E. 1999. *Asymmetry and Plurinationality in Spain*. Barcelona: Institut de Ciències Polítiques i Socials.

Intxausti, J. 1990. *Euskara: Euskaldunon Hizkuntza*. Vitoria-Gasteiz: Basque Government.

Nuñez Astrain, L. 2004. *El Euskera Arcaico. Extensión y Parentescos*, Txalaparta, Tafalla, Navarra.

Petschen Verdaguer, S. 1989. *Las Minorías Lingüísticas de Europa Occidental: Documentos (1492–1989)*. Vitoria-Gastiez: Basque Parliament.

Relevant web pages on the situation of the Basque language:

Basque Government: www.euskadi.net/euskara
Behatokia (Basque Linguistic Rights Watch): www.beatokia.org
Kontseilua (The Council of Social Organisations in favour of the Basque Language): www.kontseilua.org
Argia (Basque magazine): www.argia.com

Accommodating Linguistic Diversity in Hungary's Education System

Judit Solymosi

According to the census of 2001, some 3.2% of the Hungarian population belong to one of the 13 national and ethnic minorities living in the country. However, scientific research and minority organisations estimate that the real proportion is higher, accounting for some 8%–10% of the population. In Hungary, there is no system of registering ethnicity, as data on ethnic affiliation are considered sensitive and qualify for enhanced protection.

The *Hungarian Act on the Rights of National and Ethnic Minorities* covers only traditional minorities, that is, ethnic groups that have lived on the territory of Hungary for at least 100 years. The Act lists the minorities recognised, which are the Armenians, Bulgarians, Croats, Germans, Greeks, Poles, Roma, Romanians, Ruthenians, Serbs, Slovaks, Slovenes and Ukrainians. They speak 14 different languages, as the Roma community has two mother tongues: Romani and Beash, the latter an archaic dialect of the Romanian language. Details of Hungary's minorities based on the 2001 Census are presented in Figures 1 and 2. Figure 1 presents the data by each of Hungary's 19 counties and Budapest; Figure 2 presents the data at national level and makes comparisons with the 1991 Census. The data shows the impossibility of drawing regional maps of minority language use in Hungary.

Main Characteristics of the Minority Communities

1. Minority communities are scattered throughout the country. They typically live in rural areas, in villages and, in general, constitute a minority even within those settlements. Of the 3,145 settlements in Hungary, there are only 235 where no one declared minority affiliation. As responses to the questions on the census form were anonymous and voluntary, the data are indicative.
2. Minority communities are very different in size. The Roma community probably amounts to more than 500,000 people, while there are also very small communities numbering only one or two thousand members. In most cases, those, too, live scattered across different regions.
3. Historically, the biggest minority communities arrived in Hungary in the seventeenth and eighteenth centuries. In general, they left their home region before the development of a standard literary language and therefore speak an archaic and dialectal version used centuries ago. The communities have reached a high level of linguistic assimilation. Currently, there is a shift from the native language to the use of Hungarian. In most minority families, the language is no longer passed on to the next generation, and Hungarian has become the dominant language. On the other hand, there is also a shift from a dialect-type mother tongue to the standard language of the mother country. Learning in schools is not based on local dialects but provides education in the standard language. As a result, there is a linguistic gap between the school and the home as well as between the different generations.
4. Parallel to such linguistic assimilation, it is interesting to note that people's awareness of their minority background is increasing. That means that minority communities profess stronger feelings of identity, but their knowledge of the

Map of Hungary and the surrounding countries

mother tongue is weaker. That also means that their willingness to use their mother tongue in administration and before the courts, but also in everyday communication, is not obvious. Hungary accords minorities extensive rights to use their mother tongue, but individual members of the communities do not often avail themselves of them. It very rarely happens that a member of a minority group submits a document to the local authority in his or her language or asks to use that language before a court.

After that overview of this complex situation, we should like to take the problems one by one and see what solutions have been developed to address them.

Anonymity

As minority affiliation is a sensitive private issue, local municipal government will organise and provide minority education only on the initiative of parents. According to the law, a request by the parents of eight pupils belonging to the same minority is sufficient, and it obliges the municipality to organise a class with minority education. In this case, declaring one's identity is voluntary, and it helps people avail themselves of certain additional rights.

Geographical Dispersal

Geographical dispersal can cause problems, mainly at the level of secondary schools. The number of pupils wishing to attend a minority secondary school may not be

42   Judit Solymosi

Figure 1: Minority population per county in Hungary in the light of the 2001 census

Minorities

County	Bulgarian	Roma	Greek	Croatian	Polish	German	Armenian	Romanian	Serbian	Slovak	Slovenian	Ruthenian	Ukrainian	Total	County
Budapest	784	12273	1522	771	1185	7042	364	1205	996	1528	359	430	1425	29884	Budapest
Bács-Kiskun	28	6026	13	1695	83	4476	6	175	307	614	66	34	257	13780	Bács-Kiskun
Baranya	54	8552	75	4608	125	14205	13	155	324	70	46	22	139	28388	Baranya
Békés	22	4989	13	30	47	964	19	3233	316	5022	113	19	144	14931	Békés
Borsod-A.-Z.	55	45525	136	16	185	1159	8	137	18	1150	57	168	285	48899	Borsod-A.-Z.
Csongrád	40	2844	57	129	91	560	18	441	580	359	43	25	192	5379	Csongrád
Fejér	16	3755	324	65	122	2151	23	162	69	133	45	37	195	7097	Fejér
Győr-S.-M.	16	1368	26	1954	95	1808	8	99	36	84	77	11	138	5720	Győr-S.-M.
Hajdú-Bihar	21	10836	32	15	74	319	20	669	16	48	32	32	208	12322	Hajdú-Bihar
Heves	9	12095	16	6	61	219	5	145	7	222	18	23	98	12924	Heves
Jász-NK.-SZ.	18	11679	16	12	49	218	4	112	16	70	26	21	155	12396	Jász-NK.-SZ.
Kom.-Eszt.	32	2337	37	40	126	5119	5	140	28	2795	30	22	133	10844	Kom.-Eszt.
Nógrád	10	9209	6	9	34	744	5	58	3	1778	29	11	73	11969	Nógrád
Pest	187	11252	177	344	355	10343	52	557	884	3472	193	116	601	28533	Pest
Somogy	7	9440	11	720	68	965	14	101	71	29	44	19	112	11601	Somogy
Szab.-Sz.-B.	21	25612	13	6	47	727	20	121	12	146	31	29	472	27257	Szab.-Sz.-B.
Tolna	11	4783	8	84	43	6660	14	126	82	72	27	12	99	12021	Tolna
Vas	5	1378	8	2321	36	1023	6	73	11	29	1706	16	76	6688	Vas
Veszprém	14	2054	11	61	97	3077	10	224	22	60	33	36	186	5885	Veszprém
Zala	8	4039	8	2734	39	454	6	62	18	12	39	15	82	7516	Zala
Total	1358	190046	2509	15620	2962	62233	620	7995	3816	17693	3014	1098	5070		

Based on the data of the Central Statistical Office
Prepared by the Office for National and Ethnic Minorities
Numbers above 1,000 are highlighted with grey

Accommodating Linguistic Diversity in Hungary's Education System 43

Figure 2: RESULTS OF THE 2001 CENSUS

Minority group	Assumptions of mother tongue			Assumptions of minority belonging			Number of those attached to minority culture and traditions	Number of those using the language with friends	Proportion of language users as compared to mother tongue
	1990	2001	Change %	Number 1990	2001	Change %	2001	2001	2001 %
Bulgarian	1370	1299	-5.2	...	1358		1693	1118	86.1
Gypsy/Roma	48072	48685	1.3	142683	190046	33.2	129259	53323	109.5
Greek	1640	1921	17.1	...	2509		6140	1974	102.8
Croatian	17577	14345	-18.4	13570	15620	15.1	19715	14788	103.1
Polish	3788	2580	-31.9	...	2962		3983	2659	103.1
German	37511	33792	-9.9	30824	62233	101.9	88416	53040	157.0
Armenian	37	294	694.6	...	620		836	300	102.0
Romanian	8730	8482	-2.8	10740	7995	-25.6	9162	8215	96.9
Serbian	2953	3388	14.7	2905	3816	31.4	5279	4186	123.6
Slovak	12745	11816	-7.3	10459	17692	69.2	26631	18056	152.8
Slovenian	2627	3187	21.3	1930	3040	57.5	3442	3119	97.9
Ruthenian	674	1113			1098		1292	1068	96.0
Ukrainian	(together)	4885		...	5070		4779	4519	92.5
Total	137724	135787	-1.4	213111	314059		300627	166365	122.5
Budapest		16061			29884		35372	21958	136.7
Countryside		53973			115262		115520	66920	124.0
Villages		65754			168914		149735	77488	117.8

Based on the data of the Central Office of Statistics
Compiled by the Office for National and Ethnic Minorities

sufficient in one settlement to provide a secondary school or minority class or study group for them. However, in that case, too, at the request of the parents of eight pupils, the state is obliged to organise their schooling. That can result in running one or two secondary boarding schools which draw pupils from a larger region or from all over the country. Altogether, there are 26 secondary grammar schools and 14 technical schools or vocational training centres providing minority education or teaching a minority language.

The *Public Education Act* offers another possibility that can provide a good solution if there are fewer than eight minority pupils in a given settlement. It is a new form of schooling named "complementary minority education", which makes participation in minority education within the normal school system possible even for minorities that do not have a minority school. In this case, pupils attending normal school elsewhere have additional afternoon courses organised specifically for them in one venue – sometimes with the help of itinerant teachers – to teach them their minority language and culture. The certificate that the pupils get entitles them to pass the so-called "maturity exam" in the given subject and thus to enter higher education.

Groups of Different Sizes

The 13 minorities living in Hungary can be divided into three groups. The first group comprises the Romanians, the Croatians, the Serbians, the Slovenians, the Germans and the Slovaks. They are typically rather large communities, or used to be larger in the past, before changes to the borders of Hungary. That is why they have for decades had a well-established system of educational institutions comprising state-run schools and nursery schools. Incidentally, those are the languages for which Hungary has made commitments under Part III of the *European Charter for Regional or Minority Languages*.

The second group comprises the Roma minority. Here the main problem is not the provision of mother-tongue education, as 85% of the Roma population lost their native language centuries ago and speak only Hungarian. The Ministry of Education intends to fight the problem of segregation primarily by promoting, but also by financially supporting, integrated education. A well-established system of scholarships for Roma students is stimulating Roma young people effectively to attend secondary and higher education. As for education in the Romani and Beash languages, there are currently 8 Romani and 11 Beash primary schools where they are taught. The Gandhi Secondary Grammar School, with excellent minority education and outstanding results, has gained Europe-wide recognition, and several colleges and universities have a Department of Romology.

The third group comprises the small minorities that either do not have a network of schools, or have just one (Bulgarian, Ruthenian, Greek) – or even none (the Ukrainian, Armenian and Polish minorities). In the case of those communities, the organisation of minority education typically started only after the adoption of the Minority Act and can be made a reality only gradually. To teach the native language, they have some out-of-school courses, so-called 'Sunday schools', which constitute a special form of minority education and are organised outside the school system. In general, the organisers and operators of that form of education are the national minority self-governments, with financing from the Ministry of Education. Of course, the possibility of the "eight parents" initiative is also open to those small minorities.

Knowledge of the Native Language

Research findings from the academic year 1999-2000 show that, due to the high level of linguistic assimilation, a significant part of minority children do not speak the minority language at all, or their language skills are quite weak. According to research findings, the proportion of pupils with a minority mother tongue enrolled in minority schools is only between 5%–10% in the case of the German and Slovak children. It has to be noted, however, that his proportion reaches 60%–85% in the case of the Croatian and Serbian pupils.

To respond to that diversity, there are three types of minority education. The most frequent type are schools where the minority language is taught as a second language for at least four or five periods a week. The second type consists of bilingual schools where a significant proportion of subjects (at least 50%) are taught in a minority language, while the other subjects are taught through Hungarian. The number of schools teaching all subjects – with the exception of Hungarian language and literature – through the native language of minorities is rather low because of the lack of qualified teachers and the lack of children wishing to enrol.

Proportion of Minorities within the Hungarian Population

Here we should mention the issue of higher education. Hungary is unable to ensure higher education in minority languages in all scientific fields. We can only train teachers of minority languages and literature, and there are no courses offered in the minority language to doctors, lawyers or mathematicians; or even to teachers of other subjects such as biology and chemistry. For that reason, bilateral agreements between the kin states and Hungary ensure the full-time or part-time training of minority undergraduate and PhD students in their mother country. Diplomas obtained in the kin state are accepted in Hungary. Another solution to the problem of the insufficient number of qualified teachers of natural sciences in the minority languages is the 'importation' of teachers from the mother countries.

Such importation and the translation of schoolbooks are only a temporary solution; the development of schoolbooks more suitable to the specific needs of minorities living in Hungary is being co-ordinated by the Ministry of Education.

Higher Financial Needs of Minority Education

Public education is financed from the state budget through normative *per capita* (per child) support to municipalities. As minority education clearly contains complementary tasks to be carried out by schools, additional, so-called "minority" normative support is provided if – as we have already explained – the municipality organises minority education on the request of parents. The normative amount guaranteed is higher in the case of mother-tongue or bilingual education.

We have also mentioned that minorities typically live in rural areas and in small settlements, where the number of children is also low. Therefore, *per capita* support depending on the number of pupils may not be sufficient to cover costs. Those settlements under a certain number of inhabitants are entitled to another type of normative support, the 'small settlement normative'. If the local government of such a village organises minority education, it is entitled to a double amount.

Strengthening Identity

In the past ten years we have witnessed the gradual strengthening of the identity of minorities. The building of a democratic society, the adoption of a comprehensive Act on the rights of minorities, the ratification of international conventions in the field, the establishment of minority self-governments, and supportive measures taken by the state are all factors which have led to a more open admission of one's affiliation and to the wish for more active participation in public life.

In the field of education, that can be seen in the setting up of the National Committee of Minorities, which is the advisory body to the Minister of Education. The body has the right of veto in connection with all ministerial regulations that have an impact on minority education. They also act as an authority for approving the contents, and preparing the publication, of minority schoolbooks. The committee is convoked every month to give its opinion on the new measures and regulations envisaged.

As we have already explained, minority education is typically organised within the public, state-run education system. However, in parallel with the phenomenon of strengthening identity, we can observe an increased desire on the part of the minority self-governments either to found or to take over and run educational, cultural and research institutions, including schools. The collective right to cultural autonomy is enshrined in the Act on the rights of minorities. However, in Hungary, the practice is quite new, and its framework is still developing. It is more than simple freedom of association, as the institutions will receive state funding for their operation.

According to the regulations, both local and national minority self-governments are entitled to take over a local minority school if they conclude an agreement with the local municipal council, which as a rule maintains educational institutions. If the national minority self-government wants to take over a school or dormitory attended by pupils from an entire region or from the whole country, that agreement should be concluded with the Minister of Education. Minority self-governments – which in this way will become the patrons of such schools – receive the same form and amount of state subvention, and they are entitled to submit project proposals to the different grant-awarding agencies under the same conditions as the former patrons. Buildings and equipment will be made over to the new patrons free of charge. So far, one German and one Croatian institution have been taken over or founded by the respective national minority self-governments, and from 1 July 2004 a Slovak educational complex, consisting of a nursery school, a primary school and a dormitory, will be taken over by the Slovak National Autonomous Administration. To support those initiatives and the creation of new institutions, since 2003 there has been a new line in the state budget of *c.* €1.4 million, the use of which is managed by the Office for National and Ethnic Minorities.

We hope that it can be seen from the above that the Hungarian Government considers the conscious nurturing of the culture of the minorities not only a duty deriving from international commitments which it has undertaken but in the long-term national interest. We also try to support the preservation of minority languages and cultures through education. Hungary considers maintaining the cultural diversity of the country as a value common to all citizens.

The Sámi Languages in Education

Nils Ø. Helander

Buorit guldaleaddjit! Dahkkot miige gielaideamet gulusin ja oainnusin! Alloset dat šaddat midjiide unnán geavahuvvon giellan!

My introductory words in North Sámi were as follows: "Let us make our languages audible and visible. Do not let them become lesser-used languages for us!" As an introduction to this article on the Sámi languages in education, I shall first provide a short general survey of those elements of their geography and history relevant to our understanding of the situation today.

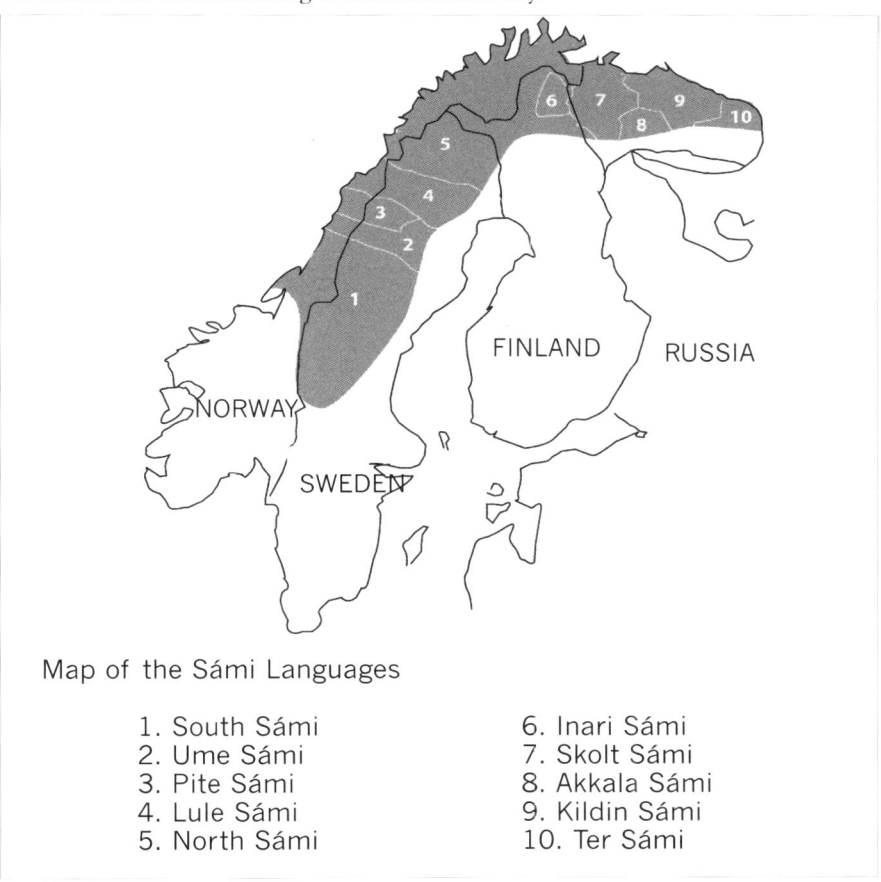

Map of the Sámi Languages

1. South Sámi
2. Ume Sámi
3. Pite Sámi
4. Lule Sámi
5. North Sámi
6. Inari Sámi
7. Skolt Sámi
8. Akkala Sámi
9. Kildin Sámi
10. Ter Sámi

The situation varies greatly for the different Sámi Languages. As the map shows, there are many different languages within the Sámi group. Geographically, they cover an extremely wide area within Finland, Norway, Russia and Sweden. Six of the languages have their own orthographies, and some are spoken in more than one country. That means that the teaching of the Sámi languages is based on the education systems of four different countries.

The situation of the languages varies regarding numbers of speakers and the use of Sámi in written form. The greatest number (more than 75%) of Sámi speakers use the North Sámi language, and North Sámi is also the language with the strongest literary tradition. It is estimated that about 25,000 people in Norway understand at least one of the Sámi languages (SEG 2000). Estimated numbers of Sámi-speakers in Finland are fewer than 3,000, with 1,000 in Russia and 7,000 in Sweden (Sammallahti 1998: 1–2).

Since the beginning of the last century, Sámi organisations have been making an effort to strengthen the languages' position, but it was not until the end of the century that they were given partial protection under language Acts in the Nordic countries. The struggle for linguistic rights started during a period when the official attitude was to prohibit the use of Sámi. After World War II, attitudes changed little by little towards toleration, and today's rules and regulations go some way towards promoting official use of Sámi.

Russia

Sámi is taught as foreign language at the boarding school, the municipal elementary school and the vocational school at Lujavri (Lovozero). There is also teaching of Sámi at Gremicha elementary school. The lack of teachers, the reduction in teaching hours and the absence of lessons at mother-tongue level cause most problems for Sámi in Russian education (Rasmussen 1999).

The Nordic Countries

In the Sámi area of the Nordic countries, education is based mainly on the Finnish, Norwegian and Swedish school systems. The Sámi themselves also contribute to relevant development through their own educational institutions.

Sweden

In Sweden there are special schools for Sámi children. From the beginning of the eighteenth century, when such schools were established, they were meant only for reindeer-herding Sámis, to prepare schoolchildren for a reindeer-herding life. The main school language was Swedish, however. It was not until the middle of the century that the idea of education in Sámi started to gain ground. Since the 1960s, such Sámi schools have also been open to non-reindeer-herding Sámis. In 1970, the estimated number of reindeer-herding Sámis was about 2,500, while non-reindeer-herding Sámis numbered about 15,000.

From the middle of the 1970s, ordinary primary and lower-secondary schools also started to give lessons in Sámi. The amount of education in Sámi, two hours a week, was of course far too little to safeguard and promote the use of Sámi. With only two lessons a week, children found it very difficult to learn to read and write Sámi. From fifth and sixth class onwards, there were four hours a week of English, but still only two hours of Sámi. It is little wonder that the result was language shift from Sámi to Swedish.

During the 1980s and 1990s, the Sámi school administration, established in 1980, made efforts to promote education in, and the use of, Sámi. At the same time, there was a strengthening of Sámi education for teachers, and nursery schools and leisure centres were also established for schoolchildren. Over the period in question, a great quantity of teaching materials in the Sámi languages have also been produced. The aim was to make Sámi children bilingual in Sámi and Swedish. Lessons were given in Sámi at the Sámi schools as a first and second language for six to eight periods a week for classes one to three, and for four periods a week for classes four to six. The ordinary primary schools and upper-secondary schools offered one to two lessons a week, although changes introduced by the school Act of 1997 stipulated that such lessons be in the mother tongue of pupils. Only one school offered teaching through Sámi. An evaluation of the school system concluded that children who did not have Sámi as their mother tongue did not become bilingual (Hyltenstam and Svonni 1990). The best progress in Sámi was found among those pupils who had received education through Sámi. (Aikio-Puoskari 2001: 102–133).

Finland

The early history of Sámi in education in Finland is in many aspects similar to that of the other Nordic countries since the 1700s. Education was part of the work of the church. There was resistance to the use of Sámi from the end of the 1700s until about 1820, when it experienced a short period of prosperity thanks to the vicar Jacob Fellman, who defied his own superiors by promoting use. When the first trained Sámi teacher started his career in 1902, he was expected to provide education through Finnish. Until about 1950, there were two types of schools, state primary schools and catechism schools. The presence of Sámi in education was often the result of a teacher's personal resistance to the wishes and demands of the authorities to stick to the use of Finnish. One result of the Finnish independence struggle was resistance to the use of Sámi in education. However, during the period there were vicars and teachers who resisted the official attitude against the use of Sámi and thus contributed to keeping Sámi alive. Ulla Aikio-Puoskari (2001: 142) writes that, after the official elementary school system was introduced as the only school for Sámi-speaking children, the language shift process accelerated.

After World War I, there was half-hearted support for Sámi cultural identity in the school system. One college of further education in Anár played a central role in the use of Sámi in education. During the 1970s, several committees discussed Sámi school issues, and although their proposals did not lead to any changes in the school Acts, some ideas were carried through at a municipal level.

During the 1980s and 1990s, provisions were changed several times in favour of Sámi as a medium of education from primary school to upper-secondary school. The use of Sámi in education should bring pupils up to the level of functional bilingualism. The provisions state that the use of Sámi as a medium of instruction promotes language knowledge much better than simply teaching the language.

Norway

In order not to make my introduction too long, I shall not dwell on the early history of Sámi in Norway. Suffice it to say that in Norway, too, the use of Sámi experienced great official resistance, especially during the century from 1850.

From the end of the 1960s, Sámi started to gain ground in education again, at first undoubtedly simply to make the learning of Norwegian easier. The Norwegian experience corresponded with that of Finland and Sweden in that it was not found possible to achieve a functionally bilingual level of proficiency in Sámi when it was taught only as a school subject to children who were not full mother-tongue speakers when they started school. Even in areas where daily use of Sámi in society is strong, it has not been possible for those pupils to achieve a functionally bilingual level of proficiency. In spite of efforts to strengthen the position of Sámi through language Acts and provisions, Sámi is far from enjoying the same position as the languages of state. The pupils' everyday surroundings, especially regarding the language of writing and broadcasting, are so dominated by the languages of state that a few lessons a week will not make them bilingual. For pupils who start school with mother-tongue level in Sámi, it will help them maintain their language, but without having the opportunity to receive their education through the medium of Sámi, they will not have the possibility to develop their language properly according to the needs of a constantly changing society.

In the municipality of Deatnu (Tana), officials are now discussing making Sámi kindergartens free of charge to get more children to learn Sámi. When children learn Sámi at pre-school age, there is a much better chance of achieving functional bilingualism, including for those who speak Norwegian with their parents.

Language use in Sámi areas is of importance regarding the possibility of motivating and strengthening use of Sámi at school, and it is also true that a strong presence for Sámi in schools will strengthen Sámi in wider society. Sámi-speaking regions are an advantage for the high number of Sámis living outside core areas who have to struggle to learn it. Today it is possible to arrange education in Sámi in so-called outlying areas where the number of pupils is at least ten.

Conclusion

To sum up, the situation regarding education in and about Sámi varies for each Sámi language. It is also different for the same language in different areas, and there are also differences owing to there being different school systems in different countries.

It is not easy to foresee the future, but we Sámis hope that the progress made by the Sámi languages in schools over recent decades will continue. The situation is most difficult for the minor Sámi groups striving to revitalise their languages. We also hope that the promotion of linguistic human rights in society in general will safeguard all so-called lesser-used languages and make them more widely used.

References

Aikio-Puoskari, U. 2001. "Saamen Kielen ja Saamenkielinen Opetus Pohjoismaissa. Tukimus Saamelaisten Kielellistä ihmIsoikeuksista Pohjoismaiden Kouluissa". *Juridica Lapponica* 25. Lapin Yliopisto.

Korhonen, M. 1981. *Johdatus Lapin Kielen Historiaan*. Suomalaisen Kirjallisuuden Seura. Helsinki.

Lund, S. 2003. *Sámi skuvla vai "Norsk Standard"? Norgga Skuvlaodastusat ja Sámi oahpahus*. Davvi Girji.

Rasmussen, T. 1999. *Språksituasjonen for Samene på Russisk Side*. Rapport til Barentssekretariatet.

Sammallahti, P. 1998. *The Saami Languages: An Introduction*. Davvi Girji OS.

SEG. 2000. *Raporta. Iskkadeapmi Sámegiela Geavaheami Birra*. Bargoaddi: Sámi giellaráddi. Sámi Ealáhus-ja Guorahallanguovddáš.

SEG. 2000. *Rapport. Undersøkelse om Bruken av Samisk Språk*. Oppdragsgiver: Sámisk språkråd. Sámisk Nærings-og Utredningssenter.

Hyltenstam, K. and Svonni, M. 1990: *Forskning om Förstaspråksbehärskning Hos Samiska Barn. Språksociologisk Situation, Teoretiska Ramar och Preliminär Bedömning*. Rapporter om Tvåspråkighet 6. Centrum för Tvåspråkighetsforskning. Stockholms Universitet.

Friulian and Other Lesser-Used Languages in Education in Friuli Venezia Giulia, Italy

Silvana Schiavi Fachin[1]

1. The Scenario

Friuli is the name of a large territory including the provinces of Gorizia, Pordenone and Udine which, together with the province of Trieste, form the region Friuli Venezia Giulia. The region which has a special autonomy is located in the north-eastern Italy, bordering on Austria to the north, on Slovenia to the east, and on the region Veneto to the west and has a total population of approximately 1.2 million (1,183,009).

Friuli is linguistically one of the most heterogeneous areas of Italy and, certainly, a unique and fascinating example of language contact in Europe. Its repertoire is rich in genetically diverse languages and presents a large range of variants and subvariants. Alongside Italian, the official state and dominant language, which is the language of instruction and covers almost all the public domains, including the church, several minority languages and Italian dialects (mostly Venetian dialects) are used by the population as home and community languages.

German varieties are spoken in the linguistic island of Sauris (Zahre) and in the peninsula of Timau (Tischlbong). Trilingual and quadrilingual communities are not unusual situations in the whole area. The German-Friulian-Italian community of Sauris and the German-Slovene-Friulian-Italian archipelago of Val Canale, near the Carinthian border, can be considered examples of remarkable and peculiar interest both from a linguistic (psycholinguistic and sociolinguistic) and an educational perspective. The Eastern border is dotted with small **Slovenian** communities where bilingual (Slovene-Italian) or trilingual (Slovene-Friulian-Italian) speakers are still not a rare exception. **Friulian**, belonging to the so-called romance or neolatin languages, is the most widely used minority language in the region with approximately 600,000 users. There are groups of Friulianophones in the region Veneto and large communities of Friulanophones exist in several European countries, in Canada, the United States and South America. Friulian was, in fact, the home and community language of the first generation of migrant workers around the world while the third generation hardly speaks it. The younger generations generally maintain an overall comprehension of the native language of their grandparents while most of them ignore Italian. The general situation in the use of languages is now that of diglossia, with bilingualism shifting rapidly to one of diglossia without bilingualism. (See also the Table on p. 53.)

Alongside these historical minorities, in more recent years multilingualism is constantly increasing as other minority groups have settled in the area, adding linguistic and cultural inlays to an already extraordinary mosaic. The influx of people from other Italian regions, from Central and Eastern Europe, from Africa and the refugees from the war-stricken areas of former Yugoslavia have created newly and uneasily multicultural and multilingual groups that neither the broader society, nor

---

[1] Silvana Schiavi Fachin, although invited to give a paper at the **Voces Diversae** conference, was unable to do so because of family reasons. However, she kindly made her paper available for publication.

Minority Language	Province	Region
Ladinophones		
Friulian[a]	Gorizia Pordenone Udine Veneto Portogruaro	Friuli Venezia Giulia
Ladins	Bozen Trento	
Slovene[b]	Gorizia Trieste Udine	Friuli Venezia Giulia
German[c]	Udine	Friuli Venezia Giulia
	Aosta	Valle D'Aosta
	Bozen Trento	Alto Adige
	Verona Vicenza Belluno	Veneto

[a] The Ladinophones, to which the Friulians are assimilated, can be also found in the provinces of Bolzano, Trento and Belluno.
[b] The population of Slovene nationality in the region Friuli Venezia Giulia is estimated around 100,000[2] and they are usually bilingual: Italian/Slovene and trilingual: Italian/Friulian/Slovene or Italian/Venetian/Slovene. In the province of Udine the Slovenes live mainly in the area of the Natisone and Torre river basins, the Resia and the Canale Valleys.
[c] Bavarian varieties of the Carinthian type can be found in the trilingual 'insulas' of Sauris/Sauras/Zahre and Timau/Tamau/Tischelwang in the province of Udine and Sappada/Pladen in the province of Belluno. "Sauris German", for example, is as it is principally because it chanced to be transplanted from the southernmost border of the Tyrolean and Carinthian German dialect area by the forebears of the present villagers over seven hundred years ago and has passed on from generation to generation. The three islands show a triglossic repertoire: the native German variety being used in communicating with fellow initiates only; Friulian with those inhabitants who are known or assumed to be Friulian speakers.

A quadrilingual situation can be found in Valcanale, near the Austrian border, where numerous inhabitants alternate Slovene, German, Friulian and Italian, using both the local varieties and the standard.

---

[2] Assessments mentioned refer to a survey conducted in 2002 by SLORI (Slovene Research Institute in Trieste) in cooperation with the nationally recognised opinion poll agency SWG based in Trieste.

the educational system can go on ignoring as they have been doing for the individual pockets of speakers of minority languages of ancient origin. The result of these migratory patterns is that teachers are faced with hitherto unknown (or either consciously or unconsciously removed) educational problems posed by an increasing number of students (especially children) who are bearers of visibly diverse languages and cultures.

The extent to which the educational system will take seriously notions such as equity and justice and promote academic achievement for all students regardless of race, class, income, religion, and language – fundamental principles written in the *Italian Constitution* – is the challenge of the future.

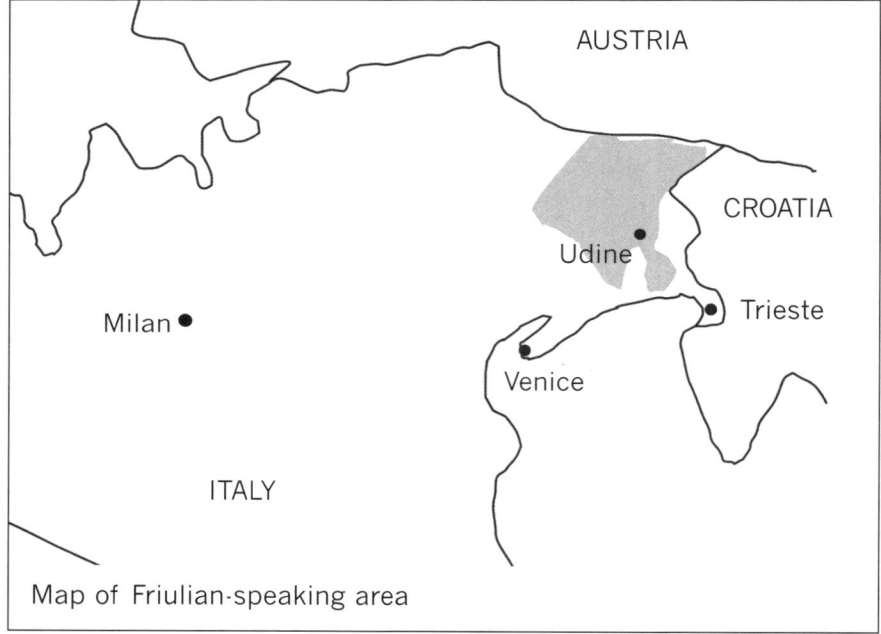

Map of Friulian-speaking area

2. The System of Education in Italy

The Italian School System is under revision and some changes will gradually take place starting from next school year 2005–06. There will be a compulsory primary level of seven years for all pupils and also a compulsory higher biennium giving access to the final vocational triennium of higher professional specialisation. This new system however is meant to be implemented gradually and will probably not become fully established before 2011.

The current educational system envisages eight years of compulsory schooling covering five years of elementary school, from the age of six to the age of eleven with a final examination leading to three years of Junior Secondary School, from the age of 11 to the age of 14. At the end of this second cycle the pupils sit an examination and they can go either to various senior secondary schools or to general, technical or vocational colleges with an average length of five years. In order to be able to enter higher education, students must sit a state examination and, after three academic years, they get a university degree (Magister). Two additional years of what is called a specialist degree lead to a doctorate.

Pre-school applies to children aged between 0 and 3 (playgroups) and 3–6 years old (kindergarten). Playgroups (crèches) are starting to be created especially in big cities or in industrial areas, but the situation is very uneven and somewhat at an experimental stage. Although kindergarten is voluntary, statistics show that about 98% of all three-year-olds attend a kindergarten.

In Italy, around 90% of schools are state schools. Private schools do not in fact play a significant role particularly at secondary level.

3. Language Use in School and Legislation

Italian is the language of instruction, and it is taught both as a subject and as a teaching tool. In a few kindergartens, first foreign language exposure takes place both in Italian and in Friuli, although the debate about the benefits of an early exposure to a second or a third language is quite lively and in favour of extending the experience to a growing number of situations. One serious obstacle, however, is the lack of competent teachers. A second handicap lies with the parents' choice which favours almost exclusively English – even in our region with two neighbouring countries which could offer plenty of opportunities of meeting people, observing foreign lifestyles and environments which are, we know, of fundamental importance in language learning and teaching. Foreign languages – the first choice goes to English; German is the second choice, and French is very rarely available – are introduced at elementary level from grade two in some schools and from grades three or four in others. The situation is, in general, very fluid for the foreign language is not compulsory, and the responsibility lays on the approval of the parents in accordance with the teaching staff. The study of a foreign language is instead compulsory at junior secondary level. Here again English is the most taught foreign language. Those schools which develop a 'lingua' programme offer two foreign languages and these, in Friulian, usually are English and German. At senior secondary level the teaching of foreign languages is compulsory but somewhat diversified, and it is difficult to give a short and systematic overview of a situation which is rather complex. At all levels, the time allotted to the teaching/learning of foreign languages is too restricted – two or three hours per week – influencing negatively the attainment of positive results.

Until 1999, lesser-used languages did not receive any recognition or any protection from the State. With the approval of the law no.482/99, *Regulations on the Protection of Historical Linguistic Minorities* the process for the safeguard and promotion of minority languages started and is very slowly underway. Articles number 4 and 5 provide regulations for the introduction of these languages in the school system at pre-primary, primary and junior secondary levels – the prominent factor for pre-primary school being the use of the lesser-used language as a means of instruction in all state schools of the territories with the presence of minority groups. The application of the law is, however, dependent on the approval of the municipalities and of the provinces to be included in the area of protection.

In primary and junior secondary schools, the introduction of minority languages in the curriculum is dependent on parents' approval. No provisions are explicitly made for the senior secondary level except for the possibility given to the schools to organise 'activities' in the area of adult education. For higher education, the universities in the regions with minority communities are entitled to offer courses in language and culture, to carry out research projects and to offer teacher training courses although without any additional grant-in-aid.

3.1 The Friulian Language in Education

Since the 1980s, we have begun to develop pilot programmes in Friulian-Italian bilingual education starting from kindergartens. At that time, I was an assistant in Modern Language Teaching in the Faculty of Foreign Modern Languages of the University of Udine, and I set up a research group which, in the early eighties, presented a bilingual partial-immersion programme to be carried out in some rural kindergartens in the province of Udine. The programme was meant for Friulian children and for the Slovene children of the Friulian Slavia as well. The Friulian parents praised the proposal immediately, while some Slovene parents rejected it.

When a teaching experiment[3] is introduced in the Italian educational system, the complicated bureaucratic procedure involves that the 'iter' has to be completed before any activity can get under way. The proposal, besides going through the inner teacher and parents bodies, was meant to be judged and approved by the provincial and regional school bodies which rejected it twice. As a consequence, it was blocked for three years; finally, I succeeded in getting the authorisation directly from the Italian Ministry of Education and in the school year 1986–87 we could start the educational activities in two Friulian kindergartens with seven teachers and 55 children aged three to five.

In the Friulian Slavia, a private bilingual kindergarten was established in the school year 1984–85 (see further paragraph 3.2) which was set up on a similar framework. I will go into some detail in describing the structure of this first programme because, in the following years, it became a 'framework of reference' for a number of contexts in which we were allowed to organize forms of bi-plurilingual education with lesser-used languages in the Region Friuli Venezia Giulia and in other Italian regions. The original scheme was always adapted to meet the specific needs and wants of each context of situation.

A simple questionnaire was used to identify the linguistic and cultural background of each child gained outside the nursery school both in the home and in the environment: the languages/dialects of the mother and father the repertoire of the migrant grandparents and relatives who, we found out, told stories, played games, and sang songs using, at times, very distant languages like, for example, Swahili or Hindi, or Chinese. Besides, the survey offered the researchers and the teachers a range of preliminary but useful data with which to analyse the level of competence of each child in Friulian, in Italian, and in other languages.

This information underwent further verification through contacts with the family and, above all, as part of the direct and systematic observation of the child's verbal behaviour during controlled communicative activities and in situations of spontaneous interaction.

The modality adopted was **'one person, one language'** which represents an

---

[3] The current word in Italian legislation is *experiment* although in the present paper the author usually refers to it using the terms *pilot project* or *experience*.

improvement of the most known mode "**one teacher, one language**" and which turned out to be one of the crucial points in the programme. Before starting the experience, all the people involved (the teachers, the headmaster, the staff, the cook, the bus driver and also the occasional visitors, in case they were bilingual), had to choose the language which they were to use – either Friulian, Italian, Slovene or German. They were supposed to stick to the language chosen in all interactions with the children.

During the first phase, that requirement was adopted even for the interactions among them when they were in front of the children. That requirement came to cause some difficulty, and so it was gradually abandoned. The researchers in fact decided that, while it was important to address the children constantly in one language, their exposure to more than one language was a natural feature of the environment which could be kept as it was.

In order to give the weaker language a well-balanced presence in the school, 50% of the activities were in one language and 50% in the second. We also chose to alternate the languages every fortnight, so that the morning activities which are prominent in the schedule of kindergartens were in Friulian, or any other lesser-used language, for two weeks, and in Italian the following two. When later on, at primary level, a foreign language was introduced, we tried, whenever possible, to 'spread' it across the curriculum. Friulian, Italian, Slovene and German songs, games, rhymes, proverbs, etc. were usually presented in contrast with foreign songs, games, stories, etc. either in (standard) German or in English, French, etc.

All the teaching-learning approach was in fact cross-curricular. The whole range of themes and topics was handled in a contrastive perspective, so that children were always faced with the analogies and differences between cultural and language systems.

Teachers were given guidelines and materials so that they could usually present a new content, new materials and new activities first in the language which the majority of children knew better, thus making input comprehensible and favour acquisition. In fact, according to Krashen (1981, 1982, and 1985), if the learner receives understandable input, language structures will be naturally acquired. This fundamental principle proved to be one of the most productive teaching strategies in language teaching. Topics such as exploring the wood or the country, learning about the seasons, the weather, using money, etc, and activities such as shopping, gardening, cooking, performing experiments, etc., first presented in one language were then partially covered also in the other language.

The programme in the two Friulian kindergartens had an official duration of six years but, with very few changes, is still going on at least in one of the two schools as the other was closed for the lack of children. The first six years were carried out within the framework of initiatives of the European Bureau for Lesser Used Languages and received financial support by the European Commission.

The European contribution was mainly used to implement the schools with teaching materials and audio-visual aids. We started to develop our own learning and teaching materials mainly in Friulian but, later on, also in the other languages of the region. Some materials have been published in several languages including lesser-used languages of other Italian regions (e.g. Occitan) and languages of wider circulation such as English, French, standard German and standard Slovene.[4] This

---

[4] See *Relé and Happiness* (1996), and *Relé goes to the Guggenheim* (2001) (Udine: Editsions Devantdaûr). Both were first created in Friulian *Relé e la felicitât* and *Relé al va al Guggenheim*. The former is published in thirteen languages, the latter both in Italian and in English. A video about the history of writing which

kind of production is actually still going on, and we have added the Friulian translation of *The Threshold Level* (Council of Europe, Strasbourg, 1975) and of the *Common European Framework of Reference for Languages: Learning, Teaching, Assessment* (Council of Europe, Strasbourg, 2001).[5] With the help of the University of Udine, the educationalists started to offer courses in teacher education and training which dealt with the fundamentals of bi-plurilingual education ranging from the theoretical component to the classroom practice.

The original framework of the project has met, during these 20 years, various difficulties when it was proposed in other contexts. The hardest thing to be overcome was the time allotted to the lesser-used language in the curriculum. The partial immersion model with 50% in Friulian and 50% in Italian was seldom accepted and realised, not even in nursery schools. At times, one or two afternoons were devoted to the lesser-used language. More often, Friulian (language and culture) integrated the Italian or the foreign language syllabus at all levels of education. When bi-plurilingual projects were developed with the support of the group of educational researchers of the University of Udine, a basic matrix (see an example in Friulian on page 59) was adopted in order to structure the theme/topic chosen, the context of situation taken into consideration, the typology of texts used, the skills engaged, the functions to be given priority, the related forms and vocabulary. In such experiences the language – native, second or foreign– was always treated as a means not as an end, taking into consideration the cultural, cognitive and affective components of the learning process.

The present situation shows, then, quite a few situations which could be considered examples of 'best practice' with teachers that have developed a high degree of professional expertise. However, they are not sufficient to cover considerable demand of Friulian education which is constantly increasing due to the Law no. 482/99 being enforced.

3.2 The German Language in Education: Three Cases

The German variety of the trilingual island of Sauris, thanks to some very keen teachers, was introduced in the local kindergarten and in the elementary school since the 1980s. The programme was restructured in the 1990s with the support of the University of Udine reaching some relevant results at school level. Nevertheless, as Norman Denison, the most renowned scholar of Sauris German, states:

> […] it seems that in Sauris the point of no return on the road of total language shift has been reached now, when, within the space of just three or four decades, Sauris German has all but surrendered the most crucial of its assets for survival: its function as the variety chiefly selected for the acculturation of preschool children (whose number have in ant case become so reduced that

---

had appeared in Friulian was then dubbed in Italian, in the Saurian and Timavese German varieties and also in Friulian with captions in English meant for the Friulian communities abroad. *Relé and Happiness* exists also in a workbook version with the Friulian or Italian story printed on the top of the page and having an empty space available for the children to write a version in their own native language. A few guidelines were added with suggestions to the teachers on how to use the material properly and effectively.

[5] *Un Nivel Sojâr* (Università di Udine, Didattica delle Lingue Moderne, 1987) and *Cuadri Comun European pes Lenghis: Aprendiment, Insegnament, Valutazion* (Udine: Consorzio Universitario del Friuli, 2004).

IL FRUT E IL SO MONT

	THEME		
TOPIC	ZUGATUI	ANIMAI	PLANTIS
	• di pêl • di plastiche • di len	• di cîl • di tiere	• di bosc • di prât
SITUATIONS	• in cjase • tal bosc • tal prât	• ors • âfs	• rôl • zanevre • jerbe

SCUVIERZI LA NATURE

Animâi	Plantis
?: dulà che a vivin ?: cemût che a son fâts ?: cemût che a si compuartin	?: dulà che a vivin ?: cemût che a son fatis
?: dal bosc ?: dal prât ?: dai paîs frêts ?: il cuarp/la vôs ?: la tane/il nît	?: dal bosc ?: dal prât ?: la struture ?: la utilitât

TEXT VARIETY: Adatament di un capitul di une storie par fruts (A.A.Milne – Winnie Puh) – tescj informatîfs – fumuts e dialics – cjantis – rimarolis – caligrams – articui giornalistics – videos – audiocasselis – enciclopediis – schedis operativis pe comprension – inmagjinis – aventaris

FUNCTIONS: Contâ – descrivi – pandi emozions, sintiments: maravee, contentece, rabie, displasê, plasê – gjavâ fûr e dâ informazions – classificâ – fâ un aventari

LANGUAGE CONCEPTS: Contâ a vôs e par scrit – dî il moment precîs di un event (cuant?) – la secuence dai fats – la durade – lis causis e i efiets – i lûcs (indulà?) – lis cuantitâts, lis cualitâts

FORMS: Discors diret e indiret – formis averbiâls e verps di timp, di lûc, di moviment – lessic: ors, âfs – rôl – businôr – splaç – mîl – zanevre – frut – niule – e v.i.

the biological survival of the community is in doubt). [...] It is ironic that precisely the time when competence in Sauris German (in the most rudimentary sense is threatened, previous diatypic restrictions on its use (for reasons of prestige)no longer inhibit its remaining speakers. It has been introduced on a voluntary experimental basis into school, for instance.[6]

Professor Denison refers to the fact that, outside the school, Saurian children do not find any opportunity to acquire the language. Native speakers in fact while co-operating enthusiastically in the school activities, never interact in Saurian with the children when at home or in the community. Denison concludes his essay with the following considerations:

> Gardner-Chloros, 1991, notes a similar readiness among Alsatian dialect speakers to set aside earlier domain inhibitions at a time when the language is ever less commonly being acquired by today's children, Sadly, the lifting of domain restrictions here too is almost certainly insufficient to offset the acquisition deficit. The resulting competence deficit leads to a drastically decreased awareness in younger speakers of the broad structural and lexical characteristics of the original 'native' strand of their pluriglossic inheritance. If we wished to give a meaning to a term like 'ethnoloinguistic shift', this might be it. (Denison, 2003: 248)

The **German Timavese** of the trilingual peninsula in the Carnian Alps of Friuli presents similar features. The kindergarten and primary school receive children having Timavese and Friulian as native languages and children with only Friulian coming from Cleulis, a small village nearby. Timavese has been introduced in bilingual programmes at pre-school level which, at elementary level, gradually approaches standard Austrian German. Friulian is also used in spontaneous interactions or during the activities dealing with materials in Friulian. Parents and other adults in Timau tend to conform to a general, now global trend to acculturate their children from birth to the mainstream culture via the mainstream language. Besides, in Timau, the present outcome is that active triglossia has become rare, having been replaced by Italian monoglossia for all practical purposes, apart from some passive competence in German and Friulian.

In the Friulian-German-Italian-Slovene archipelago in Valcanale near the Carinthian border a quadrilingual programme in all kindergartens and elementary schools of the area has been developed for over 20 years although its structure underwent substantial changes only recently. Languages were mainly taught as subjects, and the approach was somewhat traditional. In recent years, the model '**one teacher, one person**' has been adopted so that four teachers alternate in each school, offering an excellent example of team-teaching. They co-operate in developing a common syllabus for the four languages spreading them across the curriculum. They choose and adapt materials taken from the four cultural contexts and, in addition, they keep in contact with the schools of the neighbouring Carinthian and Slovenian areas with exchanges of materials and the promotion of frequent meetings among children, teachers and parents. The most prominent result is a growing interest of the

---

[6] Denison, N. 'Language Change in Progress: Variation as it Happens'. In Schiavi Fachin, S. ed. *L'educazione plurilingue. Dalla ricerca di base alla pratica didattica.* (Udine: FORUM, 2003). 229-250. (p. 247).

community for the neighbouring lifestyles and language – an outstanding result if one thinks that, after the two World Wars, the relations between the three countries were rather tense.

3.2 The Slovene Language in Education

Specific legislation regulating the Slovene minority schools in Italy is twofold: international agreements, and internal regulations. Among the international agreements mention should be made of the *London Memorandum* of 1954, providing for a Slovene school network in the province of Trieste which cannot be altered without the consent of the Republic of Slovenia. The *Osimo Treaty* (1975) entrenched the acquired rights of the Slovene minority. A *National Law* No. 1012 (1961) extended the right of being educated in the mother tongue to the Slovene citizens of the province of Gorizia.

The Trieste and Gorizia provinces have schools – from kindergarten to senior secondary level – with Slovene as the language of instruction, and Italian and the foreign language(s) as a subject. Schools in Italy with Slovene as the language of instruction constitute an integral part of the Italian school system and function under the same rules that apply to state schools of the majority. When students sit a state examination, the main language used in writing as well as in oral examinations is Slovene. The materials at all levels of instruction are selected by the teaching staff on the recommendations of the school councils; those in Slovene are offered by the Ministry of Education, Science and Sport of the Republic of Slovenia. The basic guidelines are national and adapted by the teachers under the guidance of the headmasters. There are no bilingual schools in the Gorizia and Trieste provinces.

The situation is different in the Friulian Slavia of the province of Udine. Until recently – see laws No. 482/1999 *Regulations on the Protection of Historical Linguistic Minorities* and No. 38/2001 *Regulations on the Protection of the Slovene Linguistic Minority in the Region Friuli Venezia Giulia* – Italy did not recognize the Slovenes of the Friulian Slavia and, as a result, there were never any Slovene schools established there.

The people of the community, with the support of the entire Slovene minority in Italy, decided to create a private bilingual kindergarten in the school year 1984–85 and an elementary school in the school year 1986-87 at Speter/S.Pietro al Natisone, where Italian and Slovene are the two languages of instruction on equal footing and according to the mode "**one person, one language**" (the structure has been previously described). From modest beginnings – the first group counted ten children – the school has progressed over the years and, at present, counts almost 200 pupils. In 1997 it achieved the recognition of 'equivalency' with state schools and, in 2001, it was nationalised and today covers almost half of the eligible population in the area of the Natisone river basin.

In the bilingual school, the language of education stems from the local dialect and children are gradually faced with standard Slovene in order to get them ready for bilingual simultaneous literacy. Besides, the materials in Italian and Slovene provided by the two countries, the teachers develop their own materials to support their own bilingual or trilingual projects.

The immediate perspective is obtaining their own junior secondary school because the pupils are now attending an Italian junior state school where Slovene in only taught as a subject for two hours. They are offered six additional hours of

Slovene that are optional two of which of language, two of mathematics, one of history and one of geography. These subject matters are taught through the medium of Slovene. For senior secondary schools, if the students want to go on in Slovene, they have to move to the provinces of Gorizia or of Trieste.

4. Teacher Qualifications

Until very recently, pre-primary and primary teachers did not receive any qualification at university level. The newly founded Faculty of Educational Science at the University of Udine offers some subjects: courses in Friulian/ German/Slovene language, Friulian/German/Slovene language and literature, Friulian teaching methodology. The main curriculum however is taught in Italian.

With the financial support of the region, the University of Udine in1999 started to offer training courses for Friulian teachers at pre-primary, primary and junior secondary levels in which theory and practice are combined. Besides attending lectures, the teachers are involved in developing projects for their own teaching situations, creating materials, devising learning/teaching activities and testing them in their own classes. The quality of some of the projects was particularly high, so we decided to publish them to offer the school examples of good practices that could be followed and enrich the availability of materials in Friulian.[7]

There is still no specific preparation for teaching Friulian at upper secondary level. The introduction of Friulian in Senior Secondary schools is in fact a most uncommon occurrence and it is usually offered in the form of reading sessions of either poetry or theatre. In those schools where Content and Language Integrated Learning (CLIL) is experimented in the main foreign languages (English, French, German and Spanish), Friulian has been also chosen for Electronics, Mechanics, Mathematics, Physics, Philosophy, Italian and Latin.

As for in-service training is concerned, every teacher is expected to follow a certain number of hours of in-service training every year. Some of these courses deal with the teaching of Friulian and are organized by regional school institutions or by the schools themselves.

The training of Slovene teachers takes place in Italian State Universities and only partially in the Slovene language. It is also possible to study in the universities of the Republic of Slovenia. This study is then recognized by the Italian ministry of Education, after a short procedure, as valid for teaching in Slovene schools in Italy. On the basis of the existing bilateral agreements, Slovenia organises two supplementary training courses each year, one held in summer in Slovenia and the other at the beginning of the school year in Italy.

5. Final Remarks

The very slow pace which characterises the application of the laws on the protection and the promotion of the lesser-used languages in the Region Friuli Venezia Giulia and of the other minority languages in Italy particularly in the school system, is certainly due to the lack of competent teachers and of good materials, but it must above all put down on the phenomenon of disinformation – or rather misinformation

---

[7] Schiavi Fachin, S. and A. Kersevan, eds. *Tin, Gjovanin, l'orsut e i claps* (Udine, KAPPA VU 2004), [book + CD].

– in issues such as the education of bilingual/trilingual learners.

The research data (Dolson and Linholm, 1995; Thomas and Collier, 1995) show clearly in the case of well-implemented bilingual programmes, learners from subordinated backgrounds who experience greater amounts of L1 instruction in the early grades show stronger academic achievement over time than those whose instruction has been primarily through their L2. Anybody who denies this pattern – academics, politicians and headmasters as well – has either not read the research (and I have referred to only two titles) or has chosen to ignore it because it is politically inconvenient.

References

Baker, C. 1988. *Key Issues in Bilingualism and Bilingual Education*. Clevedon: Multilingual Matters.
Baker, C. 1993. *Foundations of Bilingual Education and Bilingualism*. Clevedon: Multilingual Matters.
Cummins, J. 1979. "Linguistic interdependence and the educational development of bilingual children". *Review of Educational Research* 49: 221-251.
Cummins, J. 1981. "The role of primary language development in promoting education success for language minority students". In *Schooling and Language Minority Students: A Theoretical Framework*. Los Angeles: Evaluation, Assessment and Dissemination Center.
Cummins, J. 1996. *Negotiating Identities: Education for Empowerment in a Diverse Society*. Ontario, CA, California Association for Bilingual Education.
Dulay, H. C., Burt, M K., Krashen, S. 1982. *Language Two*. New York: Oxford University Press.
Dolson, D. and Lindholm, K. 1995. "World Class Education for Children in California: A Comparison of the Two-way Bilingual Immersion and European Schools Model". In T. Skutnabb-Kangas ed. *Multilingualism for all*. Lisse: Swets & Zeitlinger. 69-102.
Garcia, O., Baker, C., 1995. *Policy and Practice in Bilingual Education. Extending the Foundations.* Clevedon: Multilingual Matters.
Hagège, C. 1996. *L'enfant aux deux langues*. Paris: Editions Jacob.
Krashen, S. 1981, *Second Language Acquisition and Second Language Learning*. Oxford: Pergamon Press.
Krashen, S. 1985. *The Input Hypothesis: Issues and Implications*. London: Longman
Krashen, S. 1989. *Language Acquisition and Language Education*. London: Prentice Hall International.
Krashen S. 2003. *Explorations in Language Acquisition and Use: The Taipee Lectures*. London: Heinemann.
Romaine, S. .2000. *Language in Society: An Introduction to Sociolinguistics*. Oxford: Oxford University Press
Schiavi Fachin, S. ed. 1996. *Activity Packs for Language Teachers*. Udine: KAPPA VU.
Thomas, W.P. and Collier, V.P. 1995. *Research summary of study in Progress: Language minority student achievement and program effectiveness*. Summary of presentation at the California Association of Bilingual education. Anaheim, February.

First Encounters with Ulster-Scots Language, History and Culture

Hilary Avery and Andrea Gilbert

Stranmillis University College has been delighted to set up an Ulster-Scots curriculum development unit to provide first encounters with Ulster-Scots language, history and culture for pupils in primary and secondary schools. The Ulster-Scots Agency commissioned us to carry out the work in response to obligations under the *European Charter for Regional or Minority Languages* towards school pupils from an Ulster-Scots background.

The primary project began in September 2002, with the secondary and adult language projects beginning a year later. A recently appointed research officer has been assisting us in assessing the impact and added value of our teaching materials and drawing comparisons with other minority language initiatives in Europe.

Our main objective in becoming involved in this enterprise was to accord recognition to the Ulster-Scots tradition in Northern Ireland. The work that we are doing is of course part of a wider global movement to recognise and value cultural diversity in all places. In Northern Ireland, the Ulster-Scots tradition has been overlooked in comparison with the emphasis given to "British" and Irish cultures. Many school pupils in Ulster come from an Ulster-Scots background, one that has hitherto been submerged, having been seen as unacceptable, particularly at a linguistic level.

Readers will be aware that an Ulster-Scots speaker can be either Catholic or Protestant. For the less well-informed, the Ulster-Scots tongue has tended to be linked with the Protestant religious persuasion. The realisation that religious divides are not so sharp and that our cultural mix is much richer than has been simplistically supposed can only aid the development of understanding and tolerance.

We argue that the first real encounters with Ulster-Scots are at the mother's or – even more relevantly today – the grandmother's knee. Sadly, we are only too aware that the school system has hitherto largely been committed to eradicating such diversity and moulding the child into the standard Ulster English-language norm. For educators, a particular concern has been the effect that such rejection of familial language and speech patterns has had on the education of pupils from Ulster-Scots homes. A further consequence of the rejection of Ulster-Scots language has been the psychological damage to children, who found a regime at school which devalued their parents and their home life. Many Ulster-Scots can recount distress centred on the use of language in their early school experience, something that many say affected their relationship with school and learning in general. In response, the current generation of Ulster-Scots parents has largely suppressed their language and discouraged their children from speaking Ulster-Scots. That way lies the rapid extinction of a once rich language. Our work commits us to tackling that problem and raising the self-esteem of pupils from Ulster-Scots cultural areas.

We believe that we must begin by educating teachers about the origins and pedigree of Ulster-Scots language. We want to ensure that our teachers respect the language brought to school by pupils from Ulster-Scots backgrounds. We also want to make pupils in the north of Ireland aware of how they speak, and especially that many are in fact bilingual, moving from Ulster-Scots to English and back to suit

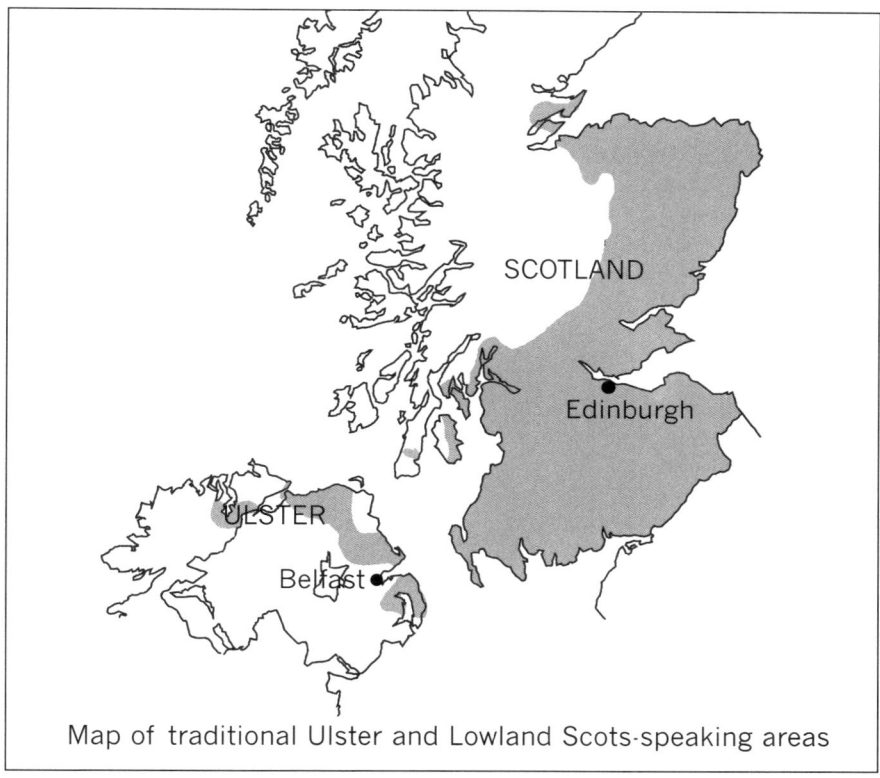

Map of traditional Ulster and Lowland Scots-speaking areas

particular occasions. We know that pupils who can identify their own use of language will enjoy choice and an extra dimension of control over their lives. Those are some of the great benefits of education for cultural diversity.

Ulster's Scots speaking areas were mapped by Professor R. J. Gregg in the 1960s and correspond with those planted by Scottish settlers in the late seventeenth century. Ulster-Scots language still has a strong presence in those areas, although it is often considered by outsiders to be of low status and an inferior way of speaking. Despite that, it continues to survive, and there are estimated to be around 100,000 Ulster-Scots speakers today.[1] Ulster-Scots is a regional variety of the Scots language, one of five main regional varieties of Scots (Central, Northern, Southern, Insular and Ulster).

In Ulster, there are three main Ulster-Scots dialect regions (in Co. Down, Co. Antrim, and across the Northern Ireland border between Co. Londonderry and Co. Donegal, with differences in vocabulary and pronunciation. The Ulster-Scots Language Society is in the process of recording and transcribing that living language, and when its text base is available there will be greater opportunities for analysis and comparison between varieties of Ulster-Scots. There is some shared vocabulary

---

[1] The only official figure for NI, from Northern Ireland Life and Times Survey conducted in 1999, is 35,000. The estimate of 100,000 speakers is put forward by the Ulster-Scots Language Society.

between Ulster-Scots and varieties of Ulster English (for example, *dander, thran, thole*) but there are Ulster-Scots language "markers" identified by Gregg which are used only by Ulster-Scots speakers. Those "markers" include the [e] in words such as *stane* and *hame*, the voiceless velar fricative [x] in such words as *licht, nicht* and *sicht*, and the familiar [u] in *toon* and hoose.

Our Ulster-Scots primary school project represents the first attempt at central production of Ulster-Scots teaching materials and integration of Ulster-Scots language, history and culture into the school curriculum. There have, however, been several interested and enthusiastic teachers who have introduced aspects of Ulster-Scots language and heritage into their classrooms through poetry, local studies and cultural activities. We hope that we have learnt from and built on that good practice by providing materials which will address the requirements of the *European Charter for Regional or Minority Languages* and the *Belfast / Good Friday Agreement* and enthuse teachers and children.

There is substantial interest in Ulster-Scots, something evidenced by cultural groups having been established in such places as County Fermanagh and County Armagh. Initial contacts with schools suggest that our teaching materials may have a place and appeal far outside the traditional speech areas mapped. It is for that reason that we are conducting a trial of the primary materials in every county in Northern Ireland, as well as in Donegal. They are being tested in both Catholic and Protestant schools and will be used as teachers in each school desire to fulfil different parts of the new Northern Ireland curricular requirements. Our materials aim to enable pupils to learn more about the Ulster-Scots tradition as a part of the diversity and mutual understanding programme; to provide pupils with opportunities to learn more about Ulster-Scots language through song, games and rhymes as part of the language and literacy programme; to provide pupils with the opportunity to sort, match and count Ulster-Scots curricular materials, and to cost a visit to Scotland as part of the mathematics and numeracy programme; to provide pupils with opportunities to learn about places in Scotland and Ulster as part of the "world around us" programme; to provide pupils with opportunities to research Ulster-Scots people who have made an impact or to research local place names as part of a cultural heritage programme; and to give pupils opportunities to investigate their own surnames as part of a personal development programme.

The primary teaching materials have wide appeal. The emphasis is on fun and enjoyment. Teachers who have used them in trials have been delighted to discover that the central theme of the new curriculum, the development of thinking skills, is an integral element of all the curricular activities produced by the primary project. In content terms, the primary materials aim simply to give a flavour of Ulster-Scots for very young children at Key Stage 1; for older children at Key Stage 2, they provide a basis for more detailed work that can be developed in the post-primary sector.

We are not teaching a language but recognising the Ulster variety of the Scots language, legitimising its status and enjoying it as an element of cultural diversity in the North of Ireland.

In the packs of teaching resources which we will be sending out to schools, we have included two explanatory booklets for the teachers. One gives a broad outline of Ulster-Scots history and culture, and another outlines the development of Ulster-Scots from the Northumbrian form of Anglo-Saxon, tracing the etymology of many Ulster-Scots words to outside influences such as the Norse and French invasions.

From that account, teachers will see that some word forms that they had supposed were merely "bad English" have much more complex origins.

We are aware that in this project we are looking at one facet of Ulster society, but, since our objective is to encourage mutual respect for others' cultures, where possible we have taken the opportunity to place Irish, English and Ulster-Scots alongside one another. In the secondary project, that has been more possible. For example, in the creative writing programme, a particular theme (such as peat-cutting) is illustrated through the poetry of James Fenton set alongside that of Seamus Heaney.

For our youngest pupils, we have produced large and very simple books with bold graphics such as *The Book of Numbers* and *The Ulster-Scots Picture Dictionary*. We have also put considerable effort into producing materials to stimulate oral activities. We have a book of traditional rhymes, such as 'Aiken Drum', which introduce Ulster-Scots vocabulary. An important resource for that age group is an *All About Me* book with activities for pupils to complete. "All About Me" activities are fairly standard classroom practice for the age group in question. The booklet that we have produced could be used by any teacher who wants a resource for the topic. Our booklet has a guide for teachers which allows the teacher to introduce Ulster-Scots language spoken in the school area. The booklet provides a range of vocabulary which covers the main regional variations of Ulster-Scots which will be found in Ulster schools. Activities can include lively discussion sessions which will reaffirm the language spoken in the homes of pupils. In the upper primary schools, Ulster-Scots language will be further accessed through songs, poems and prose. Ulster-Scots poetry and prose, which has been absent from school literature, will now find its place in the school syllabus.

The primary school project is not entirely about Ulster-Scots language: the history and culture of the Ulster-Scots is also of great importance. At a simple level, we want pupils to understand what is meant by the term "Ulster-Scot". In present-day Ireland, where so much unfortunate stereotyping occurs, it is good to be able to demonstrate that Ulster-Scots culture can act as a unifier of the two communities. Ulster-Scots people can be Protestant or Catholic. Pupils are introduced to information that clarifies those issues and teaches them about connections, both ancient and modern, between Scotland and Ireland. Pupils will be encouraged to access information through the Internet and use the Scottish-Irish connection to deliver many aspects of the new primary school curriculum.

In common with the National Council for Curriculum and Assessment curriculum in the Republic of Ireland, the new learning emphasis of the Northern Ireland Council for the Curriculum, Examinations and Assessment curriculum is on the acquisition of transferable skills. Our materials are designed to deliver such outcomes in the context of Ulster-Scots themes. In an educational conference, we would elaborate, but here it will suffice to say that, in the course of developing those skills, pupils look at some of the great Ulster-Scots such as William Ritchie (the shipbuilder), James Mackie (the engineer) and Harry Ferguson (inventor of the tractor). Pupils investigate the achievements of those men within Ireland and also consider Ulster-Scots of worldwide significance, such as those who became Presidents of the United States of America. Historical, geographical and literary themes introduced at primary level will be developed in greater depth in the secondary project. The role of the Scotch-Irish in America will be another important study area at secondary level.

In summary, we have three main objectives in our primary project: to raise the self-esteem of pupils from Ulster-Scots backgrounds; to encourage understanding and mutual respect for the cultures of others; and to show that cultural diversity can be a source of enjoyment.

As technological advancement makes the world a smaller place, it is hoped that through mutual respect and understanding between nations it will also become a safer one. It must be the responsibility of educators to offer our children a school experience that will prepare them to be the citizens of tomorrow and to contribute towards a better world – a global society.

[**Publisher's note**: On the eve of going to press, the teaching material on Ulster-Scots referred to in this paper has become available online at http://www.ulster-scots-learning.org.uk]

Developing Language Teaching Strategies: the Kalmyk Experience

Bosya Kornusova

Taking into account the advice of my European colleagues that I must assume that some of my readers or listeners may know very little about Kalmykia and not much more about the Russian Federation, I should like to refer to the most recent work in English on the Kalmyks and Kalmykia by François Grin[1] and quote from that paper. For instance, Grin writes that "Kalmykia can be described as a nation from the brink. Until a recent past, the Kalmyks were known especially for one reason: they were one of the people deported under Stalin, and permitted to return in the wake of Khrushchev's famous speech at the twentieth Congress of the Communist Party in 1956". Grin further states that "however Kalmykia deserves attention for other reasons. Apart from its highly original cultural, religious and linguistic traits, recent developments in these areas indicate a remarkably modern (some would say "post-modern") perspective on identity". I also agree with Grin that "there is little published scholarly works in English on Kalmykia, and it is useful to begin by recalling basic information".

The Republic of Kalmykia is one of 89 constituent parts of the Russian Federation. It extends over the south-east of the European part of Russia and occupies the dry steppe between the Volga and Don rivers. It borders the Republic of Daghestan and the Stavropol, Rostov, Volgograd and Astrakhan regions. Its border with the Astrakhanski region is interrupted by a narrow opening to the Volga river, and in the south-east it is washed by the Caspian Sea.

Kalmyk is a Mongolian language spoken by the eponymous nation of the Republic of Kalmykia. It is also spoken by Kalmyks living in the neighbouring regions of Astrakhan, Volgograd and Rostov, by small groups of Kalmyks in diasporas in France, Germany and the USA, and by the Oyrats[2] ('Mongols') living in China.

The Kalmyks[3] are descendents of the Oyrats, a western Mongolian people who used to live as nomadic herdsmen in a part of north-west Mongolia known as Dzungaria, which today corresponds to (Chinese) Xinjiang. At the end of the sixteenth century, they started to migrate north-west. They first appeared on the territory of Siberia in 1594–1597 and then moved westwards toward the Caspian Sea and the Volga River. The Kalmyks voluntarily joined the Russian Empire at the beginning of the seventeenth century.

Kalmykia, with its population of 320,000, is a multinational republic. The main nationality of the Republic is the Kalmyks, who make up 45.4%, and there is a large community of ethnic Russians – 37.7%. The rest of the population is made up of ethnic Darghins, Chechens, Kazakhs, Ukrainians, Belorussians, Germans, Estonians, Koreans, and so on.

---

[1] François Grin, "Kalmykia: from Oblivion to Reassertion?" *ESMI Working Paper* 10, October 2000.
[2] The Oyrat people living in China refer to themselves as *Oyrat-Mongols* and call the language which they speak *Oyrat*, although it is the same language which Kalmyks in Russia speak.
[3] The word *Kalmyk* came to replace the ethic name *Oyrats*, referring to those who had migrated to the lower Volga region in the seventeenth and eighteenth centuries.

Map of Kalmykia

Although Kalmyk is one of the languages of state in the republic,[4] it is a minority language in Russia. While legally equal, Kalmyk and Russian are not functionally equal, being divided in their spheres of application: Russian is used mainly in the official, educational, scientific and transactional domains, while Kalmyk is important in the sphere of national culture and to a small extent is still used as a household language; for only part of the population does it fulfil educational or transactional functions.

In the course of the twentieth century, as a consequence of various historic events, the Kalmyk language gradually lost many important functions and native speakers, and eventually it has become an endangered language for which survival is the most important issue today. Thus, before approaching the main topic of my paper – language-teaching strategies in Kalmykia – I should like to make a detour and say a few words about the events of the last century that brought the Kalmyk language to such a critical point.

The Modern History of the Kalmyk Language

The Great October Revolution opened a new page in the history of the Kalmyk people as well as in that of the other peoples of the Soviet Union. The introduction of socialism meant that the Kalmyk proletariat would be drawn into cultural and educational life. A Kalmyk culture "socialist in content" and "ethnic in form" was to

---

[4] The *Language Act* of 1991 declared the Kalmyk and Russian languages to be the languages of state in the Republic of Kalmykia.

be created. The Kalmyk language was therefore to undergo certain changes to be used in a new social context.

That process started with the search for the most suitable alphabet for the Kalmyk language. Thus, in 1924, the old Kalmyk alphabet (*Todo Bichig*)[5], which had been used by the Kalmyks since 1648, was replaced by the Cyrillic alphabet, then by the Latin one in 1930 and once again by Cyrillic in 1937. It was only in 1959 that a Kalmyk alphabet based on the Cyrillic script but with six additional symbols for specific Kalmyk sounds was finally adopted, and it is that which has been used since. It is obvious that a whole generation of Kalmyks grew up during the time of reform, when changes in the script were made three times in quite a short period, and subsequent generations of Kalmyk people have lost touch with their written heritage. Only a few works in the old Kalmyk orthography have so far been transliterated into the new script.

It should be emphasised that at the beginning of the twentieth century Kalmyk was the native and often the only language of the Kalmyk population, many of whom were illiterate. After the revolution, Kalmyk-medium schools were opened; textbooks, dictionaries and grammar reference books were published. Gaining access to education and communicating closely with a growing Russian population on their territory, the Kalmyks quickly became bilingual. At the same time, native speakers of Russian most often remained monolingual. It became prestigious for Kalmyks to gain a good command of Russian, as it opened opportunities for further education in vocational and higher education institutions in Moscow, Leningrad and other big cities.

The Kalmyks practise Tibetan Buddhism, which distinguishes them as one of the three Buddhist peoples of the Russian Federation, and the only Buddhist people in Europe.[6] At the end of the nineteenth century there were 62 Buddhist temples on the territory, but after the Russian revolution not a single one remained. The elimination of the traditional Buddhist religion, which helped transmit and maintain the customs and culture of the people, was also among the main reasons for the weakening of the Kalmyk language.

The deportation under Stalin in 1943 was a further and major blow to the Kalmyk language. The Kalmyks spent 13 years in exile and, during those years, the people experienced their darkest days of suffering and deprivation and endured the cruellest and bitterest trials. The Kalmyks were probably the only repressed people scattered over large swathes of territory during their exile. The deportation reduced the total number of Kalmyks to approximately 100,000. (Depending on the source, between one fifth and half of the Kalmyk population died as a result of deportation.) It is obvious that the deportation further weakened Kalmyk language and culture. The Kalmyk people were often mixed with other deported peoples and obliged to

---

[5] Until the middle of the seventeenth century, the Kalmyks used the old Mongol script, and in 1648 the (vertically written) Mongolian script was adapted for Kalmyk use by a monk, Zaya Pandita Namka-Djamtso (1599–1662), whose memory is still the object of deep respect among the Kalmyks. That alphabet was recognised by the Oyrat-Kalmyks as their national one and referred to as *Todo Bichig* or 'clear writing'. For 12 years, the author of the alphabet, who had received his education in Tibet, translated 177 religious books from Tibetan into Oyrat-Kalmyk, and his students produced translations of another 37 books. All official correspondence in Dzungaria as well as in the Volga region of the Kalmyk khanate was in that alphabet. It was used until 1924, when it was replaced by the Cyrillic script.

[6] François Grin (2000), "This culturally important feature is currently gaining increasing legitimacy in Kalmykia, and is used, along with language, to articulate a reawakening sense of identity".

use Russian, the only common language. As a result of that tragedy, a generation grew up which was not taught its mother tongue at school and acquired the language only in the family circle.

The Kalmyks were permitted to return to their native land from their 13-year exile in 1957 and to start their lives afresh, as their homes and other belongings had either been destroyed or given to Russians. On their return it was therefore not a simple matter for them to re-establish traditional lifestyles, and it took a long time to restore the education system. In the 1960s and 1970s, drastic cuts were made to native-language education, and the Soviet state applied decidedly assimilationist policies. Khrushchev himself believed that communism would be embraced faster and more enthusiastically by Russian-speaking populations, implying that other languages might be a hindrance, and russification was actively pursued under Brezhnev (Grin 2000). The last national school with Kalmyk as a means of instruction was closed in 1963. The language of instruction in all schools became Russian, with the Kalmyk language taught as a subject only for two to three hours per week. As early as the early 1970s, a generation of Kalmyks was growing up who could understand their mother tongue but could not speak it. Russian became the language of everyday communication in all spheres of life, including the family circle.

Not everything was so bad, of course, during the period. It is worth mentioning that modern Kalmyk art experienced its greatest development at the time. The Kalmyk people will always be proud of the outstanding writers, poets, singers, dancers, composers, artists and sculptors whose names became famous in the twentieth century, and especially during the years of Soviet power. Literary works by Kalmyk writers contributed a great deal to the enrichment of the language, the problem being that there were ever fewer of those who could appreciate them.

According to the 1989 census, 97% of ethnic Kalmyks reported Kalmyk as their mother tongue and, at the same time, Kalmykia became the country with the highest percentage of people fluent in Russian (88.5%). As other official statistics show, by 1985 some 93% of urban Kalmyks and 87.2% of rural Kalmyks could speak, read and write Russian, but only 27.3% of those living in towns and 45%–48% living in villages had a similar level of competence in Kalmyk (Dambinova and Korostelev 1993).

Being taught to be ashamed of their own identity and language has left a psychological scar on many Kalmyk people over 30, while the attitudes of many young people under 30 to the Kalmyk language are far from positive. Recent research in the field shows that the proportion of speakers fluent in Kalmyk does not exceed 6% among the young, and about 98% of Kalmyk pupils entering school at the age of six or seven do not speak their ancestral tongue. Most leave school without gaining any proficiency in their native language (Kornoussova 2001).

No one disputes the fact that the family and community are the primary language reproduction units, via the classic route of grandparents – parents – children. The grandparents and parents of children studying at schools today came through the deportation or were born in Siberia – the first generation that stopped speaking their mother tongue. It is therefore difficult to imagine that a native-language environment can be found in families.

Only with the beginning of *perestroika* at the end of the 1980s did it become possible to debate such issues as deportation, ecological problems and language revival. On 30 January 1991, the law *On Languages in the Kalmyk Soviet Socialist Republic* (No. 137 – IX) was adopted. According to the law, the Russian and Kalmyk languages were declared the languages of state of the Republic. Over the past ten years, several of the most important decrees of the President of the Republic of Kalmykia and Government regulations on the ethnic and cultural revival of the Kalmyk people have been adopted. They were comprehensive, concerned with all spheres of life – socio-economic development, culture, education, health, sport, mass media, and so on. Those were *On Measures for the Further Promotion and Development of the Kalmyk Language*, *On Government Support for the Study and Popularisation of the Kalmyk Heroic Epic, Djangar*, *On the "Djangariad" Republic in Traditional Sports and Games*, and so on. On 7 May 1998, the decree of the President of the Republic of Kalmykia *On Measures for the Further Revival and Development of the Kalmyk Language* was issued, followed by another decree of the President *On Measures for the Gradual Introduction of the Reformed Orthography of the Kalmyk Language*.

The new Language Act *On the Languages of the Peoples of the Republic of Kalmykia* was signed into law on 27 October 1999. Article 3 of the law declares Kalmyk and Russian to be the languages of state in the Republic of Kalmykia and "guarantees the revival, preservation and development of languages as a most important element of the spiritual heritage of the peoples living in the Republic". The Act states that the Republic of Kalmykia is the sole national-administrative formation of the Kalmyk people, and that care for the preservation, revival and development of the Kalmyk language, as the most essential of its national characteristics and the basis of its spiritual culture, is the responsibility of the administrative authorities of the Republic of Kalmykia. That is realised through the official recognition of its status, by creating conditions for its active use in the state and public spheres of life, by raising its prestige and by promoting its standardisation and dissemination.

The modern period in the development of the Kalmyk language, as P. Darvaev (2003), a Kalmyk scholar, states, can be described as the most prosperous, but at the same time as the most dramatic. Among the positive features of the period, we could mention the fact that the Kalmyk language was codified and that an attempt was made to create a unified literary language. For the first time, it was studied by scholars who were native speakers of the language, and it could be researched by those who knew its peculiarities. At last, the Kalmyk language won the status of a national or state language, assuming that it would fulfil important social functions. On the other hand, some tragic events in the history of the country and the Kalmyk people, such as the Civil War, World War II, and the deportation of the Kalmyks, brought about a drastic reduction in the numerical strength of the Kalmyk population, taking away the lives of many outstanding native speakers of the language, especially of the older generation, thus destroying the natural course of language reproduction and production. By the end of the twentieth century, the question 'to be or not to be' for Kalmyk, and consequently for the Kalmyk people, has become very relevant. So it was that in the course of a century the Kalmyk language passed through several stages, experiencing prosperity, decline and revival.

The Kalmyk Language in the Education System

It is agreed that education is absolutely central to language reproduction and production within society. Where the education system favours the minority language, a sizeable increase has been experienced in the number of children with a command of it. Teaching the mother tongue in the educational institutions of the Republic of Kalmykia has always been an area of state policy, perhaps the most successful. Education policies for Kalmyk have changed considerably over the last decade. To promote the process of mother-tongue revitalisation, *The Concept of the National System of Education* was adopted in 1993. The main achievements of the decree were the following: for the first time in 30 years, Kalmyk was once again to be used as a medium of instruction in schools in the Republic; it was also assumed that Kalmyk would be taught at all levels of the education system, starting with kindergarten, through to the higher education institutions.

What is the present situation regarding the teaching of Kalmyk? Children begin studying Kalmyk in kindergarten. According to statistics, in 2001 in the Republic's education system there were 119 pre-school institutions, with 9,368 children, among them 5,715 Kalmyk, 3,137 Russians, and 516 other nationalities. Kalmyk was taught to 8,764 (93.6%) children attending kindergarten, among them to 5,685 Kalmyks (99.5% of all the Kalmyk children attending kindergarten) and 3,615 children of other nationalities (99.0%). In addition, in 85 groups, Kalmyk was used as the medium of instruction of 1,790 children, i.e. 19.1% of all children attending pre-school settings.

In 2001, there were 181 schools with 55,113 pupils, of whom 39,705 (72.0%) pupils studied Kalmyk, including 31,488 pupils of Kalmyk nationality and 8,217 pupils of other nationalities, i.e. 79.3% of Kalmyks and 20.7% of schoolchildren from other nationalities. Of all the schoolchildren of Kalmyk nationality at school in Kalmykia (32,351 pupils), 763 pupils did not study Kalmyk (2.4%).

There are different approaches to teaching Kalmyk at school. Some students study Kalmyk as a school subject two or three times a week; some fifth- to eleventh-form students study it in advanced placement classes, with three to five lessons a week (1,777 pupils – 4.5% of all those studying Kalmyk at school); in 69 schools (38.1% of all the schools in Kalmykia) Kalmyk is used as a means of instruction for teaching 2,297 elementary schoolchildren (191 groups), i.e. 5.8% of all those studying Kalmyk at school. There are also two Kalmyk-medium schools where Kalmyk is used to teach all subjects at elementary level and some at middle school. The total number of students in those two schools is about 450.

Since 2001, ninth- and eleventh-form students have taken exams in Kalmyk language and literature. For children of Kalmyk nationality, it is a compulsory exam; for pupils of other nationalities studying Kalmyk it is elective. Of 3,611 ninth-graders, 2,449 received 'excellent' or 'good' marks (67.8%); of 2,544 eleventh-graders, 2,093 received 'excellent' or 'good' (82.3%).

Kalmyk is also taught to vocational school students. There are 17 vocational schools in the Republic, with 7,007 students, among them 4,441 Kalmyks, 2,141 Russians, and 1,426 other nationalities. Kalmyk is taught to 5,220 students (74.5% of all the students), 3,384 Kalmyks (64.82% of those studying Kalmyk) and 1,836 students of other nationalities (35.2% of those studying Kalmyk). Some 1,787 students do not study Kalmyk (25.5%).

As for higher education institutions, Kalmyk is also supposed to be taught to all students who, for whatever reason, did not study it at school. Future teachers of Kalmyk are trained in the pedagogical college (kindergarten and elementary schoolteachers) and at the Kalmyk State University (for all levels of education). In-service teacher training is run through seminars and specialised courses offered by various teacher-retraining institutions.

Besides Kalmyk language and literature, there are several other subjects concerned with studying Kalmyk culture, history and the traditional way of life. In some schools, those subjects are taught in Kalmyk; in others, in Russian. Every year the Ministry of Education organises different contests and competitions on Kalmyk language, culture and history for schoolchildren. Mass media also involve themselves in various Kalmyk-language activities. A magazine and a newspaper are published in Kalmyk for youngsters, and there are also several TV programmes.

At present, then, nearly all children of Kalmyk nationality aged from three to 18 are taught Kalmyk. Last year the first pupils of Kalmyk-medium elementary classes, started in 1993, graduated from school. In 2003, we celebrated the tenth anniversary of the national system of education. It was time to review the results of ten years of work. Everything mentioned above was named as an achievement of the development of the national education system but, at the same time, everyone understood that the present situation leaves much to be desired.

Among the problems that we have to solve, the methodology of teaching Kalmyk is often mentioned. It has become obvious that it is not enough simply to teach the native language; the way that it is taught is sometimes more important for language-learning than the number of hours. In short, it has become necessary to make the teaching of Kalmyk a more efficient process.

That problem has been the main subject of research carried out by a group of teachers of the Kalmyk, German, English and Russian languages since 1991, when the Kalmyk Centre for Instruction in Foreign Languages (KCILT) was established. Analyses of the Kalmyk-language teaching process allowed us to reveal certain contradictions:

1. between new approaches to teaching languages – the communicative approach foremost and the lack of appropriate Kalmyk language-teaching textbooks;
2. between growing demand for a level of proficiency in Kalmyk and the lack of an efficient teaching system providing the opportunity to acquire the language;
3. between the urgent need to develop students' ethnic self-awareness through learning the native language and their lack of motivation to do so;
4. between student-centred teaching and autonomous learning as factors in successful learning and the absence of the requisite conditions to realise them.

To resolve those contradictions, it was necessary to formulate relevant goals and objectives for Kalmyk language-teaching, to elaborate an efficient education system, to develop an up-to-date teaching methodology, and to write modern textbooks.

We have formulated methods of foreign-language teaching (accelerative teaching, the communicative approach, and so on), proceeding from the generally recognised fact that, for a majority of students, the Kalmyk language is no longer that of primary socialisation and everyday communication. An analysis of the modern theory and practice of language-teaching enabled us to revise the goals and objectives of Kalmyk language teaching and to determine as its main goal the achievement of **a level of communicative competence** in accordance with the Council of Europe Programme "Language Learning for European Citizenship". To achieve that goal, it is necessary to select proper linguistic materials. The 'threshold level' was of great use at this stage and helped us elaborate the Kalmyk language curriculum and the criteria for selecting and structuring teaching material. As a result of that work, a teaching set, *Uinr* (beginner's level) was developed and published, representing a new approach to Kalmyk language teaching, based on the following main principles: a communicative approach; a thematic lesson-by-lesson organisation of the material; a cyclic introduction and structuring of the material; teaching all language skills (listening comprehension, speaking, reading, writing); rich ethnocultural and linguistic material; and colourful design, games, songs, puzzles, and so on. The team of teachers and the staff of KCILT made a great effort and succeeded in opening a pilot school, *Altn Gasn*, in 1993. In its pilot programme, "Early Development and Developmental Teaching", the school focused on the following aims: to elaborate a multilingual education system; to test and evaluate new Kalmyk language teaching materials; and to develop a native language-teaching methodology. One of the components of the programme is an early start in several languages. The children begin simultaneously to learn Russian, Kalmyk, English and German at the age of five. The instruction in Kalmyk and the two foreign languages is based on similar methods and strategies. In their third form, the schoolchildren study Tibetan, which is a compulsory course until the seventh form, when it becomes optional. The study of languages is supported by courses on Kalmyk culture and history, the culture of the peoples of Russia, eastern culture and world culture and art, which are taught as compulsory and optional subjects.

The following factors were taken into consideration in the organisation of the system of multilingual education in school: the sensitive periods of a child's development; the choice of appropriate methods and techniques; and careful selection of teaching materials. The multilingual education contributed to the development of linguistic aptitude, learning strategies and skills among schoolchildren; to the development of positive qualitative changes (type and nature of thinking, memory, attention) and personality growth (communicative competence, positive 'self-image', a desire to co-operate, a tolerant attitude to participants in communication); and to the development of positive motivation to learn languages, including the mother tongue. The pilot school was also opened to test new Kalmyk language teaching materials. The first edition of the teaching set *Uinr* was successfully used, and the trial produced the conclusion that the communicative approach and the new textbooks created opportunities to achieve the desired level of communicative competence. Taking into account all the textbook's shortcomings, we developed a new version. At the moment, the team of teachers is working on a project entitled "Scientific and Methodological Guidance for the Process of Kalmyk-Language Teaching at Elementary School", carried out with the support of the Russian Scientific Foundation.

At the close of this part of the article, I should like to say that the development of the native-language teaching strategies in Kalmykia includes a communicative approach to language teaching and teaching materials design, as well as elaborating bilingual and multilingual education systems.

Conclusion

When a visitor, whether Russian-speaking or foreign, comes to the Republic of Kalmykia, he or she will easily notice that the main language spoken in the streets or in any other public place is Russian, although most of the population are of eastern appearance. That fact often surprises newcomers. If he or she asks Kalmyk people whether they speak their mother tongue, a negative answer is likely. One can easily see the presence of the unique Kalmyk culture everywhere: oriental architecture, sculptures and billboards depicting scenes from traditional Kalmyk life, signs written in the old Kalmyk vertical script, and so on. It is obvious that one will have a chance to listen to Kalmyk folklore, see national dances and even participate in some traditional celebrations. If one switches on the radio or TV, one will also be able to listen to or to watch some programmes in the Kalmyk language. It is not a problem to buy a newspaper or book in Kalmyk. However, one will hardly hear people speaking their mother tongue for daily interpersonal communication in the community. To an outsider's eye, Kalmyk remains a hidden language. Positive changes are taking place only very gradually. However, it is obvious that Kalmyk is perceived to belong mostly to the domain of language learning.

It is well known that, in dealing with the problems of the revival, maintenance and promotion of languages, the system of education is of critical importance, something quite obvious, since it is the field focusing on the part of the society which has the greatest potential – young people – and it is in school that younger generations master their mother tongue and gain a systemised knowledge of the history, culture, customs and traditions of their people. As far as the Kalmyk language is concerned, it should be added that, where a family has, through force of circumstances, stopped acting as "the nucleus of linguistic socialisation", that burden has naturally been placed on the education system. The language situation in the Republic of Kalmykia, characterised by a considerable reduction in the functional spheres of the mother tongue, an unsatisfactory linguistic environment, and low demand for the language, increases the role of schools in preserving not only the language but the speech community.

References

Dambinova, V. and Korostelev, A. 1993. "Etnoyazykovie protsessi u kalmykov" ('Ethnolinguistic Process of the Kalmyks'). In *Kalmykia: pereputie 1980h. Problemy etnokulturnogo rasvitiya* ['*Kalmykia: Cross-roads of the 1980s. Problems of Ethnocultural Development*']. Elista.

Darvaev, P. A. 2003. *Kalmytski yazik v svete teorii kulture yazika i rechi: problemy funktsionirovaniya i perspectivy razvitiya* ['*Kalmyk Language in Terms of the Theory of Language, Culture and Speech: Problems of Functioning and Perspectives for Development*']. Elista: APP Dzhangar.

Grin, F. 2000. "Kalmykia: from Oblivion to Reassertion?" *ESMI Working Paper* 10. Downloadable from www.ecmi.de/download/working_paper_10.pdf

Kornusova, B. 2001. "The Sociolinguistic Situation in Russia: the case of Kalmykia". In *Noves SL* Winter 2001. Barcelona: Directorate General for Language Policy. Government of Catalonia. http://cultura.gencat.es/llengcat/noves/index/htm

The Role of Education in Reversing Language Shift: the Estonian Experience

Mart Rannut

Current Ethnic and Linguistic Situation

Estonia is a country of 1.347 million people, with Estonians, the eponymous nation, comprising the bulk (c. 70% in 2005) of the population. Other major ethnic groups include Russians (almost a quarter of the total population), Ukrainians, Belorussians and Ingrians (Finns), with 145 different ethnic groups altogether. However, most non-Estonians residing in Estonia are immigrants or their families who came to live there after World War II, since in 1945 Estonians formed 97% of the population. More than 60% of non-Estonians reside in and around Tallinn, the capital, and almost 30% in the county of Ida-Virumaa, in north-eastern Estonia adjacent to Russia. Autochthonous ethnic minority groups are small in size, comprising Russians, mostly with Old Orthodox roots, on the shore of Lake Peipsi (c. 39,000), Jews (2,500), Germans (1,700) and Swedes (300 to 1,500). Ingrians, Roma (600 to 1,500) and Tatars (3,000) are also included among those traditional minorities.

According to data from the 2000 Census, the number of persons belonging to third nationalities has fallen considerably over the last ten years, so that they now total 81,000 persons. Fewer than 40% have maintained their ethnic language, with most others shifting to Russian and, in more recent years, Estonian. Thus, the number of Russian mother-tongue speakers is almost 400,000, which is considerably higher than the number of ethnic Russians, at the cost of third nationalities. According to estimates based on students' choice of Estonian-medium or other schools, non-Estonians should comprise one fifth of the population of Estonia in the next generation. The non-Estonian population is mainly in towns (91% of all non Estonians are townspeople), the principal concentrations (accounting for 80% of the total) being in six major Estonian towns: Tallinn, Tartu, Narva, Kohtla-Järve, Pärnu, and Sillamäe.

Knowledge of Estonian is increasing modestly. According to the census data, the proportion of non-Estonians able to speak the language has been steadily increasing over recent years, from 14% in 1989 to 37% in 2000. However, the plans had been more ambitious. Fortunately, language knowledge is much better among current school-leavers.

Speakers of Estonian and other languages are distributed unevenly in Estonia. Thus, Estonian functions in four different types of language environment (Ülle Rannut 2003, 2005). However, Estonian is the sole language spoken in various settings all over Estonia:

1. Estonian is the sole language of general communication in a major part of Estonian territory, with the exception of major cities, urban areas of Harjumaa and Ida-Virumaa, and the western shore of Lake Peipsi.
2. Estonian competes with Russian in an environment of stratified linguistic pluralism in most cities where the Russian immigrant community is situated (Tallinn, Tartu, Pärnu, Haapsalu, Kehra, Loksa, and so on). There are modest contacts between the two communities, and Russian-speaking ghettos are slowly emerging.

Map of Estonia

3. On the western shore of Peipsi (Mustvee, Kallaste), where the traditional Russian minority is situated, there is peaceful bilingual coexistence of Estonian and Russian.
4. Estonian is marginalised (being spoken by fewer than 20% of residents) in some towns of Ida-Virumaa (Narva, Sillamäe, and so on), where immigrants comprise the overwhelming majority. Altogether, Estonians form a minority in six towns and four rural communes.

A Brief History

Following the demise of the Russian Empire during World War I, the Estonian state was founded on 21 February 1918. Between the two world wars, Estonia was an independent, mainly mono-national state (Estonians comprised 89% of the total), with major officially recognised minority groups comprising Russians (8%), Germans, Swedes and Jews.

Estonia was an independent nation state until World War II, with the Soviet

Union occupying the country in 1940. The Soviet occupation lasted until Estonia regained its sovereignty in 1991.

The thus enforced totalitarian regime entailed disastrous changes to the population, including its ethnic composition, as a result of extra-judicial killings, mass deportations to Siberia and the far north, and the imprisonment (in GULAGs) of autochthonous inhabitants, with the simultaneous immigration of populations from the occupying country. For the non-Russian minorities in Estonia, no possibilities remained to promote or maintain their ethnic culture and language. All their institutions were abolished, including media, schools, societies, clubs, and so on. The net result was that by 1945 the Estonian population had decreased by one fifth. A mere 23,000 (2.7%) non Estonians remained as minorities in Estonia.

In addition to the basing of a Soviet occupation army in the country, Russian workers and collective farmers were sent to Estonia by the Soviet government. As the number of Estonians did not regain its pre World War II level, their proportion in the overall population fell from 97.3% in 1945 to 61.5% in 1989.

To make conditions more acceptable for the non-Estonian newcomers, several functional areas were Russified, and for the sake of keeping their jobs Estonians had to learn Russian. Russian was made the second language of education (not a foreign language), and in several areas, the first. Knowledge of the local language in occupied Estonia was not found necessary by newcomers, hence the low percentage with such knowledge (13%–20%) among non-Estonians. No stimuli were left for newcomers to respect the local language or culture.

In parallel with the influx of newcomers, territorial and functional language shifts took place. In several functional domains, Estonian was replaced by Russian, owing to Estonia's direct subordination to Moscow, for example, in banking, statistics, the militia (Soviet police), railway, naval and air transport, mining, energy production, and so on. Their reasons for moving to Estonia were a better standard of living (there was hunger in Russia), organised recruitment (construction work, the oil shale industry), privileged positions in certain trades where Estonians were not trusted, for example, navigation and aviation (an opportunity for Estonians to flee abroad), the railways (the risk of sabotage), communications (state secrets), and so on.

Together with the decrease in functional as well as regional areas where Estonian was used, a rapid rise in the status of Russian took place. It was caused by several factors, such as Russian compulsorily being the sole language for several functional spheres, and the construction of a parallel Russian medium network of plants, factories, offices, institutions and service bureaux as well as entertainment facilities and residential districts, providing full-scale education (including higher education, vocational schools, and so on) and services in Russian. Those structures were filled from the regular and massive influx of immigrants. As a result, a Russian-speaking environment was created in Estonia with no contacts with Estonians or Estonia, effectively hindering integration.

Soviet language policy in Estonia was implemented through a favoured immigration pattern. To consolidate immigrants on the basis of Russian, three steps were implemented: the creation of a parallel Russian-medium environment, with no need to switch to Estonian; the continuous transfer of territorial and functional domains from Estonian to Russian; and ideological incentives to prefer Russian to Estonian. Against the integrity of Estonian, other activities were implemented expanded use of Russian in administration, workplaces and mass communications; an extensive programme of translations from Russian; and a massive programme of

Russian language-teaching. During the Soviet occupation, by the 1980s, Russian had been established as the official language, while Estonian served as a minority language, and all other languages lacked any official recognition. Two major linguistic groups were formed, an Estonian-speaking and a Russian-speaking one, both identifying themselves as the majority in Estonia and taking opposite views on several crucial issues. However, owing to ever-increasing constraints on the official and public use of Estonian, the threat of further decay and, finally, death had become a reality.

Language Policy since 1988

The years from 1988 onwards reflect the gradual restitution of Estonia's independence. The conditions of Gorbachev's *perestroika* and *glasnost* provided more freedom and made totalitarian wounds visible. The Baltic republics were the most receptive to *perestroika*, taking up two main policy directions not desired by the Soviet leaders, namely, the restitution of national sovereignty and linguistic and cultural human rights issues. The two corresponding laws were the declaration of sovereignty and the language law. Estonia passed the declaration of sovereignty in November 1988, declaring the supremacy of Estonian laws over Soviet ones. The proclamation of Estonian as the official language of state in Estonia, together with its implementation through a corresponding constitutional amendment, was adopted in December 1988.

The *Language Law* was passed in 1989. It was provisional in its content, matching the needs of the transformational process under way in Estonia. Although it described Estonian as the sole official language, owing to political expediency, the main principle was the stipulation that there be Estonian-Russian bilingualism, which required that holders of certain jobs should be proficient in both Estonian and Russian (in most cases the knowledge of 800 words, i.e. elementary level, was sufficient). To reach the required level, a four-year delay was introduced in the law, so that it became effective in 1993. The law was in force until 1995, when a new language law was adopted.

The *Language Law* of 1989 should be seen as a remedy to the language problems of the time. The main problem was the catastrophic growth of Russian monolingualism owing to demographic change, the low status of Estonian in several functional and regional domains, and a lack of integrated education. The law was guided by the following principles:

- **The principle of bilingualism in the provision of services and state agencies**, with the right of customers to choose the language of communication, introduced constraints on monolingualism among clerks and service personnel, which, taking the situation into account, meant restrictions for Russians – overwhelmingly monolingual at that time – on upward mobility and on employment in positions involving contact with the public.
- **Language requirements instead of ethnic criteria**. No ethnic preferences in legislation and administration were introduced but, instead, language requirements, while providing clear language rights for speakers of other languages.(See Ozolins 1994: 168)
- **Visible signs of the new language policy**. Maurais (1997: 152) has emphasised the necessity of visible change in some language policy domains to reduce uncertainty

about the future of the language concerned through concrete manifestations. In the Estonian case, those may be public bilingual signs and information and language requirements for employment.

From the formal point of view, the Estonian language law of 1989 did not alter the former situation substantially, but rather maintained the *status quo* by granting the right to receive education in one's native language, with Estonian enjoying higher status among Estonians and Russian among Russians (*cf.* Taagepera 1990). Ozolins (1994), however, considers the modest language policies of the Baltic states a crucial element in national reconstruction and the transition from the Soviet system. The language law redefined Estonian from its *de facto* acquired minority status to full national status as the language of state and administration, and of most social discourse (Ozolins 1994: 161).

In that way, the adoption of the law signalled the redistribution of power and, alongside that, the formation of new elites in Estonia. Owing to the insignificant formal changes for most of the Russian-speaking population (the law did not concern the main bulk of it directly), the ambiguity of the situation with the two endo-majorities remained, thus causing several further conflicts and offering grounds for outside political influence. However, the main emphasis was placed on short-term visible programmes, while long-term initiatives such as education and integration programmes were either not given adequate attention or even neglected. Thus, the emerging situation was still not satisfactory, and a further qualitative step needed to be taken to improve the linguistic situation in Estonia.

Owing to the legacy of the previous period, the renormalisation policy was slow and complicated. A sophisticated set of problems concerning democracy and human rights had to be untangled, among which was the expanding confrontation between the two linguistic communities. Estonians had the right to end occupation and oppression, including at a linguistic level. At the same time, those who had immigrated during the occupation did not expect it to come to an abrupt end, meaning that they had to face obligations connected with language and citizenship, lowering their competitiveness in the employment market and worsening their relative living standards compared with those of the indigenous population. Significant attitudinal delay among the local Russian population in language and cultural issues was imminent. A feeling of "betrayal" and waiting for the return of Russian troops, together with negative attitudes towards Estonian and its speakers, was widely witnessed during the 1990s. Fortunately, those phenomena seem to have been overcome in recent years.

Acquisition Planning

The language of education has also been a concern for both Estonians and speakers of other languages, since it is inherently linked to the conflicting interests of common language promotion and minority maintenance. That dilemma is reflected in **the** *Constitution*. For educational rights, Article 37(4) of the constitution states: *All persons have the right to instruction in Estonian*. Simultaneously, the second clause guarantees the right for educational institutions established for ethnic minorities to choose their own language of instruction.

Article 6 of the *Language Law* provides for educational guarantees in Estonian and in a foreign language:

State institutions and local governments shall guarantee the opportunity to acquire Estonian-language education, according to the procedures prescribed in law, in all the educational institutions belonging to them, as well as the opportunity to acquire a foreign-language education, according to the procedures prescribed by law.

The same principle was earlier adopted in the Law on Education in 1992.

Language-teaching in other types of school is regulated by the corresponding laws. The *Law on Private Schools* gives the owner of the school the right to determine the language of the school (Article 14), requiring the teaching of Estonian from the third grade. The *Law on Vocational Schools* prescribes Estonian as the language of education (Article 18(3)). The use of other languages is determined by the patron of the school. The *Law on Universities* prescribes Estonian as the language of instruction (Article 22(8)), leaving the use of other languages to be determined by the university council.

However, challenges at a societal level have affected the education system, and several problems have also been transferred to school. The division of society on a linguistic basis has not yet been eliminated, and the attitudes and values of Estonian-speakers and Russian-speakers therefore still differ significantly, for example, attitudes towards NATO, Russia's foreign policy, historical events, Victory Day, and so on. The status shift of Russian has been recognised by the Russian community. However, learning Estonian as an adult is not a popular option, although most Russian-speakers have attended language courses and acquired valuable, though passive, language knowledge. Simultaneously, negative trends among the Russian community in Estonia have become highly visible: a high drop-out rate from the education system, unemployment, drug and HIV problems, and a high juvenile crime rate. Several Russian-speaking residential districts that used to be trendy only 15 years ago have become ghettos.

The Estonian language environment is substantially different. Since 1992 the educational level and average salary of Estonian-speakers have been higher than those of non-speakers, with the latter over-represented in prisons (c. 3.2 times), and among the unemployed and homeless. There are four times more top specialists and nine times more directors among Estonians than among Russians, while on the unofficial list of millionaires, Russian-speakers are represented marginally. Those classified as wealthy constitute 18% of the Estonian and 11% of the Russian community. Research has shown a strong connection between Estonian language proficiency and competitiveness: according to research data from 2004, those who received high grades in Estonian at Russian schools were much better off five years after graduation, even if the only reason for high grades in Estonian was a bilingual background at home.

That has had a strong impact on Russian parents' choices concerning schooling options for their children, seeking a competitive educational track. There is an increasing demand among the Russian-speaking community for increased Estonian language learning opportunities. Current teaching strategies for Estonian as a second language implemented in Russian schools have not been efficient enough. Most secondary school graduates from Russian-language schools do not have sufficient Estonian language skills to be competitive in the job market or to continue their studies in Estonian. Therefore, Estonian schools are highly valued among Russian parents, who are increasingly seeking opportunities to help their children become bilingual. Thus, there seems to be consensus regarding the best educational track. However, political *laissez-faire* in implementing educational reforms has hindered progress considerably.

For children with a non-Estonian home language, there are currently only a few entry points into the Estonian-medium education system. The main educational options are the following: Estonian-medium kindergarten, an Estonian school, or an immersion programme. In addition to those, Russian-medium schooling is available, but as an educational option that is unpopular, owing to the poor performance of its graduates.

Kindergartens and other Childcare Institutions

The proportion of children of pre-school age attending childcare institutions has been growing continuously since 1995, and 66% of one- to six-year-old children are currently covered by pre-primary education. The proportion rises significantly with the age of the children, as 85% of all six-year-old children attend kindergarten. The childcare institution for pre-school children provides children under school age with day care and the possibility of obtaining pre-primary education.

The language of instruction in a childcare institution for pre-school children is usually Estonian (78.4% of institutions). There are also 78 institutions working in Russian (13.1%), with 34 of them situated in Tallinn), and 50 (8.4%) working in both languages, accounting in total for 12,000 children in Russian kindergarten groups. Within the group, there can be only one language of instruction. The majority of institutions for Russian-speaking children are located in urban areas. Thanks to pressure from Russian parents themselves, in 1995 Estonian began to be taught as a second language to five- to six-year-olds in Russian pre-schools. In 2000, the obligation to teach Estonian as a subject was extended to the kindergarten (for children of five to six years of age) and first-grade levels. The main problem with Russian-medium pre-school educational institutions is the low competence of teachers of Estonian. There are currently more than 100 kindergarten teachers of Estonian as a second language, but as most of them (56%) do not work full-time and 30% have not completed formal training in the domain, the quality of teaching can be modest. To overcome those challenges, an extensive in-service training programme was launched for kindergarten personnel in 2003. Special teaching programmes have been designed, with the application of various language games, physical and manual activities and methods suitable for children, including some based on daily routine and TPR.

Some 74.8% of pre-school children enrolled in childcare institutions attend Estonian groups. That includes 7% of children whose home language is Russian. The reason is the wish of parents to shift to the Estonian educational track rather than a lack of suitable Russian kindergartens in the neighbourhood. At the end of 2003, some 1,114 children with a different mother tongue were attending Estonian-speaking groups in Tallinn. In recent years, the number of non-Estonian parents who choose an Estonian medium kindergarten for their child has been increasing, but Estonian-speaking kindergarten teachers do not yet have sufficient knowledge to develop and teach Russian-speaking children.

As an alternative, since 2004 total language immersion groups have been introduced in 17 kindergartens, with almost 300 children involved. That has proven a popular option and will likely grow in the near future.

Schools

Education is the most important means of guaranteeing the development and status of the language. The role of education is to provide general literacy and professional competence. Secondary education, especially compulsory education, is of fundamental importance because of its impact on language use. The requirement for an Estonian environment deriving from the Estonian constitution implies the task of providing proficiency in Estonian in the framework of compulsory education. However, several challenges are faced in the implementation of that task.

The challenges here are the large number of non-Estonian pupils and their isolation from Estonian-speakers. This is an historical legacy from the period of the Soviet occupation, when Russian-medium education expanded at the cost of Estonian. That led to students in Russian schools having an extremely multicultural background. However, it happened with the aim of eliminating all ethnic and linguistic differences and producing new Soviet citizens assimilated to Russian. At the end of the 1980s, more than 40% of first-graders in Estonia chose the Russian-medium educational track that provided only a scarce knowledge of Estonian, if at all. That implies that most Russian parents are not proficient in Estonian themselves and often harbour values and attitudes negative towards Estonian. Such a domestic affective filter may influence the performance of children in their acquisition of Estonian at school. In addition, the Russian population has been living in separate residential districts where houses were built during the Soviet period. Nowadays those have turned into ghettos, hindering communication with Estonians and integration into the mainstream.

Russians in Estonian Schools

Contemporary Estonian-medium schools have turned from *de facto* ethnic minority schools in the Soviet period to multicultural educational institutions, where the cultural background or home language of a significant portion of students differs from that of the mainstream. That covers about 5% of places in Estonian schools, accounting for over 4,000 students. However, school management is not fond of that trend, as it has resulted in a lower level of proficiency in Estonian as well as in other disciplines for all students. To avoid those negative effects, the number of Russians in Estonian-medium educational institutions has been limited, which is not a good solution either. Therefore, plans have been drafted for introducing Estonian as a second language into those schools, in accordance with the model adopted in Finland. Simultaneously, alternative programmes for Russian children are being started.

Russian Schools

According to the national curriculum, teaching of non-Estonian children is also provided in Russian. With the re-establishment of independence in 1991, the curriculum of Russian schools was harmonised with that of Estonian schools. The number of Estonian periods in Russian schools, which had been very low (twice a week, if at all) was increased dramatically.

In parallel with the corresponding demographic trend, the number of Russian-speaking pupils increased up to the year 1990, when they comprised 37% of the total.

Currently, qualitative changes are taking place in that respect. In 1993, 17% of schools used Russian as the medium of instruction. In the 2003–04 school year, there were (in addition to 521 Estonian-medium schools) 87 Russian-medium schools and 25 mixed schools. Currently, there are fewer than 40,000 pupils in Russian-medium schools, with an annual enrolment of 2,400 first-graders, a figure which decreases by 4% to 5% every year. According to the forecast, in 2009, the number of students will drop below 30,000 and the number of teachers below 2,000 (currently it is 4,000). The main reason for that drop is an extremely low birth rate (c. 3,000 children born to Russian-speaking families annually), resulting in a shortage of pupils. For that reason, several Russian schools have closed each year. The second, highly visible, reason for the decrease is Russian parents' desire to place their children in Estonian pre-school educational establishments and schools to immerse them in the language. The monolingual Russian-medium education system adopted during the Soviet occupation, with Estonian taught mainly as a subject, is still popular, but bilingual teaching has been increasing steadily. By 2005, bilingual teaching of various kinds was applied in 83% of Russian schools. To improve the situation further, since 1996 Estonian has been taught from first grade. Some Russian medium schools use Estonian as a medium for teaching certain subjects (history, geography) in the form of partial immersion.

Immersion Programmes

In Estonia, there are currently three possible points of entry into the programme – the first year of kindergarten, grade one and grade six. In the early immersion programme, 100% of instruction takes place in Estonian until the second semester of grade two, when Russian-language arts are introduced into the curriculum. Instruction through the medium of Russian is steadily increased from grade to grade. It will constitute 44% of the programme in grade six. At that point, instruction through the medium of Estonian will also constitute 44% of the programme, while 12% of instructional time will be devoted to a third language. Immersion programmes provide additional bilingual education, as they aim for functional proficiency in both the student's home language and a second language. Participation is strictly voluntary. Student selection is based primarily on a "first come, first served" basis, with a quota for the number of boys and girls (www.kke.ee).

In the late immersion programme, the grade six year of entry is viewed as a period of transition, during which only 33% of instruction is delivered through the medium of Estonian. In grades seven and eight, 76% of instruction will be delivered in Estonian. The remaining 24% will consist of third-language and Russian-language studies. In grade nine, the proportion of instruction through the medium of Estonian will drop to 60% of the curriculum (www.kke.ee).

The Estonian Ministry of Education launched a four-year implementation project in four schools in March 2000, when the total immersion programme was introduced in five classes to 134 first-grade students. That proved highly successful and has been extended every year to new schools. Currently over 1,000 students study in early immersion programmes in 12 schools. Late immersion was started in 2003 in four schools, but it has now expanded to 20 schools.

Estonian-medium Secondary Education for All

The most challenging issue in education is definitely the secondary education of Russian and other non-Estonian students in Estonia. Owing to minute numbers (c 2,000 students in Russian secondary school in 2009), full-scale secondary education through Russian is not considered expedient. Therefore, the transition to 60% Estonian-medium teaching in Russian schools will begin in the academic year 2007–08. The subjects to be taught in Estonian will be civic studies, history, geography, music and other communicative subjects that enable the creation of better conditions for further integration and access to quality education. That requires the creation of special study ware and extensive in-service teacher training, something already launched.

New Immigrant Children at School

In recent years, Estonia has created the conditions for the implementation of EU Directive 77/486/EEC, aiming at strengthening the education system and building up the necessary capacity for the education of migrant workers' children. During the process, necessary institutional structures and capacity in the area of such education were developed.

In recent years, Estonian schools have had their first experiences with newly arrived children who do not speak the language of instruction of the school. Until now, the number of those has been modest (c. 150), but that is expected to rise considerably in the near future. Legislation regulating the education of non-Estonian-speakers has hitherto been focused mainly on Russian-speakers who arrived in Estonia during the Soviet occupation. New immigrant children are immigrants and refugees who have arrived from the European Union and who have been in Estonia less than three years (www.hm.ee). Estonian legislation treats those pupils as subjects of education equal to Estonians; and all children of school age, except for the children of diplomatic representatives, are subject to the obligation of school attendance. As a starting point, a policy document concerning the education of migrant children was drafted. That document provides guidelines for national and local government and schools in accordance with which concrete actions can be taken regarding the education of migrant children, and the division of responsibilities at different levels. A handbook for teachers containing useful information on the issue of teaching migrant children and a training course for teachers, together with a textbook on Estonian as a second language at a basic level, targeted the 12 – 16 age group entering the Estonian school system (the pilot study materials *Astu sisse!* was based on the Dutch *Zebra*).

From 2004 the Estonian Ministry of Education and Research has been ready to receive migrant workers' children, providing an individual study programme; teaching Estonian as a second language on the basis of an individual study programme or in reception classes; support studies for up to three hours per week; if requested, mother-tongue studies; and admission to pre-school education and/or a school preparation group for children up to seven years of age (www.hm.ee).

Conclusion

At present, Estonian is used in all spheres of life. However, owing to political pressure and international "recommendations" from the Organization for Security and Co-operation in Europe (OSCE), education has been struggling with reforms. The past decade in Estonia seems also to have provided a major step forward here, with Estonian rising to the position of the dominant medium of education at all levels.

Expanding the training of university lecturers, teachers and educators and organising continuing education, market research for the identification of target groups and their needs, academic supervision, evaluation and modernisation of teaching materials and curricula are the main activities planned. That goes hand in hand with the increasing role of Estonian in education and the development of teaching materials that take into account the relations between Estonian and other languages of influence, establishing the national test development centre and expanding the academic learning of Estonian outside Estonia.

In spite of all the tensions, one can witness a gradual linguistic normalisation, with Estonian as the national language known by the vast majority, while minority languages are still accommodating themselves to the new conditions, including ethnic revival.

References

Maurais, J. 1997. 'Regional Majority Languages, Language Planning, and Linguistic Rights'. *International Journal of the Sociology of Language.* 127: 135-160.

Ozolins, U. (1994). 'Upwardly mobile languages: The politics of language in the Baltic States'. *Journal of Multilingual & Multicultural Development* 15: 161-169.

Rannut, Ü. 2003. 'Impact of the Language Environment on Integration and the Estonian Language Acquisition. *Proceedings of Conference "Multicultural Estonia", October 24-25, 2002.* Tallinn: Non-Estonian Integration Foundation, 125-137.

Rannut, Ü. 2005. 'Keelekeskkonna mõju vene õpilaste eesti keele arengule ja integratsioonile Eestis' ['Impact of the language environment on integration and Estonian language acquisition of Russian-speaking children in Estonia']. *Tallinna Ülikool. Humanitaarteaduste Dissertatsioonid,* 14. Tallinn: TLÜ kirjastus [Publications of Tallinn University].

Taagepera, R. 1990. 'The Baltic States'. *Electoral Studies* 9: 303–311.

Bilingual Malta: Language Teaching and the Future

Joe Zammit-Ciantar

Introduction

The Maltese archipelago is situated about 96 km. south of Sicily and 295 km. North of the African coast. It consists of two large islands, Malta and Għawdex (also called Gozo), and a number of smaller, uninhabited islands. The language used by the *c.* 400,000 inhabitants is Maltese.

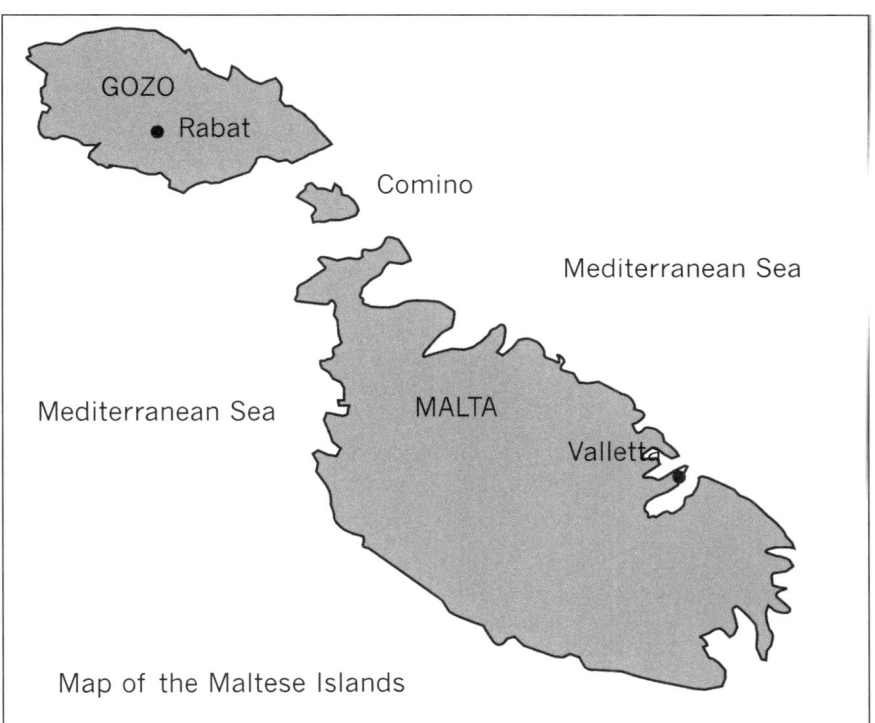

Map of the Maltese Islands

The Maltese Language

The Maltese language is a living national heritage. It derives from an Arabic dialect, which either transformed what could have been a late Punic lingering from antiquity, or was more probably brought over to the islands around AD 1050. It is used by almost all the inhabitants and by small Maltese communities that have settled in Canada and Australia. Although some Maltese who emigrated to and have settled in the USA and the UK are found to have preserved their mother tongue to a certain extent, they rarely use it outside their homes, unless with fellow Maltese migrants. All the same, it remains one of the lesser-used languages of the world.

Maltese is a mixed language. It must have evolved from a Maghrebine Arabic dialect – already mixed with Sicilian – which was used by the community that was brought over, most probably from Sicily, and re-populated the Maltese islands around AD 1048–49.[1] The two basic elements that make up the language used today are Semitic and Romance.[2] English came into contact with the Maltese language after 1800. It was first used with and by the people who worked in the Malta dockyards. Then it began to be taught as a compulsory language in schools. However, the widest and most effective contacts were brought about during the Second World War (1939–45), when British and Maltese soldiers fought the enemy side by side. Through its use in schools, in the university, and in the media, as well as in contact with the influx of hundreds of thousands of tourists who come to Malta every year, and especially with modern technology, it has become the main language source from which Maltese 'borrows' and slowly adopts lexical terms and expressions, especially in the fields of the economy, science, medicine, technology, commerce, IT, and so on. Although Malta gained political independence in 1964, because of various social, economic, and political factors, the inhabitants are linguistically still continuously in contact with, and still very dependent on, English.

A Maltese Grammar

As a written language, except for sporadic instances since the eighteenth century, with the rare exception of hundreds of place names recorded in notarial deeds,[3] and Pietro Caxaro's *Cantilena* (*c.* 1465),[4] Maltese remained unused, uncared for, and uncultivated. Contact with Italian, which was the official language of the knights of St. John for more than two and a half centuries (1530–1798), the language of the administration until late in the nineteenth century, and that which Maltese clergy and men taking up a profession studied, learned, and used when reading most of the printed material available – among themselves, and to further on their studies at home, but especially in universities in Sicily and mainland Italy – played a very important part a) through the influx of a great deal of vocabulary and syntactical structures into Maltese; b) in the creation of various Maltese alphabets used mostly between the sixteenth and the nineteenth centuries;[5] and c) in the establishment of a culture where the Maltese themselves believed that the language they could write and publish in was Italian.[6]

The first scientific Maltese grammar, *Tagħrif fuq il-Kitba Maltija*, ('Information about Writing Maltese'), first published in 1924, proved a success, and with very few

---

[1] Cf. Joseph M. Brincat, *Malta 870–1054: Al-Himyarī's Account and its Linguistic Implications*, Malta 1995, p. 20.

[2] The **Semitic** element constitutes the very basic foundation, or substructure, of the language; it manifests itself in about half of the vocabulary, and in almost all the morphological aspects of its grammar. That was eventually supplemented, especially during the period 1091–1800, by some **Romance** morphology, a very few French words, a multitude of Sicilian and Italian lexical terms, and many idiomatic and proverbial concepts; these constitute the superstructure of the language.

[3] For a study of Maltese place names encountered in Maltese notarial deeds going back to the fourteenth century, *cf.* Godfrey Wettinger, *Place names of the Maltese Islands, c.* 1300–1800, Malta 2000.

[4] Cf. Godfrey Wettinger and Michael Fsadni, *Peter Caxaro's Cantilena*, Malta 1966.

[5] For an idea of the various graphemes used at different times by divers writers in their efforts to create an alphabet for Maltese, *cf.* Joseph Aquilina, *Papers in Maltese Linguistics*, Malta 1961, especially the chapter 'Systems of Maltese Orthography' pp. 75–101b, and folding table facing p. 90.

[6] Cf. "The most significant factor of this phenomenon is that Malta created a literary culture (in its wider sense) written in Italian by the Maltese themselves." Oliver Friggieri, 'The Language Question in Malta: Consciousness of a National Identity' in *The Malta Year Book 1991,* Malta 1991, p. 414.

changes, saw Maltese accepted as an official language (second to English) in 1934,[7] entrenched in the independence constitution as the national language and the first official language of independent Malta,[8] and, very recently, accepted as one of the working languages of the European Union, with Malta confirmed a member on 1 May 2004.[9] The insularity of the inhabitants helped the totally isolated vernacular survive, and eventually develop into a distinct language. Flexibility and adaptability were and are the main characteristics that further helped keep Maltese a living and effective language.

---

[7] Regarding the use of the Maltese language in Maltese courts, *cf.* Ordinance No. XVI of 1932 (His Majesty's Letters Patent dated 14 April 1932), (*The Government Gazette* was then still printed in English and Italian), and, regarding the use of Maltese as an official language in the same Maltese courts, *cf.* "495a. (a) Subject to the ensuing provisions of this article, the Maltese language shall be the official language of the Court." Cf. Ordinance No. XXX of 1934 (His Majesty's Letters Patent dated 14 April 1934). Substitution of article 495a: (*The Government Gazette* started being printed in English and Maltese).

[8] "The national language is of course Maltese. But both Maltese and English are stated to be official languages." Cf. J.J. Cremona, *The Maltese Constitution and Constitutional History since 1813*, Malta 1994, p. 78. In the Constitution of Malta, Chapter I – The Republic of Malta, section 5, states:

"5. (1) The National language of Malta is the Maltese language.

(2) The Maltese and the English languages and such other language as may be prescribed by Parliament (by a law passed by not less than two-thirds of all the members of the House of Representatives) shall be the official languages of Malta and the Administration may for all official purposes use any of such languages:

Provided that any person may address the Administration in any of the official languages and the reply of the Administration thereto shall be in such language.

(3) The language of the Courts shall be the Maltese language:

Provided that Parliament may make such provision for the use of the English language in such cases and under such conditions as it may prescribe.

(4) The House of Representatives may, in regulating its own procedure, determine the language or languages that shall be used in Parliamentary proceedings and records."

[9] The Maltese language is already being used by Maltese official representatives participating in European Union meetings in Brussels.

The text in the *Accession Treaty* wherein the Maltese language is included states:

Institutions: Article 1

The official languages and the working languages of the institutions of the Union shall be Czech, Danish, Dutch, English, Estonian, Finnish, French, German, Greek, Hungarian, Italian, Latvian, Lithuanian, **Maltese**, Polish, Portuguese, Slovak, Slovenian, Spanish and Swedish." [My bold.]

Regarding the Maltese language becoming one of the working languages of the European Union, on 12 May 2002, the Malta Government Information Office issued the following press release, in Maltese and English:

Maltese to be EU official language

The Maltese Government has been informed that the Committee of Permanent Representatives (COREPER) at the Council of Ministers in the European Union had accepted the recommendation made by the European Commission for the Maltese language to become one of the EU's official languages on Malta's accession. The COREPER is a committee consisting of permanent representatives of the EU's member states who are responsible for preparing the work of the Council of Ministers. Moreover, when a proposal from the Commission is submitted to the Council, the same Council entrusts its examination to COREPER. When COREPER agrees unanimously with the Commission's proposal, as was the case with the Maltese language, then COREPER recommends that the Council of Ministers adopts the text prepared by the Commission.

The acceptance of Maltese as one of the EU's official languages means that the EU, after Malta's accession, will start publishing all its laws and official documents also in the Maltese language. Maltese members of the European Parliament, to be elected in June 2004 after Malta's accession, will enjoy the right to address the multi-national European Parliament in Maltese. [continued ...]

A Semitic Language

Because of its predominantly Semitic grammar, Maltese is classified as a Semitic language. It is the only Semitic language written with a Roman, or Latin, alphabet. Maltese is also the only Arabic dialect which developed into a language which now enjoys the status of a national language and, today, that of a working language in the European Union.

Bilingual Malta

The Maltese language reflects contact with the languages of the various peoples who dominated the inhabitants, beginning with the Phoenicians in c.700 BC, and ending with the British, who ruled over the islands up to 1964. That is perhaps evidenced most in the admixture of family names of the inhabitants[10] but also certainly in Maltese vocabulary.

Until 1934, when the official languages were English and Italian, the language of the administration was always that of the rulers. However, it may be assumed that in their daily intercourse, from the very remote past, the inhabitants at all times used and kept using the vernacular as a means of communication.[11] In that sense, the Maltese involved in communicating with the administrators were constrained to be bilingual; they had to learn to use at least one other language besides their own.

Maltese and English in the Constitution of Malta

Malta achieved political independence in 1964. Since then, Maltese has always been entrenched as the language of the Maltese. The latest *Constitution of Malta*, Chapter I, The Republic of Malta, Section 5, states:

> The National language of Malta is the Maltese language.
> The Maltese and the English languages ... shall be the official languages of Malta and the Administration may for all official purposes use any of such languages: [Provided that any person may address the Administration in any of the official languages and the reply of the Administration thereto shall be in such language.]

Maltese citizens would also enjoy the right to write to the European Commission in Maltese and expect to be answered in Maltese.

At present the EU has 11 official languages: French, German, Italian, Spanish, English, Finnish, Swedish, Portuguese, Dutch, Greek and Danish. The Irish Gaelic, the Luxembourgish and the Flemish (of Belgium) do not enjoy an official status in the EU. The two working languages at the Commission are English and French. The Commission will be increasing its staff by some 3,900 over the period 2004–2008 in order to meet the added requirements for translation and interpretation of new member states.

The Maltese Government has already started the translation of the 80,000 pages of EU laws into Maltese. On its own initiative, the European Parliament has a web page in Maltese and the Agricultural Directorate-General at the Commission has already published a document in Maltese. The EU Delegation in Malta has launched a web site and a newsletter in both Maltese and English.

[10] Cf. Mario Cassar, *The Surnames of the Maltese Islands*, Malta 2003.
[11] Compare with "Italian being spoken in the cities, while that spoken by the country folk is an admixture of words and forms of Arabic, [...], and Italian." J. S. Vater, as quoted by Joseph M. Brincat, *Il-Malti – Elf Sena ta' Storja*, Malta 2000, p. 155.

The language of the Courts shall be the Maltese language: [Provided that Parliament may make such provision for the use of the English language in such cases and under such conditions as it may prescribe.]

The House of Representatives may, in regulating its own procedure, determine the language or languages that shall be used in Parliamentary proceedings and records."[12]

Maltese and English in Education

After the establishment of compulsory education in 1946, both Maltese and English started to be taught in all state schools. Today, both languages are taught in all state, private, and Church schools from the earliest years of primary classes. The teaching of their use in speech, reading, and writing takes place at all levels of education. That was made compulsory by the *Education Act*,[13] drawn up by the then Minister of Education – today President Emeritus of Malta – Dr. Ugo Mifsud Bonnici, and enacted in 1989.

The Primary Schools Syllabus

Regarding the teaching of languages in primary education, the Education Act states that children should learn the Maltese and English languages, in their spoken, read, and written forms.[14]

The Secondary Schools Syllabus

The *Education Act* also provides for the further teaching of the Maltese and English languages in secondary education.[15]

The Use of Maltese and English in Tertiary Education

There is no steadfast rule regarding the delivery of academic information at a tertiary level. However, passes at 'O' Level in both Maltese and English are compulsory for entry to any of the higher secondary schools, as well as the University of Malta Junior College, where students are prepared for the 'A' Levels which enable them to proceed to university. All the same, the national minimum curriculum for post-secondary education[16] requires that "An emphasis [be placed] on the necessity of effective communication in both the verbal and the written media." That may be interpreted

---

[12] "The national language is of course Maltese. But both Maltese and English are stated to be official languages." Cf. J.J. Cremona, *The Maltese Constitution* …, p. 78.

[13] The text of the *Education Act* may be consulted in Joe Zammit Ciantar, *Education in Malta: A Handbook*, (2nd ed.), Malta 1996, pp. 42–82.

[14] Section A, 2(a), of Clause 6.3 of the National Minimum Curriculum – Primary Level (Legal Notice 73 of 1989), of the *Education Act* states: "At this level teaching should start to be formal and should be intended to achieve … [the] acquisition of the tools of knowledge and expression by the teaching of … the Maltese and English languages, in the spoken, read, and written forms."

[15] Together with mathematics, they form part of the "communicative core": section 4, B, of clause 6.4 of the national minimum curriculum – secondary level (Legal Notice 103 of 1990), of the *Education Act*. That clause further states that: "Another language at first year from those offered (Italian, French, German, and Arabic), and yet another language at third year from a wider choice which would also include Latin, Spanish, and Russian," and "particular courses in trade schools might opt for technical English in lieu of a third foreign language."

as an implied reference to the use of Maltese, but especially English, which would be extremely helpful and surely indispensable in both undergraduate and postgraduate courses taken up at university.

Ordinary Level examination papers of the University of Malta Secondary Education Certificate Board are set: in Maltese only for Maltese language and literature; in both Maltese and English for religious studies, social studies, and environmental studies; and in English only for all other subjects. Advanced Level examination papers are set: in Maltese only for Maltese language and literature; bilingually for religious studies and systems of knowledge; and in English only for all other subjects. Passes in Maltese and/or English at Intermediate or Advanced Level are required for certain undergraduate courses leading to particular degrees at the University of Malta.[17]

English at the University

The language of the university is English. That has been the case for many years now, first as part of the colonial mentality in favour of English replacing Italian, and over Maltese, and more recently to accommodate the large number of foreign students coming to Malta to take up their graduate studies at our university.

Maltese in the European Union

In the accession negotiations, Malta asked that the Maltese language be included as a legal working language – alongside those of other member countries – of the European Union. That was accepted, and Maltese has already been used by both the Maltese Foreign Affairs Minister, Dr. Joe Borg, and the Prime Minister, Dr. Eddie Fenech Adami, in their speeches in Greece, on the occasion of the signing of the Accession Treaty, in 200.[18]

English Breaks through the Barriers

The teaching of English in Malta has been going on for about two centuries now. Learning English has become an almost inherent necessity for the inhabitants. At first it could have been imposed by the rulers as part of a political programme. Then it may have been an attractive asset for any Maltese to get a 'good' job with the British administration on Maltese soil. Over time, however, it has become a great blessing,[19]

---

[16] Cf. Section 2 of the "content" of clause 6.5 of the national minimum curriculum – post-secondary level (Legal Notice 56 of 1991).

[17] The passes needed for the particular courses which may be taken at the University of Malta may be consulted in the University of Malta Special Course Requirements for Undergraduate Courses, which is published by the University of Malta around May every year. For those for entry to the University of Malta in 2005, cf. *Look ... before you leap,* Malta 2003, pp. 45–55.

[18] After 1 May 2004, when Malta officially becomes part of the European Union, all the latter's laws and official documents will also be published in Maltese. Additionally, Maltese Members of the European Parliament to be elected next June will enjoy the right to address the multi-national European Parliament in Maltese. The European Union journal will also be published in Maltese. Moreover, Maltese citizens will enjoy the right to write to the European Institutions in Maltese and expect to be answered in Maltese. [This was expressed in April 2004 and now, at time of publication, is considered past history.]

[19] To that one might add the fact that before the acquisition of English – especially in the nineteenth century – many Maltese venturing in search of a job outside Malta used to migrate to, and settle in, countries in the north of Africa such as Algeria and Tunis. They could do so because in those countries they would find it easy to work and settle using their native tongue, which has a close affinity with the

making almost all inhabitants bilingual.

Today every Maltese is conscious that without a knowledge of English we remain totally isolated and unable to communicate with the outside world. With a knowledge of English, our people can develop their cultural and intellectual capabilities even while at home. That has become a reality since English acquired international recognition, and has made us Maltese feel both lucky and proud to have gained such historic-linguistic experience. Learning English has become part of the development of our personality; it helps us break through the barriers of our geographical and linguistic insularity and feel part of a much larger world. It helps us understand the world around us, keep moving on in education for life, feel comfortable travelling to all the countries where large numbers of people can communicate through English, stand on very fertile ground in furthering our studies, have wider job choices, be competitive in every sort of market, and so on.[20]

Through a good grasp of English at home, Malta has now gained the reputation of being a very attractive centre for the teaching of English as a second language to foreigners. Besides those organised by the University of Malta, the Malta Union of Teachers, and the National Students Travel Foundation, around 22 private investors have set up schools for the teaching of English to foreigners, with courses going on all the year round. Today, those institutions cater for thousands of foreigners, especially students coming from EU member states, who come to learn English or practise the little English that they know, and of course, to experience Malta, enriched as it is by heartfelt hospitality, millennia of culture and history, a legendary climate, a healthy environment, and the wonderfully clear Mediterranean sea that bathes our shores and harbours.

Where Do We Stand?

"The civil service and public corporations now clearly need to see they employ people who are bilingual in the full sense of the word and not, as so often happens, in the sense that they speak and write tolerable or perhaps good English while they also speak and write an atrocious amalgam of Maltese, English, and Italian." This is a very recent admonishing comment, quoted from an editorial of *The Times [of Malta]*.[21] It was written after some contributors drew the attention of readers of this daily newspaper to the 'silly' and 'unacceptable' mistakes and amateurism shown in

---

dialects spoken in these countries. Later on, with the help of 'a little' knowledge of English, the Maltese started to migrate to England, and later still to Australia, Canada, and the United States of America.

[20] Knowledge of English has been beneficial also in our participation in international conferences, meetings, fora, contests (Malta will be participating in the next Eurovision Song Contest to be held in Turkey on 15 May, with a song in English, 'On again ... off again' interpreted by Julie and Ludwig), and other activities. The Maltese have grown accustomed to reading newspapers in Maltese (daily *In-Nazzjon*, *L-Orizzont*, and weekly *Il-Ġens, It-Torċa, Kullhadd, Il-Mument*) or English (daily *The Malta Independent, The Times [of Malta]*, and weekly *The Malta Independent on Sunday, Malta Today, The Sunday Times [of Malta]*).

[21] Cf. "Wanted: Translators and Interpreters", *The Times [of Malta]*, Friday, 26 March 2004. Other contributions related to this subject include George Cini, "EU looking for freelance in-house translators", *The Times [of Malta]*, Malta 18.i.2003, p. 14; Rosianne Zammit, "Full language cover in Maltese in Euro Parliament not yet possible", *ibid.*, 27.i.2004, pp. 1 and 4; Arnold Cassola, 'Let's make the best of the Maltese language in EU', *ibid.*, 19.ii.2004, p. 11; Interview with Dr. Alan Xuereb (chairman of a leading local agency which provides translation services and legal drafting) in "Lost in translation?", *The Malta Independent on Sunday*, 14.iii.2004, p. 15; (Malta Labour Party MP) Evarist Bartolo in Parliament, 'Don't make Maltese the language of Wenzu w Rozi, MP pleads', as reported in *The Times [of Malta]*, 16.iii.2004, p. 12; and (Joe Felice Pace), "'Bad Maltese' in EU website", in *ibid.*, Malta 22.iii.2004, p. 5.

the Maltese translation of the draft constitution of the EU. The debate on the professionalism of Maltese translators, proofreaders, and especially interpreters, expected to take up the required jobs in Brussels has now been going on for some time. It seems that we were not prepared for the number of qualified people required for these 'linguistic' jobs in Brussels.

It was only after that red light had drawn our attention to the situation that the University of Malta took up the challenge and started a two-year course for translators, and very recently planned a master's course in conference interpreting, to be organised jointly with the University of Malta Faculty of Arts, the Embassy of the Delegation of the Commission of the European Communities, and the Education, Youth, and Employment Ministry; that will commence next October.[25] In the meantime, some public entities[23] have decided to take the bull by the horns and themselves organise very professional courses, which, according to a participating lecturer, are leading to some extremely promising translators and interpreters. It seems that, now that awareness of this linguistically uncomfortable situation has been raised, the administration, the university, and related corporate bodies are trying to organise themselves in accordance with the linguistic needs that membership in the European Union has brought about.

Afterword

Maltese is a relatively young language. It is still developing, and there are times when translators, interpreters and authors still meet with difficulties, especially when trying to translate new expressions, ideas, and technical terms into Maltese. Globalisation, which is fast influencing the economies of countries all over the world, is impinging on the Maltese language too. The hopes of one and all interested in the use of the language in local educational programmes, and especially in harmonising EU literature for use by Maltese citizens in their own national language, may now lie in the establishment of a national council for the Maltese language, something currently being discussed in parliament. The aim of the Bill[24] is "to promote the National Language of Malta and to provide the necessary means to achieve this aim". Representation on the council of all the bodies and associations which sincerely wish and are interested in seeing that the Maltese language keeps abreast of the times and the needs of its inhabitants for effective use, be they common men, professors or creative writers, fills us with optimism. On the other hand, the learning of English is essential for one and all. However, that does not imply that we allow our attention to slip from our national language. Maltese continues to be the idiom nurtured in the family and childhood years, taught side by side with English during ten years of primary and secondary education, and used by nearly all the inhabitants as a means for communication. Above all, Maltese continues to be a beautiful, Semitic, mixed language, forming part of a European mosaic of diverse languages, and the idiom in which many Maltese authors express themselves in their works, which are part of a continuum of Maltese literature built up over the last two centuries.[25]

---

[22] Cf. 'Master's course in conference interpreting' *The Times [of Malta]*, 5.iv.2004, p. 35.
[23] Among these: 'Lexicom' and 'Euroconsult'.
[24] Bill No. 18, published in Maltese and English in *The Malta Government Gazette, Supplement*, No. 17,504, Malta 18.xi.2003.
[25] See further, Joseph Zammit-Ciantar, 'The Making of the Maltese Language'. In eds. Kirk, J.M. and D.P. Ó Baoill. *Legislation, Literature, Sociolinguistics: Northern Ireland, the Republic of Ireland, and Scotland*. Belfast: Cló Ollscoil na Banríona. 2005. 179-194

A Slavic Island in a Germanic Sea: Sorbian in Education

Leoš Šatava

Who are the Sorbs?

The Sorbs are a small Slavic nation living in the eastern part of Germany (the former GDR), close to the border with the Czech Republic and Poland. They are the last descendants of the Baltic Slavs, who have resisted Germanising influence for over a thousand years. Today about 40,000 people remain who can still speak Sorbian, a language belonging to the West Slavonic family; only approximately 15,000 to 20,000 people use Sorbian actively as an everyday language, however. The language, moreover, is divided into two standard varieties, that is, Upper Sorbian and Lower Sorbian.

After World War II, during the existence of the German Democratic Republic, many rights were secured for the Sorbs. A wide network of national institutions, schools and media came into existence. Assimilatory trends and direct measures, however, continued to be effective, and the number of users of the language went on decreasing rapidly, at the rate of about 1,000 a year.

Despite the development of Sorbian schools, media and other national institutions in the period of the socialist German Democratic Republic, the state policy towards the Sorbs can hardly be characterised as targeted and co-ordinated *language planning*. Nevertheless, that situation remained largely true even after the political changes in the 1990s. It was only at the turn of the twentieth and twenty-first centuries that new paths and models of language policy began to be actively sought by both state and Sorbian institutions. The examples of other ethnic minority groups of Europe and other continents whose revitalisation efforts have already proven successful have been of invaluable assistance.

Map of the Sorbian-speaking area

The Sorbian School System

After 1948, when, for the first time, the Sorbs were granted equality by the *Sorbian Act*, a network of Sorbian schools was created. From its very beginnings, the school system has evolved in two forms. In the part of their territory called the Catholic region (Bautzen/Budyšin and the region to the north-west) where ethnic awareness and the language have been best preserved, the **A-type schools**, that is, Sorbian-medium schools in most subjects were established. In the other part of Lusatia, Sorbian became a compulsory subject, and the schools there were referred to as **B-type schools**. Although we should not overestimate the impact of the latter fact on German pupils and students, it was nevertheless a successful outcome of the efforts that went into making bilingualism in Lusatia both real and symbolic. The expedited education of large numbers of teachers in the Sorbian Teacher Training Institute and the production of teaching materials were achieved. Between 1945 and 1950, there were three Sorbian grammar schools in northern Bohemia educating the first generation of Sorbian intelligentsia. Since 1948, *Serbska Šula* ('Sorbian School'), a journal for Sorbian teachers, has been published.

Although, until the mid 1950s, 'Lusatia will be bilingual' had been the official slogan of the political leadership of the GDR, in practical everyday life there was little political will to go by it. It was also the case for Sorbian schools: in 1962, the obligation to teach science through German was introduced. In 1964, in response to the opposition of German-speaking parents, Sorbian ceased to be an obligatory subject, and its instruction was provided only on parents' written request. The national organisation *Domowina* was not allowed to campaign for the instruction of Sorbian. Those measures resulted in the break-up of the network of B-schools and a drop in the number of pupils from 10,000 to 3,400. Not until the end of the 1960s did the number of pupils in B-schools rise to 6,000.

In the centralisation process of the 1970s and 1980s, the number of both A- and B-type schools fell; it also became quite clear that, in contrast to A-type schools, the B-type schools were not capable of 'producing' pupils able (and willing) to communicate in Sorbian. It is obvious that this fact could not be thoroughly reflected during the GDR period; owing to inertia and dilatoriness, however, hardly anything has changed since the political changes and the reunification of Germany in 1990.

At present, there are only six Sorbian primary-secondary schools (that is, *Grund-* and *Mittelschulen* covering the education from the first to the tenth class) and one Sorbian grammar school (that is, providing education from the fifth to the twelfth class) where Sorbian is the everyday language of instruction for about 1,000 pupils in total. Thus, at the turn of the millennium, only two of the above seven schools are all-A schools (that is, all classes from the first to the tenth are Sorbian-medium). In the remaining five schools, A-classes and B-classes coexist. All the schools are situated in Upper Lusatia, mainly to the west of the regional centre of Bautzen/Budyšin. That territory is now the only place where Sorbian is still the natural medium of communication for all generations. Approximately 150 children attend Sorbian nursery schools in the area. There are also a few dozen schools in Upper and Lower Lusatia with Sorbian taught as a subject (about 2,000 pupils). Two lessons a week and the casual attitude of both pupils and teachers in several cases make that rather a symbolic gesture, however.

In Cottbus/Chośebuz, in Lower Lusatia, there is also a Sorbian grammar school. However, instruction there is provided largely through German. Moreover, because of a very high degree of assimilation in Lower Lusatia, practically no Lower Sorbian mother-tongue children bring the language to school. The remaining bastion of Sorbian schooling is currently threatened by two effects:

1. After 1990, the birth rate in eastern Germany (the former GDR) fell rapidly, and, as a result, at the turn of the century several schools closed. Whereas earlier there had been about 150 pupils in each school year of A-classes at Sorbian schools, at present the total number of children from Sorbian-speaking families in one school year is only 50 to 60. It therefore seems that not even the remaining six primary-secondary schools are likely to be maintained.
2. The Saxony Ministry of Education does not fully implement specific aspects of the Sorbian system of education, and it does not accept the fact that, by closing down any of the remaining Sorbian schools, the impact on the ethnic and linguistic situation is qualitatively different from that of a closed German school. That fact stood out most clearly in the struggle for the secondary school in the village of Crostwitz/Chróścicy, which has been going on since the summer of 2002. On that occasion, which received wide media coverage, the Sorbs emerged once again as a political element after 50 years.[1]

Merger of the A- and B- Classes and the Immersion 'WITAJ' Model

At the turn of the twentieth and twenty-first centuries, as a result of the above facts, the search for new ways and models of maintaining and revitalising Sorbian and ethnic consciousness became a necessity. To maintain the Sorbian school network despite the small number of children from Sorbian-speaking families, it was necessary to persuade a part of the German-speaking parents in Lusatia that bilingual education and a knowledge of Sorbian could be an advantage for their children.

Beginning with the children in the first classes in the 2001–02 school year, the strict division into A- and B-classes was replaced with a new system of common bilingual instruction in which children from both Sorbian- and German-speaking families participate. That arrangement was applied to new classes, while the existing classes continued as A- and B- ones. However, that is the reason why there are still doubts and some fault-finding – it is feared, and to a certain extent rightly so, that the full integration of pupils from Sorbian- and German-speaking families might lead to the quick assimilation of the remaining Sorbian mother-tongue children. The officially integrated classes are, therefore, being divided in various subjects – the objective, however, is that even the children from German-speaking families will achieve full Sorbian-language competence.

The most significant innovation in this field has been (since 1998) the WITAJ ('Welcome') project, drawing mainly on the experience of the Bretons. A network of immersion nursery schools and, since 2000, first classes in some primary schools has

---

[1] Since August 2001, there have been massive protests over the government's attempt to close down one of the important Sorbian secondary schools in the heartland village of Crostwitz/Chróścicy, hitherto the only school where Sorbian is spoken exclusively. The future of the school is still open: the ministry insists on compliance with the prescribed number of 20 pupils in each of two parallel classes, as the law requires. Owing to the low birth rate over the last decade, however, that is an impossible task to fulfil. The struggle over a single school has thus become the struggle for the whole concept of the cultural life of the Sorbs in Germany and brought the Sorbian issue to an international stage.

been created in places where Sorbian is now spoken only by the older generation. Today immersion education still involves only limited numbers – there are six WITAJ nursery schools and 14 WITAJ play groups, with a current total of approximately 500 children; in addition, there are around 100 children in the first, second, third and fourth years in some schools. In nursery schools, children are brought up in Sorbian and German on the principle of '**one person, one language**' – the relationship of the two languages varies from one institution to another. Of course, the primary schools in which WITAJ classes have been set up to link preschool with school education (with the maximum of 14 lessons in Sorbian a week) do not compare with the six fully Sorbian schools. In spite of that, it is a big step forward.

Although the number of WITAJ-children is quite small, the fact that such a model has been developed and come into existence is crucial because of the very low prestige of Sorbian in many regions of Lusatia and antagonistic stereotypes among German-speaking inhabitants. It is a great achievement that in 1998 the first WITAJ nursery school was opened in the village of Sielau/Žylow in Lower Lusatia, where the tradition of Sorbian as the language of instruction had come to an end in the 1950s (Lower Sorbian spoken in the region is an ethnolect considerably different from that in the region of the main concentration of Sorbs in Upper Lusatia). Children who enrolled in the WITAJ nursery schools in Sielau/Žylow and other places are now attending the first three years of primary school. It is a considerable success that after the initial phase of scepticism to the project, there are already 30 children on the nursery school waiting list.

The rise of the WITAJ network of immersion nursery schools, however, brings several new problems that must be solved *en route*. Shortage (sometimes even non-existence) of tutors and teachers with Sorbian as a mother tongue is one example. The lack of native speakers has been at least partly solved by organising special intensive language courses and by employing other (mainly elderly) mother-tongue speakers (grandparents of the pupils in some cases). New teaching materials and textbooks (especially a primer and other books in Lower Sorbian) were badly needed.

When trying to persuade parents (the majority of whom can no longer speak Sorbian) to enrol their children in the WITAJ nursery, the following arguments are most frequently used: the resumption of the broken family and local traditions; bilingualism as an invaluable and unique regional feature of Lusatia; educational and psychological aspects of the advantages of bilingualism; and practical advantages (especially the close relation to the other Slavonic languages and the fact that the Czech Republic and Poland are becoming member states of the EU). Activists in the field of the implementation of immersion education hope to achieve a greater presence for Sorbian in the everyday life of children and young people and the enhancement of ethnic Sorbian awareness, which, in Lusatia, is closely linked with language competence.

Nevertheless, in several places there has been a noticeable change in the view of the local population (largely of Sorbian roots) regarding Sorbian and efforts at its revitalisation – from initial derision and refusal to a (cautiously) positive attitude (as in the instance of Sielow/Žylow and elsewhere). That many 'purely' German families, that is, families of German origin only or with no conscious Sorbian tradition, participate in the WITAJ initiative is also remarkable.

Some parents have noticed and appreciate the advantages of bilingual education at an early age, that is, the advantages that it brings in the sphere of abstract thinking and the general development of the intellect. It is also worth noting that the establishment of Sorbian immersion nursery schools and primary schools invited debates about the possible setting up of similar Czech and German educational institutions in Saxony's border regions; the entry of the Czech Republic to the European Union no doubt spurring the debate. Since the information about the course of the WITAJ project has to some extent overshadowed the news about the daily problems of the Sorbian schools in the Sorbian media, the need to put both in balance is being widely discussed. In that respect, the idea of 'language nests' has been introduced – Sorbian nurseries and schools and WITAJ institutions working together within a particular locality and creating a climate favourable to the ethnic and linguistic revitalisation of a given micro-region.

Within the process of restructuring Sorbian organisations, the Language Centre WITAJ was established in Bautzen/Budyšin on 1 January 2001 to co-ordinate the above, as well as other activities in the field of language planning. Its task has been to concentrate and co-ordinate efforts and activities aimed at the maintenance and development of Sorbian.

Alongside the above activities, we can also point out other innovative achievements in the field of the language, such as the modernisation of published books and periodicals, including translations from modern literature, changes in broadcasting (a stronger focus on young people, first of all in Upper Lusatia but most recently also in much more assimilated Lower Lusatia), Sorbian pages on the Internet, the start of television broadcasting in Upper Sorbian on 8 September 2001 (so far only one 30-minute programme a month plus one children's cartoon of a few minutes each week) and others.

In the field of legislation, the Sorbs have been aiming at clearer procedural regulation of the relevant laws (or possibly their amendment) and striving to achieve a schools network and law that would enable the maintenance of the existing schools, which would be based on the state agreement regarding a special regime for the Sorbian network or the existence of small schools in Saxony in general. The privatisation of some schools is also being considered at present, while the network of private Danish schools in Schleswig-Holstein is being taken as a possible model.

Conclusion

To sum up, we may conclude that after 40 years of life behind the Iron Curtain and another, rather passive, decade of looking for new forms of national life during the 1990s, visible changes in attitudes towards language policy and language planning are taking hold in Lusatia today. Those phenomena are now conceived on a more conceptual, planned and targeted basis. Nevertheless, the WITAJ immersion program has so far been the only conceptual and widely based model of language planning and revitalisation endeavour.

Today's ethnic and linguistic situation in a large part of Lusatia is comparable, for example, with that of Brittany or New Zealand in that people aged 60 and over are the predominant active users of the language.

However, even in such a situation, the above regions managed to set hopeful revitalisation efforts in motion. In the western, that is, 'Catholic' part of Upper Lusatia, however, the situation has been quite favourable so far, since the baton is still being passed on in the sphere of ethnic consciousness and intergenerational language transmission.

Will the Sorbs make use of this advantage and chance? Will it be possible, with the help of the WITAJ initiative and revitalisation practices, to succeed, replenishing the falling number of native speakers and changing the present-day form of Lusatian diglossia in which Sorbian is all too often an unequal partner of German? Only a longer-term perspective will show whether those changes will prove enough and whether the effect and success of the new forms will be strong enough to bring ongoing language assimilation to a halt, start reversing language shift or initiate the revitalisation of a small Slavonic language surviving in contact with German language and culture for over a thousand years.

Lusatia without the Sorbs or Sorbian is something many still find hard to imagine. At present, the point is to support the idea by laying solid foundations and acting consistently.

References

Šatava, Leoš. 1993. *Lusatian Sorbs in Eastern Germany*. Minority Rights Group, London, Report 1. 32–33, 45–46

Šatava, Leoš. 1994. *Minority Ethnic Groups in Europe: An Encyclopedia*. Praha: Ivo Zelezny [in Czech]

Šatava, Leoš. 1997. 'Ethnizität: Ein Danaergeschenk in neuem Gewand?'. *Lětopis*. 44/2: 3-7

Šatava, Leoš. 1999. 'Ethnic Identity and Language' / 'Culture Attitudes Among Students of the Sorbian Grammar School in Bautzen/Budyšin'. *Lětopis*. 46/1: 78-103

Šatava, Leoš. 2001. *Language and Identity of Ethnic Minority Groups. Possible Route to their Maintenance and Revitalisation*. Praha: Cargo [in Czech]

Šatava, Leoš. 2002. 'Spracheinstellung und Kulturerfahrung. Zur ethnischen Identität von Schülern der Sorbischen Mittelschulen'. *Lětopis*. 49/1: 60–82; 49/2: 45–73

Šatava, Leoš. 2005. *Sprachverhalten und ethnische Identität: Sorbische Schüler an der Jahrtausendwende*. Bautzen/Budyšin: Domowina-Verlag

A Decade of Kashubian in Education in Poland

Tomasz Wicherkiewicz

1. Introduction

Language

Kashubian (or 'Cassubian', in Kashubian: *kaszëbizna*) is a West-Slavic language spoken in northern Poland, in the province of Pomerania (*województwo pomorskie*), mainly in the counties (*powiaty*) of Gdańsk/Gduńsk, Gdynia/Gdiniô, Wejherowo/Wejrowò, Puck/Pùck, Lębork/Lãbòrg, Bytów/Bëtowò, Kartuzy/Kartùze, Kościerzyna/Kòscérzna and Chojnice/Chòjnice.[1]

The Kashubs (in Kashubian *Kaszëbë*, in Polish *Kaszubi*) inhabit an area of some 6,000 km. sq.) on the southern coast of the Baltic Sea – a tetragonal of *c.* 130 km. by 50 km.

Map of Kashubian-speaking area

Historically and paleo-ethnologically, the Kashubs are said to be direct descendants of the Pomeranians, a Slavic people that inhabited the Baltic coast between the Vistula (*Wisła*) and the Oder (*Odra*) rivers, perhaps even as far westward as the Elbe, in the early Middle Ages, and who long constituted a serious threat to the Lekhits – the ancestors of what later became the Polish nation.[2] The modern history of Kashubian began in the mid-nineteenth century, with ideas popularised by the Spring of Nations and the pan-Slavic movement (*cf.* Majewicz 1996, Treder 1997, Wicherkiewicz 2000). Since then, the sense of ethnic, regional and language identity has been strengthened by the efforts of Kashubian writers: Florian Ceynowa,

---

[1] For the information of German-speaking readers, the corresponding historical German names of the county towns are provided: Danzig, Gdingen, Neustadt, Putzig, Lauenburg, Bütow, Karthaus, Berent and Konitz.

[2] The Kashubian-Pomeranian Association and some regional politicians are striving for a change in the province's official name to "Kashubian-Pomeranian" (*województwo kaszubsko-pomorskie*).

Hieronim Derdowski, Aleksander Majkowski, Jan Karnowski, Aleksander Labuda and Jan Trepczyk.

The Kashubian language area is nowadays situated within the Polish state and, simultaneously, within the Polish linguistic area, and it is its geographic location that has determined the history and political and social conditions of its population, mostly rural, with agriculture and fishing as main occupations, as well as the development of Kashubian and its linguistic contacts: with Polish (standard and dialectal) and German (standard High German and Low German dialects) in the past (*cf.* Zieniukowa 1997).

Kashubian has completely diversified into local dialects, the number of which is estimated by some dialectologists at over 50; they can, however, be divided into three main groups: northern, central, and southern.

Population

The area inhabited by the Kashubs has diminished significantly over the centuries. The dawn of Kashubian as an ethnic group can be sought among the Pomeranians (*cf.* above). Under the pressure of German colonisation, the Pomeranians moved eastward, and the Slavic elements east of the Oder river disappeared. Since the eighteenth century, the Kashubian territory has not changed significantly, except for certain losses in the western part (present counties of Slupsk/Slëpsk, Lębork/Lãbòrg and Bytów/Bëtowò)[3] inhabited earlier by Protestant Kashubs and their linguistic subgroup – Slovincians. Periods of Germanisation alternated with waves of Polonisation. As the Kashubs were traditionally Catholic, their nobility and middle classes assimilated with the Polish majority.

During the twentieth century, the Kashub population was estimated as follows:

1900: 102,000[4]
1910: 111,000[5]
1926: 155,000[6]
1968: 140,000 to150,000[7]
1975: 150,000 to 22,000, with *c*. 4,500 speakers of Kashubian.[8]

According to the results of the first sociodemographic and sociolinguistic research in the late 1980s, the number of Kashubs (that is, persons who regard themselves as Kashubs or 'half-Kashubs') has been estimated at 350,000 to 500,000; including 150,000 to 250,000 who knew or could speak Kashubian to some degree (Iskierski and Latoszek 1995). The region of Kashubia is inhabited by 1.5 million people altogether.

The population Census of 2002 (the first since 1931) contained two questions dealing with the questions of 'nationality' and 'home language':

---

[3] German names: Stolp, Lauenburg and Bütow.
[4] Official census of the German state.
[5] Official census of the German state.
[6] According to: Meillet, Antoine 1928. *Les langues dans l'Europe nouvelle*. Paris.
[7] According to: Kloss, Heinz and G. D. McConell 1984. *Linguistic Composition of the Nations of the World*. Vol. 5. *Europe and the USSR*. Québec.
[8] According to: Haarmann, Harald 1975. *Soziologie und Politik der Sprachen Europas*. München.

1. *Among which nationality do you rank yourself?*[9]
2. *Which language(s) do you speak the most often at home?*

The answer 'Kashubian' to the former question was given by 5,062 persons (5,053 of them were Polish citizens). The absolute majority inhabit the Province of Pomerania (4,897); the remaining persons live in the provinces of: Silesia (46), Mazovia (31), Kuiavia-Pomerania (29), Great Poland and Western Pomerania (11 each), Lower Silesia (9) and Varmia-Mazuria (8). The latter question has been answered: 'Kashubian', 'Kashubian and Polish' or 'Polish and Kashubian' (no distinct data have been published) by 52,665 persons (52,567 were Polish citizens) – *cf.* http://sp.stat.gov.pl/spis/ludnosc/tab_wynik.xls .[10]

Several thousand Kashubs live abroad; worth mentioning are Kashubian enclaves in Ontario, Canada.

Language Status

Until the 1990s, according to most linguistic sources, Kashubian had been regarded as the most distinct or one of the most distinct dialects of Polish (contemporary Polish is traditionally divided into Great-Polish, Little-Polish, Mazovian, Silesian +/- Kashubian dialects). Those who regard Kashubian as a separate language classify it as one of the West-Slavic languages (together with Polish, Upper and Lower Sorbian, Czech and Slovak), forming with Polish and the extinct Polabian a separate sub-group of so-called Lekhitic languages.

Until 1989, it was prohibited by Communist censorship to use the noun *język* (Polish for 'language') regarding Kashubian. Therefore, Kashubian scholars, writers and activists used to call their ethnolect *kaszubszczyzna* ('Kashubianness') or *mowa kaszubska* ('Kashubian speech').

Since 1989, Kashubian has significantly upgraded its linguistic status. The most important factors that contributed to its present position have been: the activities of the pan-Kashubian association *Zrzeszenie Kaszubsko-Pomorskie*, founded in 1956, the translation of the New Testament – *Kaszëbskô Biblëjô* (1992) by F. Grucza and *Swięté Pismiona Nowégo Testameńtu* (1993) by E. Gòłąbk, the agreement concerning a unified spelling system for literary Kashubian (*cf.* Breza and Treder 1984, Gòłąbk 1997); before 1996 two competing systems had been used, the continuous efforts by Kashubian activists to include the language in all legal acts pertaining to minority issues and official nomenclature,[11] the organisation of the 39th Congress of the Federal Union of European Nationalities in Gdańsk in 1994, and the organisation of the 6th International Conference on Minority Languages in Gdańsk in 1996 (*cf.* Synak and Wicherkiewicz 1997).

The 1997 *Constitution of the Republic of Poland* contains two articles that appertain directly to minority rights, including linguistic rights:

---

[9] The definition of 'nationality' was provided: *Nationality is everybody's declarative (i.e. based on a subjective feeling) individual feature which expresses one's emotional, cultural or genealogical affiliation with a specific nation.*

[10] The Census included in total 38,230,080 inhabitants of the country, of whom 37,529,751 were Polish citizens, 492,176 of the latter declared a non-Polish language to be one of the home languages used most often, and 46,559 declared a non-Polish language the only home language used.

[11] The Kashubs have successfully applied for recognition as 'ethnic minority'.

Article 27.
Polish shall be the official language in the Republic of Poland. This provision shall not infringe upon national minority rights resulting from ratified international agreements.

Article 35.
1. The Republic of Poland shall ensure Polish citizens belonging to national or ethnic minorities the freedom to maintain and develop their own language, to maintain customs and traditions, and to develop their own culture.
2. National and ethnic minorities shall have the right to establish educational and cultural institutions and institutions designed to protect their religious identity, as well as to participate in the resolution of matters connected with their cultural identity.

The 1999 *Law on the Polish Language* provides, among others, for the possibility of introducing a minority language as an 'auxiliary' language in areas with a "considerable proportion of non-Polish population", where minority languages could be used in bilingual place names, in personal first names and surnames, and occasionally in local administration. However, the law lacks appropriate executive regulations; nor does it contain any provisions for the use of minority languages in jurisdiction, or in state or central administration.

The *Framework Convention for the Protection of National Minorities* was signed by Poland in 1995 and ratified in 2000. It has, however, no impact on the legal situation of the Kashubian language, since the (majority of) Kashubs are neither regarded nor regard themselves as such.

In 2003, the government of the Republic of Poland signed the *European Charter for Regional or Minority Languages,* and its ratification will probably follow the adoption of the *Law on National and Ethnic Minorities and Regional Languages* by the Polish Parliament. Chapter 4 (Articles 17 and 18) of the most recent project of the latter contains the following provisions:

Article 17:
The regional language as understood by the law is the Kashubian language. The regulations of Articles 7 to 14 will be applied respectively.[12]

Article 18:
1. The educational rights of persons who speak the language mentioned in the Article 17 will be exercised on the base of Article 15.[13]
2. Persons who speak the language mentioned in Article 17 have the right to found and run schools and educational institutions that enable teaching of or in the language, based on the general regulations.
3. The public authorities are obliged to undertake appropriate measures in order to support all activities which aim at the preservation and development of the language mentioned in Article 17, based on the general regulations.
4. The measures mentioned in §3 may be granted from the budget of an

---

[12] The above-mentioned Articles 7 to 14 of the law pertain to the use of minority languages in the spelling of Christian names and family names, private and public life, the official sphere as auxiliary languages, information, and geographical names, names of streets, names of offices and institutions.

[13] Article 15 pertains to the rights of persons belonging to minorities to be taught their minority language and/or in a minority language, as well as the history and culture of the minority group.

autonomous territorial unit to organisations and institutions that fulfil tasks aiming at the preservation and development of the language mentioned in Article 17.

Status of Language Education

Crucial to the status of teaching of and in minority languages in Poland are the following Acts:

Law on the System of Education of 1991, which grants pupils the right to maintain their national, ethnic, religious and linguistic identity, and particularly to be given classes in or through their mother tongue, as well as their history and culture;

Decree of the Minister of Education and Sport on Conditions and Methods of Enabling Pupils Belonging to National Minorities <u>and Ethnic Groups</u> [present writer's emphasis] to maintain their national, ethnic and linguistic identity of 2002 (substituting the previous one issued in 1992, which pertained solely to "national minorities"; the former decree was applied also regarding the Kashubian language group on the basis of an ... internal amendment by the then Minister of Education).

Private and Public Education

In general, Polish educational institutions can act as public, community (*społeczne*, 'social') and private establishments. As of now, there are no private schools providing education in or through Kashubian. The existing schools are predominantly public or community ones (the first of the latter type was the Community School in Głodnica (commune of Linia).

Bilingual Forms of Education

In the 1990s, only one primary school provided bilingual education to *c.* 20 children (the community school in Głodnica, commune of Linia). Owing to financial and educational problems, the school has been transformed into one with additional (although compulsory) education in the Kashubian language (three hours a week).

Teacher Training

In December 2002, the second edition of a *Qualification course for teachers of Kashubian language and regional culture* was launched at the University of Gdańsk, in co-operation with the education section of the Kashubian-Pomeranian Association. Each course has been planned for 1.5 years (3 semesters). Some 41 people completed the first run (in 2002); the second is being attended by 51 teachers and will finish in May 2004.

At present there are: 25 qualified teachers of Kashubian, 41 graduates from the first run of the teachers' course, and 51 students of the second run (in total 117 teachers).

2. Pre-school Education

Kashubian is used in pre-school education in only two private kindergartens. An early-immersion language programme, based on the experiences of similar programmes in Wales, Brittany and Lusatia is planned to start in 2005.[14] The first workshop devoted to that method is planned for late 2004.

3. Primary and Middle Education

Structure
In March, the school board of teachers should take the decision to introduce classes in Kashubian from 1 September (the beginning of the new school year), supported by a resolution of the school board. To open a class (or class section) for the instruction of Kashubian, seven written applications from children's parents are required.

The state provides funds for the teaching of Kashubian if its weekly provision amounts to three hours of classes. The subvention rate for schools providing education in or through minority languages amounts to 120% of the rate for other schools. If the number of pupils in such a school does not exceed 42, the rate amounts to 150%. The funds for the first four months of language teaching must be paid out by the commune. In some cases, that sum may also be paid out by the Ministry of Education and Sport at the beginning of the school year. The teaching programmes for primary and middle schools providing education in Kashubian were accepted by the Ministry of Education and Sport in 2002.

Language Use
The respective subjects are named: "Kashubian language", "Kashubian language with elements of regional culture", or "Regional education with elements of Kashubian language" and are taught for one, two or three hours a week.

Handbooks
Primer: Bòbrowsczi and Kwiatkòwskô, 2000; School dictionary: Bòbrowsczi and Kwiatkòwskô, 2003; Language course-book for younger classes: Pioch, 2001; Teaching programme and materials for language teachers: Pioch 2000, and Czedrowskô, Pioch and Tréder, 2001

Statistics
In 2002–03, some 52 primary schools provided classes in Kashubian language: one school for four hours a week, 31 schools for three hours, 18 schools for two hours, and two schools for one hour a week. The classes in Kashubian language in those schools were attended by 2,951 children.

Six primary schools provided classes in Kashubian language and regional culture: three schools for three hours a week, two schools for two hours, and one school for one hour a week. The classes in Kashubian language and regional culture in those schools were attended by 358 children.

Some 13 primary schools provided classes of regional education with elements of Kashubian language: four schools for three hours a week, five schools for two hours, four schools for one hour. The classes in regional education with elements of Kashubian language in those schools were attended by 1,358 children.

In 2002–03, some seven middle schools provided classes in Kashubian language: five schools for three hours a week, one school for two hours, and one school for one

---

[14] Probably under the name *Pùfôtk* (Kashubian for "Winnie-the-Pooh").

hour a week. The classes in Kashubian language in these schools were attended by 179 pupils.

Three middle schools provided classes in Kashubian language and regional culture, all of them for two hours a week. Those classes were attended by 159 pupils.

Four middle schools provided classes of regional education with elements of Kashubian language: two schools for two hours a week, and two schools for one hour. These classes were attended by 108 pupils.

As a whole, 5,113 schoolchildren at primary and middle level were provided with a form of Kashubian education.

4. Secondary Education

Structure

In March, the school board of teachers should take the decision to introduce classes in Kashubian from 1 September (the beginning of the new school year), supported by a resolution of the school board. To open a class (or class section) for the instruction of Kashubian, 14 written applications from pupils or pupils' parents are required.

The state provides funds for the teaching of Kashubian if its weekly provision amounts to three hours of classes. The subvention rate for schools providing education in or through minority languages amounts to 120% of the rate for other schools. If the number of pupils in such a school does not exceed 42, the rate amounts to 150%. The funds for the first four months of language teaching must be paid out by the commune. In some cases, that sum may also be paid out by the Ministry of Education and Sport at the beginning of the school year.

The teaching programmes for secondary schools providing education in Kashubian were accepted by the Ministry of Education and Sport in 2002.

Handbooks

Language course-book for older classes: Cybulski and Wosiak-Śliwa 2001; teaching programme and materials for language teachers: Czedrowskô, Pioch and Tréder, 2001

Language Use and Statistics

In 2002–03, only three secondary schools provided education in Kashubian in any form. The first provided classes in Kashubian language for three hours a week for 66 students; the second provided classes in Kashubian language and regional classes for two hours a week for 232 students; the third provided classes in regional education with elements of Kashubian language for one hour a week for 14 students. As a whole, 312 students at secondary level were provided with a form of Kashubian education.

5. Vocational Education

In 2002–03, only one vocational school at secondary level provided regional education classes with elements of Kashubian language (two hours a week) for 26 students. The teaching programmes for vocational schools providing education of Kashubian were accepted by the Ministry of Education in Sport in 2002.

6. Higher Education

Since 1992, Kashubian has been taught at a language course at the University of Gdańsk, as an optional specialist topic for students of Polish Language and Literature. At the Diocesan Seminary in Pelplin, Kashubian is taught for two hours a week every year as a language course to some 15 seminarians. The so-called 'Kashubian Folk Universities' in Wieżyca and Starbienino do not organise any language courses. The only language course-book for university students was published by Cybulski, and Wosiak-Śliwa in 1992.

7. Adult Education and Language Courses

The only forms of adult education in Kashubian are the above-mentioned qualification courses for teachers of Kashubian, as well as three courses in regional and alternative education, postgraduate courses in Pomeranian studies, as well as freelance courses of reading and writing in Kashubian.

In 2002–03, courses of Kashubian language and culture were organised in three centres (Gdańsk, Kartuzy and Władysławowo) and attended by 46 participants.

8. Prospects

The recent research (*cf.* e.g. Iskierski and Latoszek 1995) provided some reliable data on the situation of Kashubian. The results of the 2002 population Census could be disappointing in that respect, but taking into consideration its pioneering character, unclear criteria and a certain lack of confidence as far as all national and/or ethnic questions are concerned, the number of 52,665 persons declaring Kashubian to be their home language is undoubtedly an important indicator for language planners and educational activists.

Taking into account the fact that Kashubian was introduced (in a very modest way and dimension) as late as 1991, the total number of 5,451 pupils taught Kashubian (in any form) by 117 teachers seems quite impressive. Over the last 13 years, the most important obstacle to education through or in Kashubian has been abolished, namely, the traditional school system. It was the school that imposed the conviction of the superiority of 'urban Polish' culture to the 'rural Kashubian' one. Pupils and parents blamed the 'backwardness' of Kashubian for the poor career prospects of their children. A change in the mentality has certainly taken place.

Further development of Kashubian education is undoubtedly conditional on efforts by regional activists and the further training of qualified teachers. Crucial in that respect will also be the ratification of the *European Charter for Regional or Minority Languages* by Poland, preceded by the internal law on national and ethnic minorities and regional languages. For more information, see Wickerkiewicz (2005).

References

Bòbrowsczi, W. and K. Kwiatkòwskô. 2000. *Kaszëbsczé Abecadło – Twój Pierszi Elemeńtôrz* ['Kashubian ABC – Your First Primer']. Gdańsk: Dar Gdańska.
Bòbrowsczi, W. and K. Kwiatkòwskô. 2003. *Kaszëbsczi Słowôrz* ['Kashubian Dictionary']. Gdańsk: Dar Gdańska.

Bobrowski, Marcin M., M. Kwidzinski and H. Toby eds. 2003. *Cassubia Slavica. Internationales Jahrbuch für Kaschubische Studien* 1. Hamburg: Cassubia Slavica e.V.
Borzyszkowski, J. 2002. *Die Kaschuben, Danzig und Pommern*. Gdańsk-Wejherowo: Instytut Kaszubski, Muzeum Piśmiennictwa i Muzyki Kaszubsko-Pomorskiej.
Borzyszkowski, J. 2004. *The Kashubs, Gdańsk and Pomerania* (translated by T. Wicherkiewicz). Gdańsk: Instytut Kaszubski.
Borzyszkowski, J. and D. Albrecht eds. 2000. *Pomorze – mala ojczyzna Kaszubów* [*Historia i wspólczesność*]. *Kaschubisch-Pommersche Heimat* [*Geschichte und Gegenwart*]. Gdańsk-Lübeck: Zrzeszenie Kaszubsko-Pomorskie, Instytut Kasuzbski, Ostsee Akademie.
Breza, E. ed. 2001. *Kaszubszczyzna – Kaszëbizna* ['Kashubian']. Opole: Uniwersytet Opolski.
Breza, E. and J. Treder 1981. *Gramatyka Kaszubska. Zarys Popularny* ['Popular Outline of Kashubian Grammar']. Gdańsk: Zrzeszenie Kaszubsko-Pomorskie.
Breza, E. and J. Treder 1984. *Zasady Pisowni Kaszubskiej* ['Rules of Kashubian Spelling']. Gdańsk: Zrzeszenie Kaszubsko-Pomorskie.
Cybulski, M. and R. Wosiak-Śliwa 1992. *Kaszubski język literacki. Podręcznik dla Lektoratów* ['Literary Kashubian – Handbook for Language Courses']. Gdańsk: Graf.
Cybulski, M. and R. Wosiak-Śliwa 2001. *Ùczimë sã pò kaszëbskù. Książka Pomocnicza dla klas Starszych* ['We Learn Kashubian – Handbook for Older Classes']. Gdańsk: Oficyna Czec.
Czedrowskô, W., D. Pioch and J. Tréder 2001. *Ùczba Kaszëbsczégò Jāzëka w Szkòle. Materiałë dlô Szkólnëch* ['Teaching Kashubian at School – Materials for Teachers']. Gduńsk: Oficyna Czec.
Drzeldlon, J. 1986. *Wspólczesna Literatura Kaszubska* ['Contemporary Kashubian Literature']. Warszawa: Ludowa Spółdzielnia Wydawnicza.
Gołąbk, E. 1992. *Rozmówki Kaszubskie* ['Kashubian Conversation Guide']. Gdynia: Arkun.
Gołąbk, E. 1997. *Wskôzë Kaszëbsczégò Pisënkù* ['Recommendations on Kashubian Spelling']. Gduńsk: Oficyna Czec.
Gołąbk, E. and E. Pryczkowski 1998. *Më Trzimómë z Bògā. Kòscelné Mòdlëtwë i Spiéwë* ['We Stick with God – Church Prayers and Songs']. Gduńsk: Zrzeszenie Kaszubsko-Pomorskie, ROST.
Kaszëbskô Biblëjô. Nowi Testameńt. IV Ewanjelje ['Kashubian Bible. New Testament. 4 Gospels'] (translated by Franciszek Grucza) 1992. Poznań: Hlondianum.
Labuda, A. 1960. *Słowniczek Kaszubski* ['Little Dictionary of Kashubian']. Warszawa: PZWS.
Labuda, A. 1981. *Słownik Polsko-kaszubski. Słowôrz Kaszëbsko-Polsczi* ['Polish-Kashubian and Kashubian-Polish Dictionary']. Gdańsk: Zrzeszenie Kaszubsko-Pomorskie.
Iskierski, J. and M. Latoszek 1995. "The Kashubian Ethnic Group in the Prologue to Change: Local and Regional Perspectives". In B. Synak ed. *The Ethnic Identities of European Minorities*. Gdańsk: Uniwersytet Gdański. 141–153.
Kossak-Główczewski, K. 199. *Edukacja Regionalna Mniejszości Narodowych i Etnicznych* ['Regional Education of National and Ethnic Minorities']. Gdańsk: Uniwersytet Gdański.
Majewicz, Alfred F. 1996. "Kashubian Choices, Kashubian Prospects: A Minority Language Situation in Northern Poland". *International Journal of the Sociology of Language*. 120: 39–53. [Issue on *Minority Languages in Central Europe*].

Majewicz, Alfred F. and T. Wicherkiewicz. 1990. "National Minority Languages in Media and Education in Poland". In D. Gorter *et al.* eds. *Fourth International Conference on Minority Languages*. Vol. II. *Western and Eastern European Papers*. Clevedon-Philadelphia: Multilingual Matters. 149–174.

Mistarz, R. 2003. "Zasady Nauczania i Finansowania Nauczania Języka Kaszubskiego" ['Principles of Education and Financing of Education in Kashubian']. http://www.zk-p.pl/misc/rm_orgnaucz.htm

Neureiter, F. 1973. *Kaschubische Anthologie*. München: Verlag Otto Sagner.

Neureiter, F. 1991. *Geschichte der kaschubischen Literatur. Versuch einer zusammenfassenden Darstellung*. München: Verlag Otto Sagner.

Pioch, D. 2000. *Program do Nauczania Języka Kaszubskiego z Elementami Wiedzy o Kaszubach* ['Programme of Teaching Kashubian with Elements of Regional Education']. Gdańsk: Oficyna Czec.

Pioch, D. 2001. *Kaszëbë – Zemia i Lëdze. Podręcznik* ['Kashubia – Handbook of Land and People']. Gdańsk: Zrzeszenie Kaszubsko-Pomorskie, Oficyna Czec.

Ramult, S. 2003. *Słownik Języka Pomorskiego Czyli Kaszubskiego*. ['Dictionary of Pomeranian, that is, Kashubian'] ed. J. Treder. Gdańsk: Uniwersytet Gdański, Oficyna Czec, Muzuem Piśmiennictwa i Muzyki Kaszubsko-Pomorskiej.

Stieber, Z. *et al.* 1964–1978. *Atlas Językowy Kaszubszczyzny i Dialektów Sąsiednich* ['Linguistic Atlas of Kashubian and Neighbouring Dialects']. Vols. I–XV. Wrocław-Warszawa-Kraków: Ossolineum.

Stone, G. 1993. "Cassubian". In B. Comrie and G. G. Corbett eds. *The Slavonic Languages*. London and New York: Routledge. 759–794.

Swięté Pismiona Nowégo Testameńtu ['Holy Scripts of the New Testament'] (translated by Eugeniusz Gołąbk) 1993. Gduńsk-Pelplin: Zrzeszenie Kaszubsko-Pomorskie, Wydawnictwo Diecezjalne.

Sychta B. 1967–1976. *Słownik Gwar Kaszubskich na tle Kultury Ludowej* ['Dictionary of Kashubian Dialects and Folk Culture']. Vols. I–VII.

Synak, B. 1995. "The Kashubs' Ethnic Identity: Continuity and Change". In B. Synak ed. *The Ethnic Identities of European Minorities*. Gdańsk: Uniwersytet Gdański. 155–166.

Synak, B. and T. Wicherkiewicz eds. 1997. *Language Minorities and Minority Languages in the Changing Europe*. Gdańsk: Uniwersytet Gdański.

Treder, J. 1997. "Polish-Kashubian". In H. Goebl *et al.* eds. *Kontaktlinguistik / Contact Linguistics / Linguistique de Contact*. Vol. 2. Berlin and New York: Walter de Gruyter. 1600–1606.

Treder J. 2002. *Język kaszubski: Poradnik Encyklopedyczny* ['Kashubian Language: An Encyclopedical Outline']. Gdańsk: Uniwersytet Gdański, Oficyna Czec.

Trepczyk, J. 1994. *Słownik Polsko-Kaszubski* ['Polish-Kashubian Dictionary']. Vols. I–II. Gdańsk: Zrzeszenie Kaszubsko-Pomorskie.

Wicherkiewicz, T. 2000. "Kashubian". In J. Wirrer ed. *Minderheiten- und Regionalsprachen in Europa*. Wiesbaden: Westdeutscher Verlag. 213–221.

Wicherkiewicz, T. 2001. "Kashubian in Poland". In P. Winther ed. *Lesser-Used Languages in States Applying for EU Membership*. Luxembourg: European Parliament. *Education and Culture Series EDUC 106 EN Rev. 1*: 92–94.

Wickerkiewicz, T. 2005. "Kashubian as a Regional Language". In Kirk, J.M. and D.P. Ó Baoill eds. *Legislation, Literature, Sociolinguistics: Northern Ireland, the Republic of Ireland, and Scotland*. Belfast: Cló Ollscoil na Banríona. 163-172.

Zieniukowa, J. 1997. "On the Languages of Small Ethnic Groups – the Case of Sorbian and Kashubian". In Synak and Wicherkiewicz 1997: 311–316.

Minority Languages in Education in Slovenia

Sonja Novak-Lukanovič

1. Introduction

Today Europe is characterised by co-operation and integration, but an awareness of the significance of preserving diversity and respect for difference, as well as the promotion and preservation of identity, is even more present. The phenomenon of multiculturalism has become an issue in many debates. In almost every society, there is an overlap of different cultures, traditions and values – something that can enrich an individual culture but has the potential to result in conflict. In such situations, questions of identity become very important, and we can ask what kind of identity – ethnic, cultural, national, political, social, regional or professional. Alternatively, it may be relevant to speak of the multiple identity of an individual in a plural society characterised by overlapping cultures.

Education plays an especially important role in the formation of ethnicity. The results of extensive research emphasise that education, along with the family, the environment, and church, exercises a great influence over the formation of a young person's identity.

In education provided in multi-ethnic or multicultural societies, a special role is dedicated to language, both majority and minority. Language and language policy are always connected with education and education policy, and so bilingual education is practised. The term "bilingual education" usually refers to the use of two languages to teach content rather than simply a language itself. There are many different types of bilingual education, and its typologies depend on the programme goals, the status of the student group (dominant or subordinate, majority, minority), the proportion of instructional time given to each language, and the sociolinguistic and sociopolitical situation in the community and wider society. Bilingual education always illuminates the complex sociopolitical context of language contact and conflict within which bilingual programmes are typically implemented. It promotes linguistic competence at both an individual and societal level (Baker 1993).

2. Minority Languages in Education: The Case of Slovenia

2.1 Ethnolinguistic Composition and Legal Framework for Bilingual Education

Slovenia, like many countries, is an ethnically and culturally plural society. The territory on which the independent state of Slovenia was created in the early 1990s was never ethnically homogeneous. The number of ethnic minorities, their size and their real economic and political power have, during various historical periods, changed in accordance with changing political boundaries. The most recent change to state borders has left Slovenia a colourful collection of non-Slovene ethnic groups. The population can be classified into 'classical' (territorial) minorities – the Italian and Hungarian minorities and the newly formed ethnic communities, mostly comprising members of the nations of former Yugoslavia, which have emerged as a result of contemporary economic immigration.

According to the last population Census data, in 2002 the total population of

Map of Slovenia

Slovenia was 1,964,036, of whom the majority declared Slovene their mother tongue (87.7% – 1,723,434), 0.2% (3,762) Italian, 0.4% (7,713) Hungarian, and 0.2% Roma. The rest of the population (8.6%) are members of ethnic groups with other mother tongues – Albanians, Croats, Macedonians, Montenegrins, Muslims, and Serbs).[1]

Minority policy in Slovenia is based on the concept of human rights protection – on the positive concept of minority protection measures ('positive discrimination'). All the structural variables, presented so well theoretically by Giles (1977) and modified by Nelde and his collaborators (Nelde et al. 1996), had been taken into account in Slovene policy-making procedures by the 1960s. With that system of measures, Slovenia aimed at establishing the atmosphere and practice of cultural pluralism in ethnically mixed regions.[2] Cultural pluralism in such ethnically mixed regions as Prekmurje (Slovene/Hungarian) and Slovene Istria (Slovene/Italian) is understood as the participation of members of both the majority and the minority.

---

[1] The data are presented in 'Manjšine v prostoru Alpe Jadran in čezmejno sodelovanje: Republika Slovenija' / 'Minorities in the region of Alps-Adriatic and transfrontier co-operation: Republic of Slovenia', eds. Novak-Lukanovič, S. and Jesih, B. The study is one of those to be published within the Working Community of Alps-Adriatic in Slovene, German, Italian and Hungarian in 2004. The study was published originally in Croat in 2001.

[2] Constitutional rights are elaborated in more detail in the statutes of the communities of two ethnically mixed territories (Prekmurje and Slovene Istria). The ethnically mixed territory in Prekmurje belongs administratively to five communities (Hodoš/Hodos, Moravske toplice, Šalovci, Lendava/Lendva, Dobrovnik/Dobronak). The ethnically mixed territory in Slovene Istria belongs administratively to three communities (Koper/Capodistria, Piran/Pirano, Izola/Isola).

[3] Results from the year-long field research within the project "Ethnic identity and interethnic relations in the Slovene ethnic territory", headed by Prof. Albina Nećak-Lük (Nećak-Lük and Jesih eds. 2000) showed that in ethnically mixed regions in Slovenia the processes of language accommodation run as much in the direction of convergence as divergence from the language of collocutors. The strategy of language accommodation is above all marked by the ethnicity of the speakers. In most cases this is an asymmetrical convergence, most often marked only by the speaker, a minority member. The latter in formal language situations usually favours the strategy of divergence to the majority language over that of language preservation. One-way language accommodation underlines the unbalanced social language situation in which diglossia prevails (Novak-Lukanovič 2003).

On a linguistic level, cultural pluralism is manifested in two-way language accommodation.³

Special rights designed for the Italian and Hungarian national minorities (the 'classical' minorities) are of a dual nature, being collective and individual rights simultaneously. The recognition of the dual nature of minority rights and the implementation of the "positive concept of protection of minorities" in Article 64 of the *Constitution*[4] of the Republic of Slovenia establishes an obligation on the State to assure the realisation of those special rights, morally and materially.

For the second group of ethnically non-Slovene inhabitants, the *Constitution of the Republic of Slovenia* also guarantees expression of their ethnicity. According to Article 61 of the Constitution, they may establish ethnic organisations and associations, use their language and script, and express and develop their specific ethnic culture (Komac 2003).

2.2 Application in Practice: Models of Bilingual Education

Owing to various historical circumstances and socio demographic conditions, as well as some international arrangements, there are two models or types of bilingual education in nationally mixed regions in Slovenia which embrace pupils of majority and minority nations:

---

[4] Article 64 of the *Constitution* (*Special Rights of the Autochthonous Italian and Hungarian Ethnic Communities in Slovenia*):

The autochthonous Italian and Hungarian ethnic communities and their members shall be guaranteed the right to freely use their national symbols and, in order to preserve their national identity, the right to establish organisations, to foster economic, cultural, scientific and research activities, as well as activities associated with the mass media and publishing. These two ethnic communities and their members shall have, consistent with the statute, the right to education and schooling in their own languages, as well as the right to plan and develop their own curricula. The State shall determine by statute those geographical areas in which bilingual education shall be compulsory. The Italian and Hungarian ethnic communities and their members shall enjoy the right to foster contacts with the wider Italian and Hungarian communities living outside Slovenia, and with Italy and Hungary respectively. Slovenia shall give financial support and encouragement to the implementation of these rights. In those areas where the Italian and Hungarian ethnic communities live, their members shall be entitled to establish autonomous organisations in order to give effect to their rights. At the request of the Italian and Hungarian ethnic communities, the State may authorise their respective autonomous organisations to carry out specific functions which are presently within the jurisdiction of the State, and the State shall ensure the provision of the means for those functions to be effected.
The Italian and Hungarian ethnic communities shall be directly represented at local level and shall also be represented in the National Assembly.
The status of the Italian and Hungarian ethnic communities, and the manner in which their rights may be exercised in those areas where the two ethnic communities live, shall be determined by statute. In addition, the obligations of the local self-governing communities which represent the two ethnic communities to promote the exercise of their rights, together with the rights of the members of the two ethnic communities living outside their autochthonous areas, shall be determined by statute. The rights of both ethnic communities and of their members shall be guaranteed without regard for the numerical strength of either community. Statutes, regulations and other legislative enactments which exclusively affect the exercise of specific rights enjoyed by the Italian or Hungarian ethnic communities under this Constitution, or affecting the status of these communities, may not be enacted without the consent of the representatives of the ethnic community or communities affected.

1. a model in which the educational process takes place through the mother tongue and in which the other or second language is compulsory. This model is practised in the Slovene Italian region in Slovene Istria.
2. a model in which the two languages – the mother tongue and the second language – are languages of instruction and school subjects. This model is practised in the Slovene Hungarian region in Prekmurje.

Education for members of the Italian and Hungarian minorities is an integral part of the general education system in Slovenia. In addition to the basic goals and tasks, education in the ethnically mixed areas has some additional ones also stipulated by special laws.[5] Members of minorities have the right to education in their mother tongue and to learn about the culture and history of their nation of origin, as well as about the environment in which they live. Both models are maintenance/enrichment models (according to the classification of Skutnabb-Kangas 1981); their social goal is cultural pluralism, while their linguistic goal is two way bilingualism (functional bilingualism). The school syllabi are adapted to specific ethnic circumstances, and elements from Hungarian or Italian history, geography and culture are added to the syllabi of Slovene schools. Second-language acquisition and knowledge of each other's history, culture and literature contribute to the development of mutual tolerance and respect (Novak-Lukanovič, Mejak 1991; Novak-Lukanovič 2003).

The law of Slovenia guarantees members of national minorities the right to participate in designing the curricula of schools at all levels and the programmes of kindergartens that operate in ethnically mixed areas of Slovenia.[6]

Special attention is also paid to co-operation with the state or mother nation of the minority in the field of in service teacher training, the organisation of field trips and the preparation of textbooks. Slovenia has signed special agreements with the Republic of Italy and the Republic of Hungary which also regulate the protection of the minorities and the assistance in providing minority education on both sides of the border.

2.2.1 The Model in Practice: Slovene Istria and the Italian Minority

The Italian minority lives in the area of three coastal communities (Koper/Capodistria, Piran/Pirano, Izola/Isola) in the Slovenian part of Istria. Italians began to settle mainly in towns during the Austro Hungarian monarchy, and in particular after the year 1920, since, according to the Rapallo Treaty (12 November 1920) a large part of western Slovenia was ceded to Italy.

---

[5] The Law on the Special Rights of the Italian and Hungarian Ethnic Communities – *Official Gazette*, 11.05.2001, No. 35, pp. 4044–4047 – deals with the implementation of the rights of the Italian and Hungarian ethnic communities in the field of pre-school education, elementary education, lower and secondary vocational training, secondary technical or vocational training and general secondary education. The law defines the goals, the programme, the kindergarten and school network, the establishment and management of kindergartens and the management of public kindergartens and schools, the status and tasks of employees, the documents issued, and the consulting as well as financing of public kindergartens and schools with Italian as their teaching language, plus bilingual public kindergartens and schools. According to the law, the state (Ministry for Education, Science and Sport) provides funds for extra costs related to bilingual classes (extra teaching materials, teacher training in parent states, co-operation of schools with schools and institutions in parent states), for teachers in charge of bilingual programmes, for original textbooks and for bilingual documentation.
[6] Council of Experts of the Republic of Slovenia for General Education, Commission for the Education of Minorities.

After the World War II, the area of three coastal communities formed part of Zone B of the Free Territory of Trieste (administered by the Yugoslav Military Government). The *Memorandum of Understanding and the Special Statute*, designed as an annexe (October 1954), regulated the status of both national minorities (the Italian in Yugoslavia and the Slovene in Italy), and especially the organisation of the school system in ethnically mixed territories. The *Memorandum of Understanding* and its annexes, especially the special statute, represented a framework of standards for minority protection. The stipulations of the memorandum were confirmed by the *Osimo Treaties* in 1977, and by the *Slovene Italian Agreement* in 1992.

In the Slovene Italian ethnically mixed area in Slovene Istria, owing to various historic circumstances, children attend pre-school institutions, primary and secondary schools and colleges where Slovene or Italian is the language of instruction and the second language is an obligatory subject of the curricula.[7] Therefore, pupils are educated in their mother tongue – Slovene or Italian – but learning the second language (Slovene or Italian) is compulsory. The so-called coastal model of second-language teaching in primary schools was established in 1959. Over the years some new methods in teaching second languages have been introduced. A case study on the enhancement of Italian language-teaching at a primary level has been undertaken to determine the most appropriate model for language-teaching in the territory of Slovene Istria (Čok 1995).

In the schools where Italian is the language of instruction, teaching staff and other school personnel are native Italian-speakers, and Italian is the language of oral and written communication, including with parents and broader society. Textbooks, manuals and other teaching materials are prepared either in Slovenia or imported from Italy in accordance with Slovene regulations on the adoption of instructional materials.

2.2.2 The Model in Practice: Prekmurje and the Hungarian Minority

The Hungarian minority is concentrated in the ethnically mixed territory of Prekmurje, the region beyond the river Mura, situated in the north-eastern part of Slovenia along the Hungarian border. The ethnically mixed territory belongs administratively to the communities of Lendava/Lendva and Murska Sobota. The ethnically mixed character of the region originated during its thousand year-long attachment to the Hungarian state, which determined the political, economic and cultural development of Prekmurje. After the decline of the Habsburg monarchy, in the year 1919, Prekmurje became part of the newly founded Kingdom of Serbs, Croats and Slovenes. According to the Treaty of Trianon (4 June 1920), a part of the Slovene population remained within the state of Hungary, and a part of the Hungarians remained within Prekmurje in Slovenia. The treaty determined the rights of the minorities to use their own language in school.

In the ethnically mixed area of Prekmurje, the educational process is bilingual at

---

[7] Kindergartens with Italian fall within the framework of primary schools with Italian. In the school year 2001–02, kindergarten with Italian was attended by 268 children. The network of elementary schools with Italian covers the entire ethnically mixed territory (one autonomous, two parent schools and six succursal schools) and was attended by 434 children. Secondary schools with Italian as teaching language had 278 pupils enrolled in the school year 2001–02, which means that 980 children enjoyed education in Italian.

[8] In the school year 2002–03, bilingual education was practised in four elementary schools (eight years), attended by approximately 1,300 pupils per year. Approximately 312 pupils per year attend bilingual secondary school (Nećak-Lük 2003: 70).

all grades (kindergartens, primary schools, different types of secondary school) and for all pupils, irrespective of their ethnicity or individual wishes.[8] Bilingual education in Prekmurje has been functioning since 1959.

In each lesson the concurrent method is applied, with language-switching. Bilingual education is characterised by contact between the two groups and the two languages. Such contact is not coincidental, but permanent, at least in a certain period of an individual's life. The success of bilingual communication during lessons in all curriculum subjects depends on various linguistic, pedagogic and psycholinguistic factors. A child's ability to participate actively in bilingual instruction is closely connected with his or her language proficiency in the mother tongue, and with second-language competence. Owing to there being language-switching in all classes, it is obvious that a child must acquire, for active participation and to understand new content, a certain degree of language competence in the second language. In all lessons, a child may always answer or talk in his or her mother tongue, except during lessons in the second language itself.

According to the law, teachers and other personnel in the bilingual school must be bilingual. All external signs on the school, announcements and school documentation (grade books, timetables, school reports) are bilingual. Communication between the school and parents (parent-teacher meetings, announcements to parents) and most textbooks are also bilingual.

At a vocational and secondary level, the position of the minority language of Hungarian varies. The difference in possibilities derives from the legal status of the minority, which is based on the territorial principle. The minority language at secondary level can be the medium of instruction and a compulsory subject (bilingual programme) or can be an optional subject within the school (with Slovene as the language of instruction). In the ethnically mixed region of Prekmurje some bilingual programmes are offered at a vocational and secondary level (teacher training, humanities, business).[9] Outside that area, it is possible for pupils to attend only optional lessons in Hungarian.

According to the law, teachers and the other personnel in the bilingual school must be bilingual. All external signs on the school, announcements and school documentation (grade books, timetables, school reports) are bilingual. Communication between the school and parents (parent-teacher meetings, announcements to parents) and most textbooks are also bilingual.

3. Minority Language in Education and Bilingual Education Policy in Slovenia

3.1 Interethnic Relations and Ethnic Identity in the Slovene Ethnic Area

The empirical research investigation entitled "Interethnic Relations and Ethnic Identity in the Slovene Ethnic Area" and undertaken by a research team of the Institute for Ethnic Studies in Ljubljana[10] was conducted in 1994 and 1996 in the ethnically mixed Slovene-Italian region in Istria – the Coastal Region – (in the town of Izola/Isola) and also in 1991, 1994 and 1996 in the ethnically mixed Slovene-Hungarian territory in Prekmurje (in the town of Lendava/Lendva).[11] The sample was randomised, and the aim of our questionnaire was to cover the major spheres of

---

[9] Ibid. 8.
[10] For a detailed presentation of the research data, see Nećak-Lük and Jesih eds. (2000).
[11] In Lendava, the sample was: 1991: N = 678; 1994: N = 333; 1996: N = 320. In the Coastal Region, the sample was: 1994: N = 697; 1996: N = 264.

life in the ethnically mixed territories. We were interested mostly in the characteristics of life in the area, attitudes towards ethnicity, the evaluation of cultural activities, attitudes related to the mass media, opinions on bilingualism in public life and on the status of the Slovene and minority languages, views on the concept of bilingual education, and attitudes towards the status of the Hungarian and Italian ethnic communities.

3.2 Languages in the Education System in Ethnically Mixed Areas

In ethnically mixed areas, the education system, as described in previous sections, creates conditions enabling individuals to comprehend the complex and contradictory nature of society and thus form relationships characterised by tolerance and an understanding of diversity. Taking into account all those facts, we were interested in determining the perceptions and views of the population regarding the role of minority languages in education and its opinion of bilingual education. In the present article, the analyses of only two questions from the research questionnaire are presented.

A. To what degree do you consider it necessary for Slovene children to gain an equally good command of Slovene and the language of the minority (Hungarian/Italian)?
B. To what degree do you consider it necessary for Hungarian/Italian children to gain an equal command of Slovene and Hungarian/Italian?

The respondents could choose from the following options: 'very necessary', 'rather necessary', 'irrelevant', 'mostly unnecessary', 'completely unnecessary' and 'I don't know'.

The respondents were asked the question over a period of time, thus indicating any pattern of change or trends in their views. At the same time, it is necessary to point out that the use of the term 'equally good command' is quite a demanding condition, and that it is highly unlikely for majority and minority members to be equally fluent in both languages.[12] Our purpose was primarily to ascertain respondents' degree of perception of the significance of having an equally good command of the two languages on the part of majority and minority. The results are presented in Table 1 and Figure 1.

In Lendava, respondents kept changing their views. The results indicate that, in 1991, a majority (almost 70% of respondents) were of the opinion that it is 'very necessary' or 'rather necessary', respectively, for Slovene children to gain an equally good command of Slovene and the minority language. In 1994, the number of those respondents had decreased, while the proportion of those believing it to be 'mostly' or even 'completely unnecessary' increased. In 1996, the proportion of respondents in favour of 'very necessary' or 'rather necessary' had gone up again, thus approaching the results from 1991.[13]

A rather high percentage of respondents was of the opinion that it is 'mostly unnecessary' or even 'completely unnecessary' for Slovene children to have an equally good command of the two languages. Rejecting the learning of Hungarian means

---

[12] The concept of two-way bilingualism is described in theory but is a very rare phenomenon in practice, which is why I did not even expect that it could be implemented in Slovenia.
[13] Similar trends showing different views regarding cultural diversity at certain points can be seen in many other questions analysed – see Novak-Lukanovič (2002).

Table 1: The Acquisition of Slovene and the Minority Language (Hungarian/Italian)[14]

	It is more important for minority children to learn the two languages than for Slovene children	It is more important for Slovene children to learn the two languages than for minority children	It is equally important for minority and for Slovene children to learn the two languages	p (Wilcoxon test)
Lendava 91 Slovenes	192	20	151	< 0.001
Lendava 91 Minority	101	8	104	< 0.001
Lendava 91 Others	44	7	45	< 0.001
Lendava 94 Slovenes	133	10	40	< 0.001
Lendava 94 Minority	62	7	32	< 0.001
Lendava 94 Others	32	5	6	< 0.001
Lendava 96 Slovenes	103	8	64	< 0.001
Lendava 96 Minority	56	5	38	< 0.001
Lendava 96 Others	21	2	15	< 0.001
Obala 94 Slovenes	79	49	266	0.002
Obala 94 Minority	26	22	130	0.325
Obala 94 Others	17	13	72	0.435
Obala 96 Slovenes	36	8	104	< 0.001
Obala 96 Minority	16	5	46	0.028
Obala 96 Others	7	7	27	1

Figure 1: The Acquisition of a Good Command of both Slovene and the Minority Language (Hungarian/Italian)

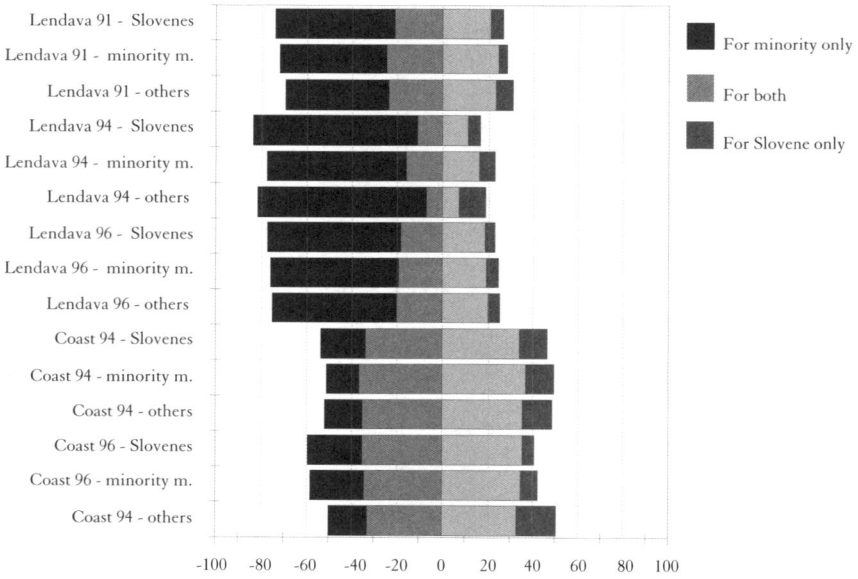

[14] Respondents' answers to the two questions regarding the scale of answers (from 'very necessary' to 'not

that some, especially Slovenes, do not understand or accept a bilingual setting. However, unwillingness to learn Hungarian does not necessarily imply that they reject a bilingual setting or diversity; it may mean only that they are not motivated to learn Hungarian.

The respondents' view that minority children should gain an equally good command of the two languages differs in the case of Slovenian children. Only a few individuals believe that an equally good command of the two languages is unnecessary for minority children.

In the Coastal Region, the results are somewhat different from those in Lendava. The differences regarding the importance or meaning of language in education cannot be clarified with a different educational model. The result is not a sufficient basis for an answer regarding which of the two models is better. The results of the questionnaire indicate that the role of the individual language in international communication is highly important, affecting an individual's wish to learn the language. The strongly held opinion that Slovene children of the Coastal Region should gain an equally good command of the two languages in school had greatly increased by the second occasion. A majority of respondents in the region believe that minority and Slovene children should be equally fluent in the two languages (see Table 1).

The results in Table 1 show statistical discrepancies between Lendava and the Coastal Region, or rather between opinions regarding the need for a command of Italian and Hungarian. Thus, in the Coastal Region, the need for an equally good command of Slovene and Italian is equally distributed between the majority and the minority.

In Lendava, the proportion of respondents – at least on the basis of statistical analysis – believing that Slovene children do not need an equally good command of both languages is relatively high; that means that the possibility of mutual (two-way) language accommodation is decreasing (see Table 1).

In Lendava, there are statistically significant differences between individual groups regarding who should be learning the two languages ($p < 0.05$). In the Coastal Region, minority members and the group 'others' make no distinctions regarding who should be learning the two languages at school (indicating value $p > 0.05$).

The difference between the Coastal Region and Lendava can be found in the status of the language itself. The Italian language has a specific advantage over Hungarian (viewed from a strictly practical point of view). That advantage refers to the following indicators: Italian is 'more useful' in world communication, economic co-operation with Italy is highly developed, and in the entire area Italian is strongly present in media such as television and radio.

3.3 Bilingual Education

The importance of children in Lendava and the Coastal Region gaining an equally good command of the two languages is also related to respondents' views on the bilingual model of education. The analysis of statements indicates statistical differences between groups, which underlines the fact that individuals ascribe varying significance or importance to individual assertions or statements. Irrespective

---

necessary') are brought together into three views. The Wilcoxon test compares the answers of a single respondent. Numbers in Table 1 show how many respondents answered the two questions regarding the importance of language acquisition for the respective groups.

Table 2: Respondents' Views on Bilingual Education in Lendava (a lower value indicates stronger agreement with the assertion)

	Slovenes	Hungarians	Others
BS* brings pupils of Slovene and Hungarian nationality closer together	1.96	1.54	1.98
Children like learning Hungarian	3.40	2.66	3.21
Teachers have an adequate command of Slovene	2.46	2.05	2.33
More Hungarian should be spoken in classes	3.57	2.29	3.27
Learning other foreign languages would be preferable to Hungarian	2.84	3.95	2.98
Children like learning Slovene	2.11	2.15	2.11
More Slovene should be spoken in classes	2.37	3.25	2.69
Teachers have an adequate command of Hungarian	2.58	2.71	2.50
BS provides satisfactory knowledge for further schooling	2.63	2.06	2.58
Hungarian culture should be given more space in the curriculum	2.94	2.03	2.59
The use of two languages in classes is distracting	2.68	3.51	2.95
BS should be attended by Hungarian pupils only	3.53	4.27	3.56
Monolingual classes would be more appropriate	3.03	4.08	3.27

*BS = bilingual school

of ethnicity, everybody in Lendava strongly agrees with the statement that bilingual schooling brings pupils of Hungarian and Slovene nationality closer together. Equally, the majority disagrees with the statement that only members of the Hungarian minority should attend bilingual school, or that monolingual classes would be more appropriate.[15] Although in Lendava the prevailing view is that an equally good command of the two languages is of greater importance for minority members, everyone agrees with the assertion that bilingual schooling brings children together, which proves that the majority accepts diversity and respects it in the education system. Table 2 shows respondents agreeing with individual views.

In the Coastal Region, views differ less statistically between individual groups regarding individual statements than in Lendava. Among assertions accepted by the majority are those referring to teachers' good command of Slovene and Italian, that Slovene children like learning Italian, and that Italian-language school provides sufficient knowledge for further schooling. Table 3 shows respondents' views on the concept of bilingual schools in the Coastal Region.

4. Conclusion

Individual views on minority languages in the education system are an important

Table 3: Respondents' Views on Bilingual Education in the Coastal Region (a lower value indicates stronger agreement with the assertion)

	Slovenes	Italians	Others	Total
The present model brings Italian and Slovene pupils closer together	2.13	2.03	2.21	2.11
Slovene children like learning Italian	1.97	2.09	2.13	2.03
Teachers have an adequate command of Slovene	1.71	2.02	1.74	1.79
The number of Italian lessons in Slovene school should be higher	3.03	2.11	2.87	2.76
Learning other foreign languages would be preferable to Italian	3.27	4.07	3.57	3.54
Italian children like learning Slovene	2.57	1.93	2.48	2.34
The number of Slovene lessons in Italian school should be higher	2.32	2.76	2.68	2.49
Teachers have an adequate command of Italian	1.93	2.45	2.07	2.10
Italian-language school provides adequate knowledge for further schooling	1.94	1.68	1.96	1.87
Italian culture should be given more space in the Slovene-language school curriculum	2.88	1.83	2.54	2.53
Slovene culture should be given more space in the Italian-language school curriculum	2.33	2.06	2.38	2.26
Italian-language school should be attended only by Italian children	3.46	3.64	3.78	3.55
Bilingual classes would be more appropriate	3.37	3.35	3.10	3.32

factor, as they affect the maintenance or loss of the language of a minority community living in daily contact with another language group. The view of the minority language (Italian or Hungarian) in the education system is reflected in individuals' perceived need for language acquisition (the subjective dimension), and marking strategies of language accommodation in ethnically mixed territories in Slovenia.

In Lendava, Slovenes and Hungarians have different views on the assertion that children like learning Hungarian. Slovenes are less in favour of that statement than Hungarians. In the Coastal Region, however, results indicate that Slovenes – more than Italians – believe that Slovene children like learning Italian (see Tables 2 and 3).

Statistical data regarding minority language-learning indicate differences in the respective motivation to learn Hungarian and Italian. The difference in the status of the individual language affects views on learning, which means Italian is in an advantageous position. Nevertheless, differences in views on the concept of bilingual education in Lendava do not mean that individuals do not accept the learning of the two languages because they reject diversity and multiculturalism, but mainly because they are pragmatic and do not see the same scope for international communication in

Hungarian.

The empirical results of the long-term project "Interethnic Relations and Ethnic Identity in the Slovene Ethnic Area", concerning the minority language in education and bilingual education, proved that, in spite of some criticism, bilingual education in those two areas is acceptable to the majority of respondents regardless of their ethnicity and is considered to be successful, providing sufficient knowledge for further schooling (Novak-Lukanovič 1998, 2000). The fact that schooling and education are important for the implementation of ethnic equality is proven by the fact that, according to respondents in the research, school is the very place where the right of the Hungarian and Italian minority to use their languages is exercised regularly and daily. In a way, that underlines the fact that use of the minority language is mostly restricted to school and less frequent in other spheres of a person's social life. That can lead to a thesis that, in ethnically mixed territories, functional bilingualism is formally or legally guaranteed but not practised and that diglossia is occurring. That thesis has also been confirmed by previous studies (Mejak, Novak-Lukanovič 1991; Dular 1987).

Statistical analyses of the data also show that the present type of bilingual education in Prekmurje in the coastal area has a very important influence on the formation of an individual's ethnicity. At the same time, according to our respondents, bilingual education in ethnically mixed areas in Slovenia has a significant role in interethnic relations, which, they feel, regardless of ethnicity, are characterised by coexistence, tolerance and the acceptance of diversity (Nećak-Lük and Jesih 2000).

References

Baker, C. 1993. *Foundation of Bilingual Education and Bilingualism*. Clevedon: Multilingual Matters.
Čok, L. 1995. "Zgodnje učenje in poučevanje drugega jezika-umestitev pouka drugega jezika na razredno stopnjo osnovne šole". Ljubljana: *Uporabno Jezikoslovje* 4: 59–76.
Dular, J. 1987. "Jezikovni položaj, dvojezičnost v javnosti, vzgoja in izobraževanje". In *Madžari in Slovenci: sodelovanje in sožitje ob jugoslovansko-madžarski meji*, Inštitut za narodnostna vprašanja, Ljubljana. 207–265.
Giles, H. 1977. *Language, Ethnicity and Intergroup Relations*. London, New York, San Francisco: Academic Press.
Lian, K. F. 1982. "Identity in Minority Group Relations". *Ethnic and Racial Studies* 5: 42–52.
Mejak, R. and Novak-Lukanovič, S. 1991. *The participation of parents, school and the social surrounding in the implementation of the concept of bilingual education*, Institute for Ethnic Studies, Ljubljana.
Nećak-Lük, A. 1992. "Literacy Acquisition in a Bilingual School". *Razprave in Gradivo*. 26–27: 110–117.
Nećak-Lük, A. 1993. "The language component of interethnic relations issues in the ethnically mixed regions along the Slovene Hungarian border". *Razprave in Gradivo / Treatises and Documents* 28: 28–37.

Nećak-Lük, A. 1995. "L1 and L2 Language Learning and Use in the Slovene-Hungarian Context", Report on Workshop 5B "Learning and Teaching Languages in Pre-school and Primary Bilingual Contexts (age three to four up to 12 to 13)", Council of Europe, Strasbourg, CC-LANG. 95: 38–51.
Nećak-Lük, A. 1993a. "Medetniāni odnosi v slovenskem etniānem prostoru". Ljubljana: RIG. 15–28.
Nećak-Lük, A. 1993b. "Language Education for Intercultural Communication in Slovenia". In Ager, D., Muskens G. and S. Wright eds. *Language Education for Intercultural Communication*, Clevedon: Multilingual Matters. 181–192.
Nećak-Lük, A. and Jesih, B. ur. 2000. *Medetnični odnosi in etnična identiteta v slovenskem etničnem prostoru – urejanje medetničnih odnosov v Lendavi*. Ljubljana: Inštitut za narodnostna vprašanja. 208 str.
Nećak-Lük, A., Muskens, G. and Novak-Lukanovič, S. ur. 2000. *Managing the Mix Thereafter: Comparative Research into Mixed Communities in Three Independent Successor States*. Ljubljana: Institute for Ethnic Studies.
Nelde, P. *et al*. 1996. *Euromosaic*. Luxembourg: Office for Official Publications of the European Communities.
Novak-Lukanovič, S. 1993. "Dvojezična vzgoja in izobraževanje: vloga v družbi in stalisča posameznikov". RIG. 38–45.
Novak-Lukanovič, S. 1998. "Stališča do večinskega in manjšinskega jezika v vzgoji in izobraževanju na narodnostno mešanem območju v Sloveniji. V I. Štrukelj ur. Jezik tako in drugače". Ljubljana. *Društvo za uporabno jezikoslovje*. 91–96.
Novak-Lukanovič, S. 2000. "Pogled na dvojezično vzgojo in izobraževanje". In: Nećak-Lük, A. and Jesih, B. eds. *Medetnični odnosi in etnična identiteta v slovenskem etniānem prostoru. Urejanje medetničnih odnosov v Lendavi*. Ljubljana: INV. 149–164.
Novak-Lukanovič, S. and Jesih, B. eds. 1999. *Manjšine v prostoru Alpe Jadran in čezmejno sodelovanje: Slovenija. Delovna skupina za manjšine* Alpe-Jadran: v tisku.
Sussi, E. 1990. "L'influenza dei fattori di socializzazione sull' identita'". In *Vzgoja in izobraževanje v večjezičnem okolju. Problematiche educative in ambiente plurilingue*. Trieste: IRRSAE.

Khakas in Education and Ethnic Identity

Tamara Borgoyakova

The Republic of Khakassia is situated in the southern part of Siberia in central Russia. During Soviet times, Khakassia had various levels of autonomy: *ujezd*, *okrug*, self-governing *oblast*. In 1991, it was granted the status of republic. The Khakas language belongs to the Khakas group of the *ujgur-oguz* branch of the Turkic language family (Baskakov 1963) and is the native language of the indigenous population of the republic. According to the census data, in 1989 the Khakas people numbered 78,000 and made up 11% of the population of the republic. They have been in a minority (less than 20%) since the 1950s, and by the early 1990s language shift to the dominant Russian was gathering pace. Although about 60% of the indigenous people live in the countryside, there are very few villages with a homogeneous Khakas population where Khakas is still used as the primary language. According to the Khakas *Constitution* (1995) and the *Language Law* (1992), Khakas became the second official language of the republic after Russian. Efforts have been made in the republic to maintain and strengthen the use of Khakas in the domains of education, the mass media, cultural and social events and as a family and community language. Owing to its official status, Khakas has experienced a kind of revival in education over the last ten years.

Khakas as a Subject

There has been an increase in the number of schools, classes and children learning the language as a subject (both as a required course and as an option), showing considerable growth from 50% of Khakas children in 1994 to 70% in 2004. More importantly, Khakas became the language of study in some *urban* schools and kindergartens. According to the *Language Law* of the republic, Khakas children have the right to study their native language, but it is not obligatory. Today about 35% of Khakas children living in Abakan study it in different forms in eight high schools (of 24 city schools). In City School No. 28, some 26 children are of non-Khakas origin. All learn the Khakas language.

When children start to learn their native language at school, the level of their language competence varies from fluent to zero. However, as they are few, they are usually in the same group. The number of native language lessons is one to three periods per week if they are optional, and four if they are on the curriculum. School No. 28 is the only urban municipal 'national' (ethnic) school for Khakas children. It was opened in 1996 for the purpose of creating better language-learning conditions. Today, 88% of all schoolchildren there are Khakas, and all the children study the Khakas language. Only 32% of them are fluent in the mother tongue (The division into language study groups is based on their language competence, and study groups have fewer children). According to the curriculum, there are four Khakas language classes a week at elementary level, and five classes a week at middle level (grades five to six). Apart from language classes, those children participate in various cultural events. According to a survey, parents sent their children to the school because of the opportunity to learn the mother tongue (55%) and ethnic culture (36%).

Map of Khakassia

Pre-school Level

Since the early 1990s, Khakas classes have been introduced at pre-school level in some kindergartens in the city of Abakan. The children are not divided into different groups according to their ethnic origin, so Russian children also learn Khakas words, songs and poems. In 2004, about 300 children were studying the language in ten kindergartens (out of 30) in Abakan.

Higher Education Level

The established tradition of using both Khakas and Russian as languages of instruction is still used in the training of Khakas language teachers in the undergraduate programme at the Institute of Sayano-Altay Turkology of Khakas State University. That programme has been available for Khakas high school graduates for 60 years. Its graduates form the majority of schoolteachers and journalists working in the Khakas mass media (the republic's newspaper *Khakas Chiri*, Khakas radio and TV programmes).

Table 1: The Khakas Language in Abakan Municipal Schools in 2000–01.

Schools in Abakan	Number of Khakas children	Learn Khakas (per cent)	Number of children in grades									
			1	2	3	4	5	6	7	8	9	10
No. 1	201	109 (54)	25	26	22	-	14		22			-
No. 2	50	32 (64)	10	5	10	7	-	-	-	-	-	-
No. 3	125	37 (29)	11	-	15	-	8 + 3		-	-	-	-
No. 10	99	20 (22)	8	12	-	-	-	-	-	-	-	-
No. 11	125	38 (30)	12	12	14							
No. 12	100	21 (21)	-	-	-	-	-	-	4 + 7		10	-
No. 14	153	69 (45)	17	15	17	-	10		10			
No. 20	168	33 (20)	-	21	12	-	-	-	-	-	-	-
No. 22	250	149 (60)	15	11	14	-	18	15	14	21	27	14
No. 24	351	153 (43)	-	-	21	-	22	23	25	21	26	15
No. 28	259	273* (100)	44	49	51	-	45	50	34	-	-	-
	1756	934	142	151	176	7	117	98	84	56	72	31

The Language of Instruction

The use of the Khakas language as a language of instruction is decreasing. Until the early 1960s, it was used as the language of instruction in most rural middle and elementary schools. Later, owing to the official policy of the ethnolinguistic assimilation of national minorities in the USSR, education in Khakas in rural schools was reduced to an elementary level. In 1995–2001, some 7%, or 600 children, in rural elementary schools of the republic were taught in their mother tongue. Today, that number has fallen to 100 children, and instruction is in both Khakas and Russian.

Language Competence

According to our survey of groups of Khakas children studying the mother tongue in 2001, there is an obvious difference in the level of language competence within the age subgroups of schoolchildren. The biggest difference in understanding and speaking skills is found between the senior and junior subgroups. It is necessary to mention that passive forms of language competence are better developed in comparison with active ones in all subgroups.

Children in the senior age group (group four) use their mother tongue with their grandparents and parents almost three times more often than the youngest, group one. Children aged from seven to ten, for example, use only Russian, speaking with their parents (38.8%), grandparents (39.2%) and with their friends (79.9%), in comparison with 12%, 22% and 55% in the senior group (see Table 3).

Table 2: Levels of Language Competence of Schoolchildren and Students Aged 7–20 (%).

Age group	Degrees of language competence											
	Understand			Speak			Read			Write		
	G*	L*	0	G	L	0	G	L	0	G	L	0
1 (7-10)	31.7	58.6	9.7	28.8	61	10.3	36.3	59.6	4.1	41.5	53.1	5.4
2 (11-14)	36.8	58.7	4.4	29.8	59.4	10.8	58	39.8	2.2	57.6	39.2	3.2
3 (15-17)	43.8	52.2	4.0	34	50.8	15.2	62.1	34.9	3	54.7	41.6	3.7
4 (18-20)	72.6	22.2	5.1	64.1	22.2	13.7	76.9	12	11	69.2	13.7	17.1
Average	46	47	5	39	48	12.5	58	36	5	55	36	7

* G = good, L = limited

Table 3: Language Use with Parents, Grandparents, Friends (%).

Age groups	Communication with mid-age generation			Communication with elder generation			Communication with friends		
	R*	R&Kh*	Kh*	R	R&Kh	Kh	R	R&Kh	Kh
7-10	38.8	46.3	15	39.2	41.9	18.9	79.9	16	4.2
11-14	29.3	57.6	13.1	23.4	44.7	31.9	70.7	27.7	1.6
15-17	36.9	41.6	21.5	23	41.8	35.1	67.2	27.7	5.1
18-20	12.8	42.7	44.4	11	22.9	66.1	29.1	68.4	2.6
	29	47	23	24	37	38	61	35	3

* R= Russian, R&Kh = Russian and Khakas, Kh = Khakas

Emotional Attitude, Language Competence and Ethnic Identity

Our recent study also shows that an overwhelming majority of schoolchildren and students from both Abakan and various rural districts of the republic (more than 90% of about 1,500 respondents) have a positive emotional attitude to the mother tongue as part of their ethnocultural identity and express a readiness to take part in language preservation and development activities.

More than 68% of them consider Khakas to be their mother tongue, 7.4% think that it is Russian, and 24.3% named both Russian and Khakas. That proves that, despite the process of language shift from Khakas to Russian, the Khakas language remains a valued symbolic marker of the Khakas ethnic group and contributes to the maintenance and persistence of ethnicity across generations within rapidly changing social contexts (Edwards 1994). According to the anonymous questionnaires, the majority of both urban and rural Khakas residents want their children to learn their native language at school and express their wish to help preserve and develop the mother tongue. The score for positive attitudes is a little higher among urban residents.

We have studied the correlation between language competence and the ethnic identification of Khakas schoolchildren. Three different types of schools with Khakas as a subject were chosen. The first group consists of rural senior schoolchildren from Askiz and surrounding settlements with an ethnically mixed population, with 33% fluent in Khakas. Some 83% of respondents named Khakas their mother tongue, while 12% named both Khakas and Russian.

The second group is represented by the graduates of the Republican National Boarding School in Abakan, coming from practically all towns and rural districts in the republic. In that group, 26% are fluent in the mother tongue, and 47% have limited language competence. Some 70% of them named Khakas as their mother tongue, and 24% named both Khakas and Russian.

Graduates of Abakan High School No. 22 represent the third group. Their families live dispersed in the capital, where the Khakas make up 8% of the population. Those children learn their native language as an optional subject. Only 19% are fluent in all the forms of language competence. However, more than half (56%) name Khakas as their mother tongue, and 38% name both Khakas and Russian. Russian alone was given as the mother tongue by only 3% of school graduates (2.7% of the graduates in the first group, 3.7% in the second, and 3% in the third) and Khakas by 95%. According to the census data from 1994, some 73% of Khakas respondents name Khakas as their mother tongue. That shows growing positive attitudes to the native language that do not depend on the level of language competence of young Khakas people (Borgoyakova 2002).

The increased use of Khakas in education is mostly of a quantitative nature. It deals with the increase in urban schoolchildren studying Khakas as a subject (more often than not as an optional one). Qualitative measures including the development and publication of language textbooks, dictionaries, visual aids and so on for all forms and levels of education do not meet contemporary requirements. Devolved language law does not support the return of the language to the domains of administration, the economy, legislation or the community. It is unlikely that Khakas will become fully functional or be acquired as a first language by a majority of the ethnic group. However, the high degree of language loyalty among young people may help slow language shift and preserve Khakas as a (mainly passive) component of bilingualism with the dominant Russian.

References

Baskakov, N. 1963. *Introduction to the Study of Turkic Languages*. Moscow.
Borgoyakova, T. 2002. *Socio-linguistic Processes in the Republics of Southern Siberia*. Abakan: Khakas State University, Institute of Linguistics of the Russian Academy of Science.
Edwards, J. 1994. *Multilingualism*. London: Routledge.

Language Reforms in Tatarstan's Education System and the Ethnolinguistic Orientation of Young People

Yagfar Garipov and Marina Solnyshkina[1]

Introduction

The democratic transformation of Russia raised the legal status of its national[2] republics, resulting in the possibility of the latter pursuing their own – in many respects, independent – language policies. A period of ethnic language renaissance began in the late 1990s. For the last 10–12 years, the Republic of Tatarstan has achieved significant success in the functional development and revitalisation of the language of its eponymous people.[3] Some 51% of Tatar children are nowadays being schooled in their native language, while 12 years ago such children accounted for only 12%. At that time only 10.6% of Tatar children were being taught through their native language in pre-school educational institutions, but that figure has now increased to about 65%. The introduction of Tatar as a school subject is extremely important. Tatar and Russian, as the languages of state (government) in Tatarstan, are taught on an equal basis in secondary schools. Nearly 100% of schoolchildren in the republic study Tatar at school. That is a very important step towards realising the idea of legal equality between languages. A polyethnic, multilingual civil society is being formed in modern Tatarstan. Pupils can be instructed in seven different

Map of Tartarstan

---

[1] Although not participants in the **Voces Diversae** conference, Dr. Yagfar Garipov and Dr. Marina Solnyshkina kindly supplied the present paper for inclusion in the proceedings volume.

[2] In the former Soviet Union, the term *nationality* (*natsionalnost*) was used to refer to what might be considered ethnic differences in other parts of the world.

[3] In 2000, some 51.4 per cent of residents in the republic were Tatars and 41.3 per cent Russians.

languages. Some 100% of Russians, 76% of Udmurds, 57% of Chuvashes, 49% of Maris, and 11% of Mordvinians are taught in their native languages, while Jewish children study Ivrit (Hebrew). In addition, 28 Sunday schools function at ethnic cultural centres, where more than 2,000 children are taught their native language.

Ethnic Socialisation in Tatarstan: Ups and Downs

The ethnic socialisation of a person is influenced by many factors. The system of education in Tatarstan as a social institution leaves much to be desired, since it does not play the role that it is supposed to play. Tatar is still not the working language of higher and professional education. The Tatar public insists on creating an independent Tatar ethnic university financed by the state. The concept of such a higher educational establishment has been worked out, and its necessity is acknowledged by the powers that be in the republic. The ethnic university would become an elite educational establishment forming an ethnic intellectual elite and the ideological foundation of ethnic revival.

After the Gossovet (Parliament) of the republic adopted the Law *On the Restoration of Latin Script to the Tatar Alphabet* in 1999, the national school of Tatarstan underwent important transformations. The transition to Latin script was planned to start in 2001 and last ten years. As part of the experiment, 60 schools in the republic began teaching Tatar in Latin script. However, the transition of all Tatar national schools to Latin script is being hampered. The federal government called the transition to Latin script "political separatism" and "a threat to Russian security". Some Russian politicians in the State Duma began speaking about the possible violation of a single cultural space and the estrangement of the Tatar population from Russians. In all fairness, we have to state that Russians do not read Tatar texts, even in Cyrillic. Thus all interested parties have the chance to learn the new written language together with the Tatars. However, the talk of the weakening of Tatar and Russian ties is absolutely unfounded, as there is no way one could imagine the life of the Tatar people outwith the Russian economic, cultural and educational ambit.

The ethnicity and socialisation of the personality begins in the family. It is the language and cultural environment in which a person acquires social experience and the socially significant qualities of mentality and behaviour. Language is the most important means of the socialisation of the personality.

When a person considers a language his or her native one, that quite often does not mean that he or she really speaks it, and, of course, it does not mean that he or she uses it in all its functions. What people actually declare is their ethnic or national consciousness. The micro-census of 1994 proved that 97% of Tatars considered Tatar their native language. At the same time, only 81.6% used it at home, which means that for a fifth of the Tatar population of the republic, the native language had ceased to be the language of communication even in the family. Although Tatars make up a little more than half of the population of the republic – 51.4% (1994), the Russian-speaking population prevails (62% to 65%). It is quite evident that active Tatar-speakers are even fewer. At home about 35% of young Tatar city-dwellers speak Russian or mainly Russian, while in the villages 9% of young Tatars speak Russian at home. Tatar, or mainly Tatar, is the language of a quarter of young Tatar city-dwellers, and more than 60% of young Tatar villagers. Tatar and Russian are spoken equally by 41% of city-dwellers and 20% of villagers (see Table 1).

The choice of native language by a person is determined mainly by the language

Table 1: Language of Communication in the Home

	Languages of home communication	nation	
		Russians	Tatars
City	Tatar	0.0	24.1
	Russian and Tatar	1.9	41.4
	Russian	98.1	34.5
Village	Tatar	0.0	70.7
	Russian and Tatar	1.7	20.3
	Russian	98.3	9.0

Table 2: Native Language versus Language Spoken in the Home

What language do you consider your native one?	What language do you speak at home?				
	only Tatar	mainly Tatar	Tatar and Russian equally	mainly Russian	only Russian
Tatar	100.0	86.1	75.3	45.8	20.5
Russian	–	–	3.3	13.5	45.5
Both languages	–	13.9	20.9	40.6	34.1

of the family, that is, home communication. The native language is considered the language acquired in early childhood in the process of the person's socialisation and ethnocultural orientation.[4] There is no socialisation without natural communication. Probably the language of the person's first socialisation determines the ethnicity of the socialisation itself, as this it is an important objective quality of the *ethnos*.

The type of family language environment forms a picture of the native language. Young people raised by their parents in Tatar considered it their native language, while only a fifth of Tatar young people (20.5%) with a Russian family socialisation considered Tatar their native language, and more than 74.5% considered Russian their native language. (see Table 2).

To a certain degree, the family language environment determines the attitude of a person to the language of his or her people and the development of linguistic consciousness. An absolute majority of young people from Tatar-speaking families consider speaking the language of their people important (97.9%). Not all young people from Russian-speaking Tatar families where people speak mainly or only Russian share that viewpoint (83.0% and 78.6% respectively).

The functional prevalence of the native language in family education and its development in family communication become more important in the linguistic consciousness of the ethnic community if the native language functions in an environment where another language enjoys social superiority. We consider that it is the family that makes real and active native speakers – language 'entrepreneurs'. There is no need for special decrees permitting the extension of 'family' functions of the language. What we need is the will, together with a certain degree of effort from each of us in the practical use of the native language. Today it is extremely important to realise the value of what at first sight is an insignificant personal contribution to

---

[4] See *Ethnic and Ethnosocial Categories*. Moscow, 1995: 157 [in Russian].

Table 3: What does the native language mean to you?

No.		Nation	
		Tatars	Russians
1.	The native language is a means of communication.	31.1	59.4
2.	The native language is a part of my nation's culture.	37.7	16.9
3.	The native language is the foundation of the development of my nation's spiritual life.	13.5	6.9
4.	The native language is the guarantee of the existence of my national community.	15.7	16.4

the real functioning of the language. An approach to the native language from the position of a consumer bearing in mind nothing but its possibilities as a means of communication and social advancement testifies to a rather low level of linguistic consciousness. We still have to state that for a majority of the Tatar people, as well as the ethnic elite and intellectuals, the native language is nothing more than an ethnic symbol.

The interest of the academic public has lately been focused on the development and realisation of the concept of the language rights of the personality. By that we understand the right to choose, study and use the language, not only in one's personal life but social life too. At present, the language rights of the personality are formulated quite well. However, an ability to provide for the language rights of a quantitative or social minority in a polyethnic society is unlikely without the concept of language duties.

The functional reconstruction of the language in its full scope, together with its wide diffusion among the entire ethnic community, is possible with an effort on the part of the people themselves, followed by turning all potential language-speakers into active users. Conscious use of the language and language entrepreneurship are important. In the circumstances of direct interaction and contact, a language survives, according to A. Martinet, "not because of its inner qualities, but because its speakers are more bellicose, fanatic, cultural, better entrepreneurs". Unfortunately, our attitude to the native language contains a feeling of inferiority, and we still lack the developed skills of natural freedom while using the native language in a foreign environment.

We may speak about certain levels and, consequently, about the sociological measurement of the language consciousness of both an individual and the ethnic community as a whole. Probably we may presuppose that the language consciousness of native peoples of the Baltic republics is much higher than that of us Tatars. The language consciousness of Tatars, in its turn, is higher than that of the Chuvashes, Mordvins, Karels, and so on.

While studying the sociocultural problems of young people in oil regions of the republic, we tried to evaluate the significance of the native language among them using a rank scale (see Table 3). The versions of answers to the question "*What does the native language mean to you?*" are ranked. Only one possible answer is chosen. N = 1034, Year = 2000.

Table 4: What language do you speak at home?

Preferred teaching language at university or college	What language do you speak at home?				
	only Tatar	mainly Tatar	Tatar and Russian equally	mainly Russian	only Russian
Russian	18.4	51.3	60.0	69.1	86.0
Russian and Tatar	65.0	43.4	32.6	27.7	11.6
Tatar	16.5	2.6	1.1	1.1	–
Other		2.6	6.3	2.1	2.3

As we see from Table 3, the native language significance for Tatars turned out to be 21%, and for Russians 17.9%, so the difference is small. The rather low index for Tatarstan's Russian young people can easily be explained by the functional development of the Russian language in all spheres of life and the absence of any noticeable problems with its application in future. At the same time, the low index for Tatar young people testifies to an absence of adequate understanding of the importance and significance of the language, the seriousness of the status situation of their native ethnic language, and the problems of its functional development.

The answers to the question "What makes you closer to the people of your nation?" vary; the majority (72%) replied "language". However, at the same time, 55% of Tatars in the city and 22% in villages admit that with people of their nation they speak only or mainly Russian. Thus we have to admit that Tatars have a low level of linguistic consciousness. Any real extension in its functions is impossible without action by language entrepreneurs, native Tatar-speakers. Two thirds of city-dwelling Tatars consider Tatar their native language, together with 85% in villages. About 10% of city-dwelling Tatars called Russian their native language, and 2% in the villages. At the same time, there is a noticeable ethnic marginalisation of Tatars expressed in a double ethnic identity. Some 23% of city-dwelling Tatars consider that they have two native languages, Russian and Tatar, while the proportion of such people in villages is 13%.

Language alone does not determine ethnic identity. That phenomenon consists of many components and dimensions.

In its potential, Tatar is not inferior to the super-languages of the world. However, during the twentieth century, because of various, mainly political, reasons the language was moved to a secondary place, and its functional sphere was deliberately narrowed. Probably because of that, a majority of respondents formed an incorrect impression regarding the potential and perspectives of the Tatar language, and that is the reason behind contemporary orientations and viewpoints. About 60% of Tatar city-dwellers and 37% of villagers think that professional education should be provided only in Russian.

Research testifies to the important role of the family in the ethnic socialisation processes. The answer to the question *Who or what influences your national feelings more?* of 59% of young people was 'parents, family', and 53% pointed to the mass media; only 18.5% mentioned school. It is that very factor that explains the noticeable influence of the family language environment on the ethnolinguistic

Table 5: What state languages of the Republic of Tatarstan must the following speak?

	Both languages of state (Tatar and Russian)		Tatar only is enough		Russian only is enough	
	Tatars	Russians	Tatars	Russians	Tatars	Russians
President of the republic	91.9	83.1	1.0	1.1	2.1	8.2
Officials, civil servants	87.1	71.0	2.7	1.6	2.9	15.6
Tatars inhabiting the republic	82.5	61.7	8.1	11.9	2.1	8.4
Russians inhabiting the republic	67.5	39.3	1.3	1.8	17.9	42.2

orientation of Tatar young people in professional education. The majority of Tatar-speakers by birth prefer to receive professional education in two languages (65.0%), and every sixth intends to apply for enrolment to a higher educational establishment or college. It is obvious that an absolute majority of Tatar young people from Russian-speaking families prefer professional education through Russian (86.0%).

These figures speak for themselves. The National Tatar University could become an educational establishment of a new type, able to revive both the language and culture of the 7 million population. Then it would be followed by a change in the public mindset. Even Russian respondents admit the possibility of receiving education in Russian and Tatar. It is considered by 11% of Russian city-dwellers and 14% of Russian villagers. Some young Russians would like to speak the two languages of state, although it is obvious that the majority of Russian young people would like to receive professional education in their native language of Russian (85.5% of city-dwellers and 80.4% of villagers).

The beginning of democratisation and language reform in the education system in Tatarstan led to the opening of Tatar-Turkish secondary schools. The foreign languages teaching level there is much higher, and it gives its leavers a better chance of continuing their education in foreign educational establishments. It is noteworthy that Russians make up 30% of secondary school students.[5]

Differences in the educational establishments' degree of influence in forming the national feelings of Russian and Tatar young people testify to the fact that they have still not become ethnic cultural centres. Here we do not mean specialised Tatar grammar schools where national education programmes are being successfully realised.

All stages of the educational system should participate in solving the sociocultural and spiritual problems of national revival and achieve the following aims: to transmit ethnic culture; to form national consciousness in new generations; and to make available neighbouring peoples' cultures to harmonise transnational relationships in our republic.

In December 2001, the newspaper *Vechernya Kazan* set up a hotline with the

---

[5] Republic of Tatarstan, 22 December 2000.

Ministry of Education authorities to discuss the problems of Tatar language-teaching in schools. Some parents doubted the demand for Tatar in the professional development of young people and recommended holding a poll among parents. The answers to the poll question[6] are quite thought-provoking.

It is remarkable that Tatars' and Russians' views on the necessity of speaking two languages of state for the President and officials are very close. About 40% of Russians consider it necessary to speak the language of the eponymous nation.

As part of our research, we also tried to determine the language preferences of young people. The results of the poll are reflected in the preference scale, which is informative as it is. Respondents were asked to enumerate the languages that they would like to speak (Tatar, Russian, any European language, Turkish or Arabic). Both Tatars and Russians accorded first place to their native language, which is quite natural and only to be expected. Tatars accorded second place to the Russian language, and Russians to the Tatar language. In general, it is an extremely positive characteristic of the polyethnic community of Tatarstan, which testifies to the presence of language tolerance among young people. The preferences for foreign languages coincide. Both Tatars and Russians place European languages first. There are pragmatic reasons for that; English is the language of international communication today. Arabic and Turkish yield to European languages.

Conclusion

Language preferences among Tatar young people are to a great degree determined by the language policy of the state and the functional revival of the native language. It is necessary to consider two levels of that policy, institutional and individual. On an institutional level, the language policy of the Republic of Tatarstan is orientated towards providing for equal bilingualism, with legal and functional equality in various social spheres. However, on an individual level it is necessary to provide for prioritising the native language in socialisation. Only a personality that has been formed mainly in its own linguistic and cultural environment and received education through its native language is able to raise linguistic consciousness to the requisite level to provide for the real functioning of the language in all spheres of social life (education, power structures, science) and become the foundation of the preservation and development of the native language.[7]

---

[6] See *Cultures of Tatarstan Peoples* (in Russian).
[7] The research presented here is financially supported by the Russian Humanities Scientif Fund (Project Code is 05-03-03531à), to which grateful acknowledgement is made.

Un Aperçu de la Récuperation de la Langue Catalane pour l'Enseignement et la Formation du Professorat

Joaquim Arenas i Sampera

Considération préalable.

Le catalan est la langue propre à la Catalogne. Elle est officielle en Catalogne et, au même titre que le castillan ou l'espagnol, elle procède du latin. Elle est l'expression d'une culture universelle qui compte sur des personnalités de la notoriété de Gaudí, Dalí, Pau Casals, Ramon Llull ou Verdaguer. La langue catalane n'est pas seulement parlée dans la Principauté de Catalogne, elle est également parlée à l'intérieur de l'Etat espagnol dans les territoires d'Aragon, dans le Pays valencien, dans les îles Baléares et, à la limite des Pyrénées Orientales, situées dans la République française, elle est aussi la seule langue officielle de l'Etat indépendant de la Principauté d'Andorre, et se parle aussi dans la ville italienne d'Alghero, en Sardaigne. La langue catalane est reconnue dans la Constitution espagnole et dans le statut d'Autonomie de la Catalogne (loi régionale).

La *Constitution espagnole* dans son article 3 dit littéralement:

> 1. Le castillan est la langue officielle de l'Etat. Tous les Espagnols ont le devoir de la connaître et le droit de l'utiliser. 2. Les autres langues espagnoles seront également officielles dans les différentes Communautés autonomes selon leurs statuts.

Conformément au texte constitutionnel, le statut d'Autonomie de la Catalogne fut rédigé en 1979. Il est décrit dans son article 3:

> 1. La langue propre à la Catalogne est le catalan. 2. Le catalan est la langue officielle en Catalogne, tout comme le castillan, qui est officiel dans tout l'Etat espagnol. 3. La Generalitat de Catalunya – le gouvernement autonome – garantira l'usage normal et officiel des deux langues.

Principes fondamentaux de la normalisation de l'usage du catalan dans l'école et dans la société.

Il faut mettre en relief deux faits transcendantaux et qui propagés et pratiqués par la Generalitat ont permis les résultats obtenus grâce à l'opportunité du moment (l'année 1978) et à la clarté de leurs contenus: premièrement, la volonté politique du gouvernement autonome de généraliser la connaissance du catalan dans l'ensemble de la population de la Catalogne; deuxièmement : La définition de la personnalité linguistique que devait avoir les centres d'enseignement non universitaires de la Catalogne. Cette définition disait : "L'école sera catalane par la langue utilisée dans l'apprentissage, par les contenus des programmes avec un apprentissage poussé du castillan (espagnol) et d'autres réalités linguistiques de type universelles ".

Dans ce sens, les modèles européens du bilinguisme appliqués par les états modernes ne répondent pas aux nécessités de la Catalogne en ce qui concerne l'aspect sociolinguistique. Et surtout, ils ne répondent pas aux nécessitées des sociétés qui veulent récupérer leur langue après une longue persécution politique, une langue que doit être restituée à leur place d'utilisation sociale comme langue hégémonique.

L'application du concept de bilinguisme en vigueur et officiellement adopté en Europe a eu comme base : l'apprentissage de la langue et de la culture de l'Etat et l'étude de langues étrangères de caractère majoritaire : anglais-français, italien-français, etc. Ou, dans le meilleur des cas, l'apprentissage scolaire de la langue minoritaire immigrée était imposé comme une transition en vue de l'acquisition de la langue de l'Etat.

Ainsi donc, le système éducatif catalan, dispose d'une ordonnance qui indique l'apprentissage de trois ou de quatre langues: le catalan, première langue de l'école, le castillan ou espagnol, seconde langue scolaire, l'anglais et le français ou une autre langue vivante, troisième et quatrième langues d'apprentissage.

Les grandes lignes d'action normalisatrice de la langue.

Il y existe un programme d'action visant à incorporer la langue catalane dans l'enseignement qui repose sur trois grands points : le législatif – décrets, lois – l'actualisation linguistique du professorat et l'information techno-pédagogique pour atteindre un enseignement de qualité et moderne.

1. Le corpus législatif

Les décrets, les ordres et les lois ont été un support réel et décisif à la dynamisation et au développement de la langue catalane et de son incorporation dans l'enseignement, de la même façon que ces lois ont été décisives pour leur prohibition il y a trois cents ans. Un bref coup d'?il au développement de cette action normalisatrice qui a été si positive pour la normalisation du catalan fait suite:

En 1978, l'apparition du Décret de 2092 daté du 23 juin et de l'Ordre du 18 septembre, lesquels ont établi : l'incorporation obligatoire du catalan dans les Plans d'Étude de l'Ecole Maternelle, l'enseignement obligatoire, l'enseignement secondaire ; la reconnaissance aux établissements scolaires de la possibilité d'enseigner en catalan de manière optative et avec une autorisation préalable ; la création de chaires de langue catalane dans les Écoles universitaires de formation au professorat.

En 1981, et déjà dans le cadre de la Generalitat Statuaire, apparaît un nouveau Décret (D 2089 du 3 octobre) qui rend effectifs les transferts de compétence en matière d'enseignement du Ministère du gouvernement de l'Etat à la Generalitat de Catalogne.

En 1982, intervient l'incorporation obligatoire dans les curriculum scolaires de l'enseignement en catalan dans deux matières aux moins. Cela implique que le catalan est la langue du professeur, du livre de texte, des exercices des élèves et de la notation.

En 1983, la Loi du 7/1983 de Normalisation linguistique de la Catalogne est consolidée dans le processus législatif. Essentiellement le contenu est celui-ci : Le catalan est la langue propre à l'enseignement en Catalogne. Les enfants ont le droit de recevoir les premiers enseignements dans leur langue habituelle, qu'il s'agisse du catalan ou du castillan. Les langues catalane et castillane doivent être apprises obligatoirement à tous les niveaux non universitaires. En accord avec les exigences de leur mission d'enseignement, les professeurs doivent connaître les deux langues officielles.

En 1990, la Loi de l'Etat (LOGSE) qui change les Plans d'Etudes et qui doit se développer et être appliquée par les gouvernements autonomes rend possible que tout l'enseignement soit véhiculé en catalan dans tous les établissements scolaires de Catalogne.

En 1998, une nouvelle Loi du Parlement de la Catalogne (L.1/98) régissant la Politique linguistique de la Generalitat, vient à confirmer les principes établis et appliqués à l'enseignement du catalan depuis 1980.

2. L'actualisation linguistique du professorat.

Le manque de préparation du professorat a été une des difficultés objectives que l'on a dû surmonter pour parvenir à faire du catalan la langue scolaire. Il fallait préfigurer un plan de perfectionnement qui facilite et encourage un corps enseignant compétent.

En 1978, 52% seulement des instituteurs d'écoles maternelles et d'enseignement primaire de la Catalogne parlaient le catalan et le pourcentage était de 46 % dans le département (province) de Barcelone.

Un ambitieux programme de recyclage du catalan pour les professeurs a été mis en place avec l'objectif de renforcer la formation personnelle et pédagogique qui, jusqu'alors, avait été réservée aux professeurs. Cette actualisation linguistique a été recommandée aux Instituts des Sciences de l'Education des universités catalanes.

Dès le début, des milliers de professeurs participèrent à ce recyclage linguistique, qui connut son point culminant au cours des années 1981-82, avec 18.150 enseignants inscrits, dont 7.074 avaient le castillan comme langue maternelle. Il fût organisé 923 cours dans 23 points territoriaux. Il s'agissait là d'une véritable faculté universitaire répartie sur toute la Catalogne (Il y avait 350 emplacements où les cours étaient dispensés).

Le développement de ce recyclage a abouti à deux sortes de diplôme. L'obtention du Certificat donnait droit à enseigner le catalan jusqu'à la cinquième années de l'école primaire et à donner les cours sur toutes les matières de la totalité de l'enseignement primaire en catalan. L'obtention du Diplôme universitaire de "Maître de Catalan" qui permet d'enseigner la langue et de donner les cours en langue catalane à l'ensemble de l'Enseignement général obligatoire.

Ces deux diplômes comprenaient les matières suivantes : langue catalane, pédagogie, histoire de la Catalogne, géographie catalane, et littérature catalane. L'expérience a prouvé que le contenu des programmes de cette opération était excessif et que les matières de « traitement didactique de la langue » et d'«histoire et géographie catalanes » faisaient perdre l'efficacité de la compétence communicative, élément indispensable pour le professeur qui avait besoin d'utiliser de façon spontanée et correcte la langue qu'il doit enseigner.

En réponse à ce problème, une restructuration a eu lieu en 1989 qui, sans faire varier l'objectif final, a modifié les contenus. Ce nouvel aménagement a mis en place trois modules ou groupes d'étude: **Le Module 1** qui comprend : l'initiation à la langue écrite, tout en consolidant l'usage oral ; la pédagogie de la langue ; et la connaissance de la Catalogne. **La Module 2** prétend permettre au professeur d'affirmer ses connaissances concernant la langue écrite et de se consacrer aux contenus des sciences sociales qui traitent de la Catalogne et de sa culture.

D'autres modalités ont été conçues mais ne sont pas en vigueur aujourd'hui.
1. Les cours de **formation permanente institutionnelle (FOPI)** avaient un caractère intensif. Un jour par semaine, les maîtres-élèves abandonnaient leur travail d'enseignants et assistaient à une session d'une durée de huit heures. Chacun d'eux était remplacé par un maître assigné par l'administration. L'objectif des FOPIs est de faire en sorte que les maîtres acquièrent la compétence linguistique, orale et écrite leur permettant d'enseigner en catalan.
2. Notons également la mise en **pratique d'un programme d'Immersion pour les professeurs (PIP)** permettant de recycler les professeurs qui n'ont pas encore de compétences linguistiques en catalan. Les résultats ont été excellents, puisque ces professeurs, à la fin de l'activité s'exprimaient en catalan non seulement quand un interlocuteur leur parlait en cette langue mais aussi lorsqu'ils conversaient entre eux.

Pour maintenir la capacité communicative en catalan les maîtres-élèves en langue maternelle castillane ayant suivi les cours intensifs de langues FOPI ou PIP disposent sur le lieu même de leur travail, de **Cours de Conversation** chaque semaine. Après vingt-trois ans d'offre de diverses modalités permettant l'actualisation linguistique du professorat au Système Educatif Catalan, celui-ci présente la situation suivante:

ÉCOLES PRIMAIRES

Cours scolaire	Avec accréditation	Sans accréditation	Total
1986-1987	64,91%	35,09%	36.128
1989-1990	73,58%	26,42%	30.884
1992-1993	88,03%	11,97%	31.327
1995-1996	93,29%	6,71%	40.636
2001-2002	95,03%	4,97%	44.540

Les cours de formation linguistique pour les professeurs d'enseignement secondaire sont organisés de manière différente que ceux que nous venons d'expliquer et qui sont réalisés pour les enseignants de l'école primaire, c'est à dire, pour les maîtres.

Pour l'enseignement secondaire, les cours ont été organisés dans les mêmes Lycées dans le cadre d'un horaire en-dehors du temps scolaire. Ces cours sont dispensés par des professeurs d'universités ou par des professeurs spécialisés en Langue et Littérature Catalanes du même Lycée. Voilà ici un résumé de l'évolution des cours de langue catalane dispensés depuis 1986:

ÉCOLES SECONDAIRES

Cours scolaires	Nombre de cours	Elèves-professeurs	Nombre de certificats
1986-1987	72	518	114
1989-1990	260	2.456	595
1992-1993	302	3.233	1.958
1995-1996	97	1.165	421
2001-2002	34	415	198

Ces données nous indiquent que depuis 1986, à peu près 10.000 professeurs d'enseignement secondaire qui sont spécialistes en matières non linguistiques ont obtenu le certificat de connaissance du Catalan

3. L'information technique et le soutien didactique au professorat

L'école catalane, de langue et contenus catalans, doit se baser sur une forme authentique de faire et de créer une école. C'est pour cette raison que l'Administration de l'éducation a lancé des programmes visant la catalanisation scolaire et la qualité de l'enseignement. La langue et les contenus des Programmes sont importants, mais tout au long de l'histoire du pays, la qualité et la catalanité ont existé dans le domaine éducatif. Ainsi donc, un vaste programme d'assistance destiné aux professeurs et aux écoles a été mené à bien dès le rétablissement de la Generalitat.

Après plus de vingt ans, une équipe de personnel assesseur, au nombre de cent-dix à peu près, ont été disséminés dans l'ensemble du pays catalan pour offrir, à chaque nouveau cours scolaire, des centaines de Séminaires d'assessorat didactique aux enseignants des écoles primaires, en accord avec les besoins de leurs établissements scolaires.

À L'Enseignement Primaire on appliqua un Programme spécifique réalisé par la convocation de Séminaires et le Plan d'application est accompli suivant les deux modalités suivantes :
Une formation technique ponctuelle qui fournit de connaissances sur les bases psycholinguistiques, pédagogiques et sociologiques du curriculum, ainsi que, du traitement didactique initial que les enseignants devront appliquer. Elle est réalisée en une ou deux sessions afin que les maîtres prennent pleine responsabilité de l'éducation et qu'ils l'assument en pleine connaissance de cause.
Séminaires périodiques d'assistance de niveau. Il y en a de deux sortes:
Séminaires thématiques. Il s'agit d'une information technique longitudinale pendant toute la durée des cours scolaires et d'une périodicité bimensuelle. Au cours de ces séminaires, on étudie les propositions didactiques qui devront être incluses dans le programme d'activités éducatives de la classe ; par exemple : comment appliquer l'immersion linguistique dans cette école. Les professeurs disposent pour leur application de plusieurs instruments élaborés depuis les unités de langue écrite selon les directives les plus à la pointe dans le domaine de la Psychologie et de la Pédagogie.
Séminaires d'école. Il s'agit de sessions de formation dans lesquelles participent, soit tout le professorat d'un établissement scolaire, soit une équipe concrète de ce professorat. L'objectif est offrir une formation qui puisse aider les professeurs à approfondir leur propre pratique scolaire et à incorporer des nouveautés pédagogiques permettant une amélioration des résultats d'apprentissages linguistiques.

Dans L'Enseignment Secondaire (Collèges, Lycées), il y a une différence considérable dans la situation du professorat, puisque les professeurs qui enseignent la langue catalane aux élèves sont tous accrédités par les Universités, le reste du professorat ayant besoin d'aide pour communiquer en catalan, une langue que, souvent, ils n'ont pas appris à l'école. L'information technique doit se diversifier selon deux modalités, en fonction du destinataire: La formation des professeurs de langue et littérature catalanes; et l'appui didactique donné aux professeurs qui enseignent d'autres matières ou qui ont des responsabilités de gestion du centre éducatif et qui devront utiliser la langue catalane comme langue véhiculaire. La majorité des actions d'information technique qui se sont développées en Catalogne, en rapport avec la normalisation linguistique, sont dirigées vers les professeurs de langue et de littérature catalanes. Cette activité a quatre objectifs:

Formation des professeurs formateurs des autres et responsables du recyclage et des cours complémentaires.

Motivation à la lecture parmi les élèves des écoles secondaires avec le **Programme "le plaisir de lire" (El gust per la lectura)**. Il s'agit d'une activité qui englobe la formation des professeurs, une proposition d'activités pour les élèves, et à la fin, un acte collectif de tous ceux qui ont participé. Dans chaque cours scolaire, on prend des oeuvres littéraires différentes et on apprend à connaître l'auteur : sa personnalité, sa vie, son ?uvre.

Les **"Ateliers de Langue et de Littérature catalanes"**, réunion d'échange entre tous les professeurs de ces matières qui a lieu tous les deux ans. Jusqu'à l'heure actuelle, 12 "Ateliers" ont été tenus avec des sujets monographiques pour chacun d'eux et avec plus de trente propositions d'activités chacun.

Séminaires de didactique de la Langue pour les élèves ayant des difficultés d'apprentissage, en particulier pour ceux qui arrivent en provenance d'autres pays et qui ne connaissent pas la langue ni la culture. De plus en plus, ces séminaires se diversifient d'après les situations des différentes collectivités d'immigrés et également de diverses situations scolaires d'accueil.

Pour les professeurs d'autres matières, on a organisé des cours d'une durée de trente heures sur l'amélioration de certains aspects de la langue en leur matière tels que le perfectionnement de l'expression orale, du texte écrit et du discours de l'enseignement, du langage administratif, des nouveautés en langue normative et en langue standard.

Considération finale

Cet ambitieux programme d'assistance didactique a été développé pendant vingt-quatre ans successifs, avec des résultats très positifs pour l'incorporation du catalan dans les écoles, objectif primordial de notre société au moment de la récupération des libertés démocratiques. Au début, ces séminaires donnaient réponse au besoin d'assurer la qualité de l'enseignement, face à un changement généralisé de la langue scolaire en vue d'aider les professeurs à utiliser le catalan comme langue véhicule, de faciliter les instruments didactiques nécessaires à l'enseignement de cette langue, si longtemps proscrite de la vie officielle et de la vie académique, et qui devrait être connue par tous les enfants, un bon nombre desquels ne parlant pas le catalan chez eux. Lors des derniers cours scolaires, les besoins ont changé en même temps que l'école changeait également en parallèle avec l'évolution logique de notre société, dans laquelle, il faut le dire, est intervenue une amélioration des conditions sociolinguistiques avec une plus grande connaissance de la langue catalane dans l'ensemble de la société. Aujourd'hui, une bonne partie de cette actualisation du professorat est dédiée aux nouvelles méthodes d'accueil des enfants qui arrivent à l'école en provenance d'autres pays et d'autres continents, résultat des mouvements migratoires prévalents de nos jours. L'incorporation de ces élèves dans nos écoles, ou de la langue usitée, qui n'est pas une langue de l'état, offre plus que des difficultés didactiques, voire des difficultés d'ordre politique et social, de prestige de la langue et d'acceptation de cette réalité, tout cela préconise maintenant la prise en charge d'un travail pédagogique très qualifié, et malgré cela, il est encore nécessaire de s'occuper de l'information technique des professeurs.

Coláiste Ollscoile Naomh Muire, agus Túsoideachas do Mhúinteoirí Lán-Ghaeilge

Gabrielle Nig Uidhir

Tá dúshraith fianaise le hardchaighdeán agus ardchailíocht an oideachais lán-Ghaeilge in Éirinn. Is é a chuireann mianach leis an fhianaise sin ná méadú agus leathnú an tsoláthair, torthaí measúnaithe, taifead dul chun cinn na ndaltaí, taighde ar ghnéithe den tumoideachas (Gallagher agus Hanna, 2002), bunachair sonraí agus eolas eile á dtaifeadadh ag Comhairle na Gaelscolaíochta, Gaelscoileanna agus An Chomhairle um Oideachas Gaeilge agus Gaelscolaíochta. Meastar go leanfaidh den dul chun cinn seo ó dheas (Mac Donnacha, 2004).

Ó thuaidh, tá Comhairle na Gaelscolaíochta agus Iontaobhas na Gaelscolaíochta freagrach as pleanáil straitéiseach earnáil an Ghaeloideachais. Léiríonn straitéis fhorbartha na Comhairle treisiú an tsoláthair lán-Ghaeilge atá á phleanáil agus á chur i bhfeidhm ar fud na sé chontae. Is é an toradh is mó atá le fás agus forbairt na ngaelscoileanna, atá ábhartha don pháipéar seo, ná ráchairt ar sholáthar múinteoirí cáilithe don earnáil lán-Ghaeilge.

Cuireadh tús le hOideachas Tosaigh do Mhúinteoirí Lán-Ghaeilge i gColáiste Ollscoile Naomh Muire, Béal Feirste, i Meán Fómhair 1996. Ón dáta sin ar aghaidh, cláraíonn mic léinn (iníonacha léinn) fochéime gach bliain ar chúrsa Bhaitsiléir an Oideachais (le hOnóracha) a mhaireann 4 bliana agus cláraíonn mic léinn iarchéime ar an chúrsa bliana, 'Teastas Iarchéime san Oideachas' (TICO). Is gné thábhachtach de sholáthar acadúil an Choláiste iad an dá chúrsa ghairmiúla seo. Tugann an soláthar lán-Ghaeilge sainaitheantas don institiúid mar sholáthróir dátheangach agus mar ionad saineolais sa tumoideachas. Is le leas na hinstitiúide chomh maith le leas na scoileanna agus leas an phobail a oibríonn an pháirtíocht seo.

Ar feadh dhá bhliain roimh 1996, d'fhostaigh an Coláiste Oifigeach Taighde chun cúrsa lán-Ghaeilge a dhearadh ab fhéidir a mhúnlú isteach sa B.Oid. agus a d'éascódh soláthar sainoideachais d'iarchéimithe tumoideachais le cur leis an chúrsa iarchéime a bhí á reáchtáil ag an am sin don earnáil lán-Bhéarla. Bhí an tionscnamh taighde sin dúshlánach de thairbhe athbhreithniú na Céime B.Oid. a bhí á ullmhú le linn na tréimhse sin.

Cúlra: fás agus borradh ráchairte

Ba ré chruthaitheach, fhuinniúil, dhinimiciúil san earnáil lán-Ghaeilge í an tréimhse sin ó bhunú na chéad bunscoile i mBéal Feirste (1971) a d'oscail le naonúr daltaí, go dtí an tréimhse sin ag tús na nóchaidí nuair a tháinig méadú suntasach ar an ráchairt ar oideachas múinteoirí. Sa bhliain 1991, bunaíodh an chéad mheánscoil lán-Ghaeilge. Sa bhliain chéanna, bunaíodh eagras tacaíochta agus forbartha do mhúinteoirí agus thuismitheoirí lán-Ghaeilge a thabharfadh faoi thionscnadh na hearnála ar fud na sé chontae.

Faoin am ar cuireadh tús leis an taighde ar thúsoideachas lán-Ghaeilge sa Choláiste (1994), bhí dhá mheánscoil agus naoi mbunscoil sa tuaisceart, á gcothú ag 19 naíonra. Scoileanna saorscartha ab ea an chuid is mó díobh siúd. Ach bhí tús curtha le bunú aonad lán-Ghaeilge taobh istigh de scoileanna na Comhairle Caitlicí (CSCC) agus bhí pleananna le haghaidh bunscoile satailíte forbartha agus réidh lena gcur i bhfeidhm. Bhí cúigear de na scoileanna seo maoinithe ag Roinn an Oideachais ó thuaidh, ag an phointe sin. Díríodh cuid mhaith d'fhuinneamh an phobail lán-Ghaeilge ar bhunú scoileanna agus ar fheachtas maoinithe agus ar phróiseas comhairlithe le Roinn an Oideachais. Bhí béim mhór ar staitisticí – líon na scoileanna, cóimheas múinteoirí-daltaí agus critéir inmharthanachta. Bhíodh frustrachas ar na múinteoirí lán-Ghaeilge a bhíodh ag tnúth leis an am nuair a thiocfadh leo an infheistíocht ama agus airde sin a athdhíriú le fócas ní ba ghéire ar shaincheisteanna oideachais mar mheasúnú, modhanna teagaisc, áiseanna agus, ar ndóigh, ar oideachas múinteoirí agus chúrsaí inseirbhíse. Mar sin féin, léiríonn doiciméid, miontuairiscí agus comhfhreagras a bhaineann leis an tréimhse sin go raibh tús maith curtha leis na spriocanna sin go léir agus gur spreag borradh na scoileanna agus dul chun cinn oideachasúil na ndaltaí agus an nasc leis an phobal dearcadh dearfach folláin san earnáil go ginearálta (Gaeloiliúint, 1993a).

D'fhoilsigh Roinn an Oideachais athbhreithniú ar thúsoiliúint múinteoirí i dtuaisceart na hÉireann (ROTE, 1993) a spreag díospóireacht faoi Oideachas Múinteoirí go ginearálta. Cé nár luadh oideachas lán-Ghaeilge sa doiciméad seo, chruthaigh sé deis thráthúil do mhúinteoirí agus phríomhoidí lán-Ghaeilge teacht le chéile agus riachtanais oiliúna na hearnála lán-Ghaeilge a phlé agus moltaí forbartha a phleanáil (Gaeloiliúint, 1993b). Mar thoradh ar an phlé seo, scríobhadh litreacha chuig institiúidí tríú leibhéil ag iarraidh orthu aghaidh a thabhairt ar dhearadh agus ar sholáthar cúrsaí cuí d'ábhair múinteoirí lán-Ghaeilge. Fuarthas freagra dearfach ar an iarratas seo ó Choláiste Ollscoile Naomh Muire, Béal Feirste.

Bonn Taighde agus Pleanála

Mhaoinigh Roinn an Oideachais an saothar taighde a bhí de dhíth chun cruth a chur ar thúsoideachas do mhúinteoirí lán-Ghaeilge. Ó rinneadh an cinneadh tabhairt faoin tionscnamh taighde sin (1994-96), léiríodh tacaíocht agus dea-thoil agus dearcadh oscailte faoi chomhlíonadh na riachtanas oiliúna agus oideachais sa chomhthéacs seo. Baineadh tairbhe as flaithiúlacht comhleacaithe in institiúidí eile, áit a raibh eiseamláir cleachtais le feiceáil nó taithí ábhartha á tógáil.

Is é an bunsmaoineamh a bhí ag údaráis Choláiste Ollscoile Naomh Muire sular thosaigh an obair seo ná go ndearfaí modú(i)l nó cuid de mhodú(i)l a thabharfadh tuiscint ar an tumoideachas do na mic léinn agus d'fhorbródh caighdeán ard Gaeilge. Faoi lár na chéad bhliana, thuig pobal an Choláiste go raibh gá le hionchur lán-Ghaeilge a bheadh fite trí ábhar na céime agus a bheadh mar fhráma don chúrsa iarchéime chomh maith. Ní leor foghlaim <u>faoin</u> tumoideachas amháin. Ba ghá bunfhealsúnacht agus oideolaíochtaí an tumoideachais a chur i bhfeidhm i saol acadúil na mac léinn lán-Ghaeilge, ag eiseamláiriú an chur chuige oideachasúil agus teangeolaíochta seo i saol an Choláiste. Ba léir gur chuí staidéir churaclaim a dhéanamh trí mheán na Gaeilge chun an taithí lán-Ghaeilge a chur ar fáil do mhic léinn, go háirithe dóibh siúd nach bhfuair an taithí sin ag leibhéal na bunscoile nó na meánscoile iad féin.

Bhí buntáistí eile leis an tréimhse taighde a caitheadh roimh thosú ar na cúrsaí lán-Ghaeilge. Tugadh faill agus am le riachtanais na mac léinn a aithint. Mar shampla, cé go raibh obair ar siúl ag múinteoirí bunscoile ag cruthú áiseanna teagaisc, ní raibh áiseanna ar bith ar fáil do mhic léinn tríú leibhéal. Mar sin, cuireadh tús le hullmhú cuid de na háiseanna a bheadh de dhíth sna cúrsaí. Bunriachtanas eile a bheadh ann timpeallacht dhearfach, fhorásach a bheith ar fáil san institiúid féin. Le linn an phróisis chomhairlithe a tharla i gcomhar le gach roinn ábhair agus ar fud phobal an Choláiste (leabharlann, riarachán, srl.) dáileadh eolas ar an chóras tumoideachais agus tuiscint ar an oideachas lán-Ghaeilge. Fuarthas amach go raibh léachtóirí ar an fhoireann, taobh amuigh de roinn na Gaeilge, a raibh Gaeilge acu, ach í meirgeach, nó a raibh suim faoi leith acu san oideachas lán-Ghaeilge. Tógadh bealaí cumarsáide idir léachtóirí (lán-Bhéarla, dátheangacha, lán-Ghaeilge) a thacódh le cur i bhfeidhm rathúil an tsoláthair lán-Ghaeilge.

Le linn na tréimhse taighde seo, aithníodh an tábhacht le critéir áirithe a thacaigh le cur i bhfeidhm éifeachtach an tsoláthair lán-Ghaeilge:

1. *Timpeallacht dhearfach san institiúid 3ú leibhéi*l

Bhí Gaeilge ag lucht bainisteoireachta an Choláiste agus chuidigh sin le hardú phróifíl agus stádas na Gaeilge. Bhí léachtóirí le Gaeilge i gceithre roinn taobh amuigh de roinn na Gaeilge. Chuir an buntáiste sin bonn maith faoin soláthar lán-Ghaeilge trasna an churaclaim. D'iarr baill eile den fhoireann forbairt ghairmiúil chun feabhas a chur ar a gcuid Gaeilge. Cuireadh suas comharthaí dátheangacha san fhoirgneamh chun tacú le timpeallacht dhátheangach. Rinneadh socruithe a d'éascódh seirbhís aistriúcháin chun áiseanna teagaisc agus ábhair eolais a chur ar fáil sa Ghaeilge.

2. *Maoiniú*

Bhronn Roinn an Oideachais deontas neamhspleách chun an tionscnamh taighde a mhaoiniú. Fógraíodh buiséid neamhspleácha a d'íocfadh as ceapachán acadúil lán-Ghaeilge agus costais bhreise an tsoláthair. Aithníodh go raibh tábhacht leis an chéim sin, ag an phointe ama sin, chun teannas ar bith a d'imreodh droch-thionchar ar thionscnamh nua a sheachaint.

3. *Lárnú na tsoláthair lán-Ghaeilge*

De réir struchtúr sholáthar an Oideachais Tosaigh do Mhúinteoirí ó thuaidh, tá cúraimí ainmnithe faoi leith ar na hinstidiúidí tríú leibhéal. Tá dualgas sonraithe ar Choláiste Ollscoile Naomh Muire soláthar túsoideachais do mhúinteoirí bunscoileanna lán-Ghaeilge a chur ar fáil ag leibhéal na céime B.O. agus ag leibhéal an teastais iarchéime, TICO. Is buntáiste ag na mic léinn lán-Ghaeilge go bhfuil an soláthar seo suite in aon ionad amháin a éascaíonn pobal lán-Ghaeilge mar chuid de phobal iomlán na hinstidiúide. Is tábhachtach an ghné sin d'oideachas agus d'fhorbairt na mac léinn a spreagann cumarsáid idir chomhscoláirí lán-Ghaeilge taobh amuigh den léachtlann. Tá an tacaíocht seo ríthábhachtach sa tréimhse ullmhúcháin roimh thaithí scoile i ngaelscoil, mar shampla. Is buntáiste ag na mic léinn agus ag an fhoireann teagaisc go bhfuil an tÁisaonad Lán-Ghaeilge suite sa Choláiste agus gur áit í ina bhfuil obair chruthaitheach ag dul ar aghaidh ag cruthú áiseanna do na scoileanna.

An soláthar faoi láthair

Maidir le líon na n-iontrálacha iarchéime, cloíonn an Coláiste le cuóta a ardaíodh ó 5 mac léinn sa chéad bhliain den Teastas go 20 iarchéimí i 2004. Ní rialaíonn an córas céanna i gcás na bhfochéimithe mar thig le mac léinn ar bith le Gaeilge cur isteach ar an chosán lán-Ghaeilge, uair amháin a thugtar áit dóibh sa Choláiste. Athraíonn líon na bhfochéimithe ó bhliain go bliain, ach de ghnáth bíonn idir 10 agus 15 fochéimí lán-Ghaeilge i ngach bliainghrúpa. Bíonn aird na mac léinn lán-Ghaeilge dírithe ar earnáil an tumoideachais agus is gnách do na mic léinn nuacháilithe post a aimsiú i scoil lán-Ghaeilge agus fanacht sa chóras sin.

Léiríonn Tábla 1 imlíne de phróifíl eispéireas na teanga ar an dá chúrsa (gan léachtaí ar an teanga Ghaeilge san áireamh).

Tábla 1: Dúshláin i soláthar Túsoideachas Múinteoirí don earnáil lán-Ghaeilge

Codanna den chúrsa a dhéantar trí mheán na Gaeilge nó le hionchur Gaeilge		
	Staidéir Phroifisiúnta (Oideachas agus Curaclam)	Taithí Scoile
TICO	Litearthacht, uimhreas, an domhan thart orainn, creideamh; Réamhscolaíocht / luathbhlianta / Eochaircheim1; Saincheisteanna an tumoideachais.	2 bhloc de Thaithí Scoile i scoil lán-Ghaeilge; 1 bhloc de Thaithí scoile i scoil lán-Bhéarla.
B. Oideachais 1&2	Litearthacht, uimhreas, an domhan thart orainn; Staidéir Teagaisc..	Taithí i scoileanna lán-Bhéarla.
B. Oideachais 3	Curaclam na bunscoile; Soláthar iomlán Gaeilge nó dátheangach.	Taithí Scoile i scoil lán-Ghaeilge.
B.Oideachais 4	Curaclam na bunscoile: Soláthar iomlán Gaeilge nó dátheangach; Saincheisteanna an tumoideachais.	Taithí Scoile i scoil lán-Ghaeilge.

Is féidir dúshláin an tsoláthair a anailísiú sa fhráma thíos:

Forbairtí 3ú leibhéil:	*Acmhainn ar fáil:*	*Forbairtí sna scoileanna:*
athbhreithniú ar oideachas tosaigh múinteoirí; athbhreithniú na céime; dearadh modúlach cúrsaí.	líon na foirne teagaisc;	curaclam nua, reachtaíocht nua, forbairt naíonraí, pleanáil iarbhunoideachais, fortheilgean folúntas.

Is minic a chluintear múinteoirí ag tagairt do na síorathruithe agus do na tionscnaimh nua is gá dóibh a chur i bhfeidhm ar bhonn leanúnach. Bíonn an patrún céanna le sonrú ar fhorbairt agus ar fheidhmiú an tsoláthair ag leibhéal an oideachais tríú leibhéil. Tá beirt léachtóirí tumoideachais lánaimseartha sa Choláiste. Cé go bhfuil na freagrachtaí teagaisc roinnte ar fhoireann ildánach leathan, caithfidh méid na croífhoirne tionchar a imirt ar thosaíochtaí agus ar theorainn na forbartha. Mar shampla, is laige í nach bhfuil múinteoirí cáilithe fostaithe i mórchuid na naíonraí lán-Ghaeilge. Ag an am céanna, dá mbeadh níos mó naíonraí ag cuardach múinteoirí

Coláiste Ollscoile Naomh Muire, agus Túsoideachas do Mhúinteoirí Lán-Ghaeilge 149

Léarscáil de Ghaelscoileanna i dTuaisceart Éireann 2002-03

cáilithe, ba dhoiligh freagairt do mhéadú ráchairte gan foireann léachtóirí níos fairsinge. Gan amhras, is í an chonstaic is mó a imríonn tionchar ar an soláthar ná líon teoranta na croífhoirne teagaisc.

Is dúshlán eile atá romhainn amach anseo ná monatóireacht a dhéanamh ar an ghaol idir líon na bhfolúntas post agus líon na n-iontrálacha. Castacht bhreise a tharlaíonn mura n-aimsítear cothromaíocht chuí idir líon scoileanna agus líon na mac léinn is ea líon na n-áiteanna atá ar fáil i scoileanna lán-Ghaeilge don Taithí Scoile. Nuair a bhronntar céim nó teastas iarchéime ar mhic léinn lán-Ghaeilge an Choláiste, tá patrún láidir ann go gcuardaíonn siad poist san earnáil lán-Ghaeilge. Bíonn buntáistí ag baint le cuid mhaith de na dúshláin a chuirtear roimh lucht lán-Ghaeilge an Choláiste. Mar shampla, ba ghá soláthar Oideachais Tosaigh Múinteoirí a athbhreithniú i gcomhthéacs athbhreithniú an Churaclaim. Ceann de na buntáistí a bhaineann leis an phróiseas sin ná daingniú na bpáirtnéireachtaí idir an Coláiste, na scoileanna agus eagrais eile.

Ceann de na hathruithe is suntasaí i bhforbairt an tsoláthair seo ná méadú líon na mac léinn lán-Ghaeilge a d'fhreastal ar naíscoil, ar bhunscoil agus ar mheánscoil lán-Ghaeilge roimh thosú ar Oideachas Tosaigh Múinteoirí trí mheán na Gaeilge. Is cuí an fhorbairt seo a chur san áireamh mar fhianaise bhreise den rath atá ar an earnáil lán-Ghaeilge ar fud na tíre.

Leabharliosta

DENI. 1993. *A Review of Initial Teacher Training in Northern Ireland*. Bangor: Department of Education.
Gaeloiliúint 1993a. *Nuachtlitir Ghaeloiliúin*t. Meitheamh 1993.
Gaeloiliúint 1993b. *Nuachtlitir Ghaeloiliúint*. Samhain 1993.
Gallagher, A.M. and Hanna, E, 2002. Outcomes for Pupils Who Received an Irish-Medium Education. Research Report Series No. 26. Bangor: Department of Education.
Mac Corraidh, S. 2001. *An Ghaelscolaíocht in Oiliúint Tosaigh Muinteoirí do Chéim Bhaitsiéir an Oideachais. Taighde agus Teagaisc*, Vol. 1. Béal Feirste: Coláiste Ollscoile Naomh Muire.
Mac Donnacha, J. 2004. 'The Role of the University in meeting the needs of Linguistic Communities: An Irish Case Study'. Paper presented at Workshop A: Positive Models of Language Policy and Planning. Dialogue on Language Diversity, Sustainability and Peace, Barcelona, 20 to 23 May 2004. http://www.linguapax.org/congres04
Nig Uidhir, G. 1996. Oiliúint Múinteoirí do Scoileanna Lán-Ghaeilge. A Report on the Commencement of an Irish-medium Pathway in St. Mary's University College, Belfast, June 1996. Belfast: St. Mary's University College [unpublished].
Nig Uidhir, G. 2002. 'Initial Teacher Training for Irish-Medium Schools'. In eds. J. M. Kirk and D.P.Ó Baoill. *Language Planning and Education: Linguistic Issues in Northern Ireland, the Republic of Ireland, and Scotland*. Belfast Studies in Language, Culture and Politics 6. Belfast: Cló Ollscoil na Banríona. 65-75.

St. Mary's University College and Irish-Medium Teacher Training

Gabrielle Nig Uidhir

There is substantial evidence for the high standard of Irish-medium education in Ireland. Examples of that evidence include the increase in provision, assessment results, the progress of pupils, research in aspects of immersion education (Gallagher and Hanna, 2002), databases and other material recorded by Comhairle na Gaelscolaíochta, Gaelscoileanna and An Chomhairle um Oideachas Gaeilge agus Gaelscolaíochta.

There are strong indications that such progress will continue both in the Republic of Ireland (Mac Donncha, 2004) and in Northern Ireland, where Comhairle na Gaelscolaíochta and Iontaobhas na Gaelscolaíochta are responsible for strategic planning for the Irish-medium sector. The development strategy of the Comhairle outlines the further planned expansion and enhancement of Irish-medium provision throughout the six counties of Northern Ireland. An important result of the growth and development of Irish-medium schools is the demand for qualified teachers for the Irish-medium sector.

Initial training of teachers for Irish-medium education began in St. Mary's University College, Belfast, in September 1996. Since that date, undergraduate students have been able to undertake a B.Ed. (Hons.) bilingual course, which lasts four years, while postgraduate students can choose a one-year Irish-medium course, Teastas Iarchéime san Oideachas (Postgraduate Certificate in Education). Those two vocational courses are an important aspect of the academic provision of the college. Irish-medium provision helps to identify the college as a bilingual provider and as a centre of expertise in immersion education. That provision benefits the institution, the community and the schools concerned.

Between 1994 and 1996, the college employed a research officer to design an Irish-medium course which could be incorporated into the B.Ed. That research project was made more challenging by the fact that the B.Ed. degree was under review during the period. Another aim of that project was to plan for the provision of an Irish-medium initial teacher education certificate, at postgraduate level, offering specialist insights into immersion education.

Background: Growth in Demand

During the years following the foundation of the first Irish-medium primary school in Belfast in 1971, demand for Irish-medium teacher education increased. It was a period of creativity, energy, and dynamism in the Irish-medium sector. In 1991, the first Irish-medium secondary school was founded. In the same year, an organisation was set up by the Irish-medium community in order to support the development of the schools in a more planned and co-ordinated way (Gaeloiliúint).

By the time the research project at St. Mary's College began (1994), there were two secondary and nine primary schools and 19 nursery classes in Northern Ireland. Most of those schools were free-standing, but some had been founded as units within schools managed by the Catholic Council for Maintained Schools (CCMS), and plans for a satellite primary school had also been developed and were ready to be implemented. At that point, five of those schools were funded by the Department of Education in Northern Ireland. Much of the energy of the Irish-speaking community was channelled into the foundation of new schools and into funding campaigns. Huge emphasis was placed on statistics - the number of schools, teacher-pupil ratios, and viability criteria. Irish-medium teachers found it frustrating that so much of their time was devoted to the provision of basic materials and that their teaching was not supported by suitable assessment tools and other resources. They were developing their own specialist teaching methods, addressing current educational questions without specialist training in Irish-medium education at initial teacher training level. Even so, documents, minutes and correspondence dating from that time show that initiatives to address that situation were being planned. The increase in the number of Irish-medium schools, the progress of the pupils and the strong sense of partnership between schools and their communities inspired a positive outlook in the sector as a whole (Gaeloiliúint, 1993a).

The Department of Education published a review of initial teacher training in Northern Ireland (DENI, 1993) which sparked a general debate on teacher education. Although Irish-medium education was not mentioned in that document, it created a timely opportunity for teachers and principals to meet and discuss the training needs of the Irish-medium sector, and to plan development proposals (Gaeloiliúint, 1993b). As a result of that discussion, letters were written to third-level institutions requesting the design and provision of courses which would train teachers for the sector. St. Mary's University College, Belfast, responded positively to that request.

A Planning and Research Base

The Department of Education funded the research project at St. Mary's (1994-1996), and from the outset a supportive attitude and goodwill were evident among college staff. The generosity of colleagues from other institutions was also of great value and made an important contribution to the work.

The original plan of the authorities in St. Mary's University College was the design of a module or part of a module which would give an understanding of immersion education to the students and which would foster a high standard of Irish. At a very early stage, the college community realised that elements of the degree and postgraduate courses would need to be based upon the immersion approach, modelling good practice in immersion pedagogy. It is not sufficient to learn about immersion education only. The basic philosophy and educational science of immersion education would have to be experienced by the students in a practical way. In order to give students, especially those who had not been through the Irish-medium system themselves, a meaningful Irish-medium experience, the curriculum would have to be studied through Irish.

The initial period of research yielded other advantages. It gave time and opportunity to identify the needs of the students. For example, although primary teachers had created their own teaching resources, there were no materials in Irish available for third-level students. The research officer began to address that need. Preparation of some of the resources to be used on the courses began. Another basic requirement for a successful outcome was the existence of a positive, progressive environment within the college itself. During the consultation process, carried out in collaboration with every subject department and across the college community (library, administration, resources, etc.) information was disseminated about the immersion system and about Irish-medium education. It was discovered that some of the lecturing staff, outside the Irish department, knew Irish or were especially interested in Irish-medium education. A support system was put in place to encourage and assist lecturers (English-medium, bilingual, Irish-medium) to contribute to the Irish-medium provision.

During that research period, specific criteria were identified which supported the effective implementation of the Irish-medium provision:

1. *A positive atmosphere in the third-level institution*

Some members of the senior management team in the college were competent in Irish, and that helped to raise the profile and status of the language. There were also Irish-speaking lecturers in four departments outside the Irish department. That supported the Irish-medium provision across the curriculum. Other members of staff requested professional development in order to improve their Irish. Bilingual signs were erected in the building to promote a bilingual atmosphere. A translation service to provide teaching resources and information in Irish was made available.

2. *Funding*

The Department of Education awarded an independent grant to fund the research project. The introduction of Irish-medium provision required a separate budget in order to avoid any tension which would adversely influence the new initiative.

3. *The centralisation of Irish-medium provision*

At an early stage during the introduction of Irish-medium B.Ed. and PGCE courses, the areas of responsibility in each of the universities and colleges were redefined.
St. Mary's University College was given the specific responsibility of providing training for Irish-medium primary and nursery teachers. It was beneficial for the Irish-medium students all to be based in one centre, within a supportive linguistic environment. It also gave them the opportunity to communicate in Irish outside the lecture theatre - working on coursework, preparing classes, sharing resources and carrying out everyday social interaction. That experience would prove to be very important in the period of preparation leading up to school experience in an Irish-medium school. It was an advantage for the students and for the teaching staff that the Irish-medium resource unit was also based in St. Mary's.

Provision at Present

Student intake is a subject of great interest within the sector and is closely monitored by principals and by Comhairle na Gaelscolaíochta. The quota of postgraduate entries in the college has risen from five in the first year of the certificate to 20 postgraduates in 2004. The same system does not apply at undergraduate level, as any student competent in Irish can apply to do the Irish-medium option, once accepted by the college. The intake varies year to year, but there are normally between 10 and 15 Irish-medium undergraduates in each year group. The Irish-medium students are particularly interested in the immersion sector, and following graduation they usually gain employment in that sector and remain in it.

The linguistic profile of the courses is outlined in Table 1 (not including lectures on Irish as an academic subject).

Table 1: Course comprising elements carried out through the medium of Irish or bilingually

Course comprising elements carried out through the medium of Irish or bilingually		
	Professional Studies (Education and Curriculum)	School Experience
PGCE	Literacy, Numeracy, The World About Us, Religious Education; Early years issues in Irish-medium; Issues in immersion education	2 blocks of school experience in an Irish-medium school; 1 block of school experience in an English-medium school.
B.Ed. 1 and 2	Literacy, Numeracy, The World About Us; Teaching Studies.	Experience in English-medium schools
B.Ed. 3	Primary Curriculum – all subject areas.	Experience in an Irish-medium school.
B.Ed. 4	Primary Curriculum – subject areas experienced through Irish or bilingually; Issues in immersion education.	Experience in an Irish-medium school.

Challenges in the provision of teacher training for the Irish-medium sector

Key challenges can be analysed within the framework below:

Third level developments:	*Resource available:*	*Developments in schools*
review of initial teacher training, degree review, modular design of courses.	number of teaching staff.	new curriculum, new legislation, nursery development, post-primary planning, vacancy projection.

Teachers are often heard referring to the pace of change and new initiatives which must be implemented on an ongoing basis. The same pattern exists in the development and implementation of the provision at third-level education. There are

Map of Irish-medium Schools in Northern Ireland, 2002-03

two Irish-medium lecturers in St. Mary's University College. Although teaching responsibilities are shared staff across disciplines, the number of specialist staff members must impact upon the priorities and the parameters of the development. For example, the limited number of statutory nurseries is a weakness within the Irish-medium sector. At the same time, if nurseries were seeking more qualified teachers, it would be difficult to respond to such a demand without more lecturing staff available at St. Mary's. Without doubt, the limited number of lecturing staff is a key factor influencing future developments.

Another challenge ahead is the monitoring of the number of vacancies and the student intake number. A further complication arises if an appropriate balance is not achieved between the number of schools, student intake and the number of places available in Irish-medium schools for students on school experience. The falling numbers of primary school pupils in general may also impact upon the Irish-medium provision, even though that is still an expanding sector.

Teachers are often heard referring to the changes and new initiatives which must be implemented on an ongoing basis. The same pattern exists in the development and implementation of the provision of third level education. There are two immersion lecturers in the College. Although teaching responsibilities are shared among a broad multi-talented team, the amount of staff must impact upon the priorities and the parameters of the development. For example, it is a weakness that many of those employed in Irish-medium nurseries are not qualified teachers. At the same time, if nurseries were seeking more qualified teachers, it would be difficult to respond to such a demand without a broader lecturing staff. Without doubt, the limited number of lecturing staff is the greatest hindrance to enhanced provision.

Another challenge ahead is the monitoring of the amount of vacancies and the number of entries. A further complication which arises if appropriate balance is not found between the amount of schools and the amount of students is the number of places available in Irish-medium schools for students on School Experience. When a degree of postgraduate certificate is awarded to Irish-medium students in the college, there is a strong pattern that they seek jobs in the Irish-medium sector.

Many of the challenges faced by the Irish-medium team in the college also bring advantages. For example, Teacher Training provision had to be reviewed in the context of the Curriculum review. One of the advantages of that process was the cementing of relations between the College, the schools and other organisations.

One of the most striking changes in the development of this provision is the increase in the amount of Irish-medium students who have themselves come from Irish-medium nurseries, primary and secondary schools before beginning Irish-medium teacher training. This development should properly be considered as further evidence of the success of the Irish medium sector across the country.

References

DENI. 1993. *A Review of Initial Teacher Training in Northern Ireland*. Bangor: Department of Education.
Gaeloiliúint 1993a. *Nuachtlitir Ghaeloiliúint*. Meitheamh 1993.
Gaeloiliúint 1993b. *Nuachtlitir Ghaeloiliúint*. Samhain 1993.
Gallagher, A.M. and Hanna, E, 2002. Outcomes for Pupils Who Received an Irish-Medium Education. Research Report Series No. 26. Bangor: Department of Education.
Mac Corraidh, S. 2001. *An Ghaelscolaíocht in Oiliúint Tosaigh Muinteoirí do Chéim Bhaitsiéir an Oideachais. Taighde agus Teagaisc*, Vol. 1. Béal Feirste: Coláiste Ollscoile Naomh Muire.
Mac Donnacha, J. 2004. 'The Role of the University in meeting the needs of Linguistic Communities: An Irish Case Study'. Paper presented at Workshop A: Positive Models of Language Policy and Planning. Dialogue on Language Diversity, Sustainability and Peace, Barcelona, 20 to 23 May 2004. http://www.linguapax.org/congres04
Nig Uidhir, G. 1996. Oiliúint Múinteoirí do Scoileanna Lán-Ghaeilge. A Report on the Commencement of an Irish-medium Pathway in St. Mary's University College, Belfast, June 1996. Belfast: St. Mary's University College [unpublished].
Nig Uidhir, G. 2002. 'Initial Teacher Training for Irish-Medium Schools'. In eds. J. M. Kirk and D.P.Ó Baoill. *Language Planning and Education: Linguistic Issues in Northern Ireland, the Republic of Ireland, and Scotland*. Belfast Studies in Language, Culture and Politics 6. Belfast: Cló Ollscoil na Banríona. 65-75.

Issues in Minority Language Teacher Education: A Scottish Gaelic Perspective

A.G. Boyd Robertson

The Scottish Context

Gaelic-speakers constitute a very small minority of the Scottish population (*c.* 1.2%). Only 58,562 Scots classed themselves as Gaelic-speakers at the 2001 census. A further 7,000 claim to be able to read and write the language, and a total of 92,306 Scots say that they are able to understand Gaelic.

The strongest Gaelic-speaking communities are to be found in the Western Isles, particularly on Lewis, the Uists and Barra, and Skye. A substantial proportion of the Gaelic population resides in and around Glasgow, and there are significant concentrations of Gaels in Edinburgh, Aberdeen and Inverness. The Gaelic-speaking population remains skewed towards the older generation, although there are indications in certain areas that the development of Gaelic-medium education since the mid 1980s is beginning to have a positive impact on the number of young people able to speak the language.

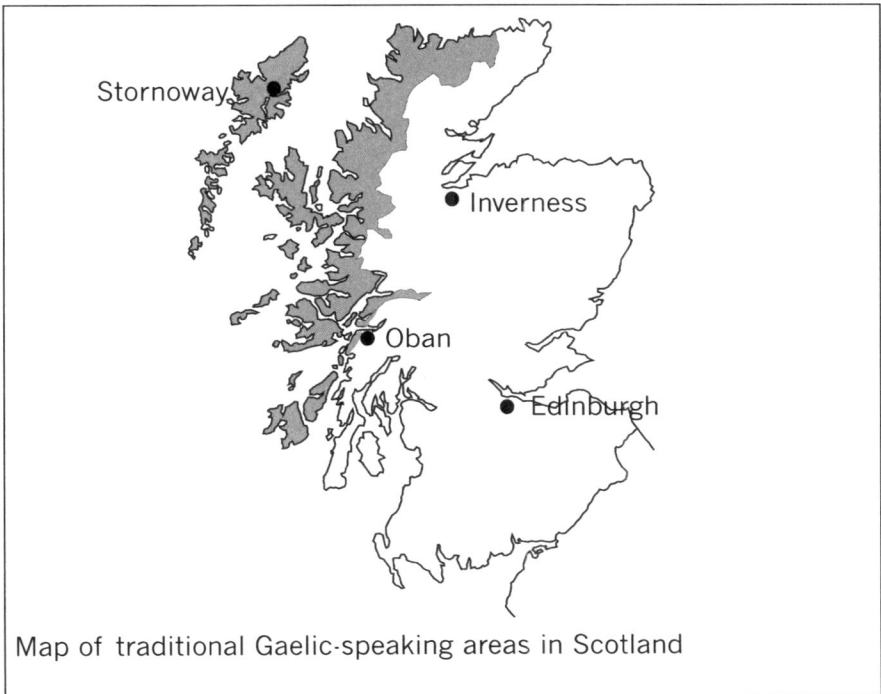

Map of traditional Gaelic-speaking areas in Scotland

There are two main routes into teacher training for the primary school sector – a four-year Bachelor of Education (with Honours) course, and a one-year Postgraduate Diploma in Education (Primary) course. Traditionally, most students have entered teaching through the BEd course, but in recent years recruitment to the PGDE(P) course has been greatly increased. The one-year postgraduate diploma course is the main route into secondary school-teaching, although there is also a concurrent degree option for students in certain subjects, for example, maths and the sciences.

Initial teacher education is available at seven teacher education institutions, or TEIs, all of which are based in universities. Three of the seven TEIs make provision for teacher education in Gaelic – the universities of Aberdeen, Glasgow and Strathclyde. My own institution, Strathclyde, and Aberdeen are the main providers.

Anyone wishing to teach in Scottish schools must obtain registration with the General Teaching Council for Scotland, GTCS. As well as regulating entry into the profession, the GTCS also validates teacher education courses. On successful completion of an initial teacher education course, students are guaranteed a one-year induction period in schools. After successful completion of that probationary period, they are free to apply for a post in a school of their choice.

Access to Training

The ease with which prospective students can access teacher education can be of critical importance in a minority-language context. In a geographically far-flung language community, the location of teacher education can be highly significant. In the Gaelic situation, teacher training was until recently confined to Glasgow and Aberdeen, meaning that only students able to spend the required time in those centres could undergo training. Potential recruits to teaching, including women with young families, were thus effectively debarred from entering the profession. Given that half the Gaelic population lives in the Highlands and Islands area, at a considerable remove from Aberdeen and Glasgow, a not insignificant number of prospective students have been denied a realistic opportunity of undertaking training.

Happily, that situation has been alleviated within the last two years with the introduction by Aberdeen and Strathclyde universities of flexible modes of course delivery and part-time study patterns. The University of Strathclyde has, in collaboration with local authorities and colleges of the University of the Highlands and Islands Millennium Institute (UHIMI) such as Lews Castle College, introduced a PGDE(P) with Gaelic course which employs a blended learning approach using video conferencing and other off-site means of course delivery.

In addition to pre-service training, there is a need for minority-language teachers to receive training on an ongoing basis while in service. Gaelic-medium teachers in Scotland can tap into the full range of professional development opportunities available through English as well as local and regional provision in Gaelic and an annual national two-day event for all engaged in Gaelic-medium teaching. Class teachers in Scotland are now encouraged to undertake a modular course of continuing professional development, or CPD, which leads to the award of chartered teacher status and an enhanced level of salary.

Status of Training

The extent to which teacher education in a minority language is recognised formally at national level is a reliable indicator of the status of training in the minority language. Where there is formal recognition, there will normally be benchmarks and performance indicators which set the standards to be met. Those will specify the competences, skill and knowledge that student teachers must demonstrate. In

Scotland, those have been published for English, but parallel criteria for Gaelic have yet to be elaborated. That was recognised by a working group which produced a report on Gaelic-medium teacher education for the GTCS in 1999. One of the recommendations of the report adopted by the GTCS was that there should be a specific qualification to teach in Gaelic. A certificate would be required for all those entering Gaelic-medium teaching, and teachers already in the system would be able to add a qualification to teach in the sector by undertaking a modularised CPD course. The new PGDE(P) with Gaelic course offered by the University of Strathclyde could be seen as a first step towards a specific Gaelic-medium qualification.

Models of Provision

Where provision is made for minority-language teacher education, it can range from additional bolted-on elements of courses through to full-scale dedicated courses in the language. At the lower end of the scale, students voluntarily subscribe to extra-curricular or twilight classes which are add-ons to the main training course. While those can be highly focused and worthwhile in themselves, they also transmit a clear signal about the status accorded to the language and make extra demands on the minority-language student.

In the middle range of provision, it is not uncommon to find minority-language inserts in courses which are delivered mainly through the medium of the majority language. The inserts may consist of periods of school experience and coursework modules, for example, on language development. One measure of the standing of those inserts is whether they are core or optional elements of a course. Placements in schools are normally core elements and carry considerable weight in student assessment.

Towards the upper end of the range of provision, one finds integrated pathways where the minority-language dimension within a majority-language course consists of a planned series of core and elective elements which offer progression and balance throughout the duration of the course. In Scotland, the operation of those pathways has fallen somewhat short of the consolidated and coherent pattern claimed.

The optimal type of provision for any minority language is a dedicated course of teacher education in that language. The size of the minority community and how that translates into student numbers, government policy and institutional economics will play a major part in determining the viability of bespoke courses in the minority language. It may be that only the strongest of minority language communities can sustain dedicated courses, for example, Catalonia, Wales and the Basque Country.

Management of Provision

The way in which minority-language provision is managed and administered by higher education institutions can have a profound effect on the nature and effectiveness of the training given. The extent to which speakers of the minority language have a role in directing and co-ordinating training in the language can be an important factor in determining the type and quality of experience gained by students. Majority-language speakers, however supportive they may be, do not have the specialised knowledge and insight that speakers of the minority language have into their own language and culture. Where the minority language forms a very small part of the overall course portfolio of a TEI, the attitudes displayed by individual members of staff and by the institution itself can be marked by a lack of understanding, scepticism, or even downright hostility. It is, therefore, vital that minority-language speakers are closely involved in managing the training and that the language itself is used extensively in course administration and assessment.

Resources and Funding

The size and strength of the minority community will be a major determinant of the resources allocated to teacher education in the language, but even in the strongest minority community the funding available seldom matches that of the majority-language provision. In small minority communities, additional costs are likely to be incurred because of the smaller scale and the consequent lower ratio of students to lecturers. In the case of Gaelic, placements are often in schools which are a considerable distance from the TEI, leading to higher travel and tutorial visit costs. Where funding of courses is at a uniform rate, the additional costs arising from minority-language training can be a strong disincentive to TEIs from engaging in the field. In such a scenario, it is highly desirable to have a specific funding mechanism provided by the government. There is a precedent in Scotland in the scheme of specific grants for Gaelic education, which affords financial support to local authorities planning new initiatives in Gaelic in school education.

Recruitment of Students

This is one of the major issues faced by Gaelic in Scotland. Where the population base is so small, the pool of potential teachers is very limited, and it becomes imperative that all possible measures be taken to address the issue. Although the difficulty has been acknowledged and discussed for over ten years, there has not yet been a concerted programme of action to tackle the problem. Several individual measures have been taken at national, regional and institutional level. For example, the Scottish Higher Education Funding Council has allocated places on courses specifically for Gaelic-medium students, and those ring-fenced quotas have undoubtedly led to more Gaelic-speaking students gaining places. However, there is still a need for a national recruitment drive and a sustained programme of targeted publicity and advertising.

The problem of recruitment is exacerbated by seepage in the system, whereby students allocated places on the basis of their Gaelic specialism elect to transfer to the English-medium training stream and to eventual employment in that sector. That is usually because of a real or imagined lack of proficiency in Gaelic.

Linguistic Proficiency

Our experience in Strathclyde has been that students enrolling on courses have a wide range of language knowledge and experience. Some are native speakers of the language, and some are products of Gaelic-medium school education, while an increasing number are adult learners who have achieved a considerable degree of fluency in the language through immersion or other forms of intensive study programmes. The latter are usually highly motivated, and their commitment to

PROVISION FOR MINORITY LANGUAGE (ML) TEACHER TRAINING

MINIMAL	MEDIAL	OPTIMAL
very limited access to training		ready access to training
restricted modes of course delivery		range of modes of course delivery
few opportunities for professional development		regular opportunities for professional development
no national benchmarks for training		national benchmarks for training
no specific qualification to teach (in) ML		specific qualification required to teach (in) ML
no certificate awarded for training in ML		certificate awarded for training in ML
training in ML restricted to add-on elements		dedicated training course(s) in ML
ML not used in course administration		ML used in all course administration
ML speakers not involved in managing training		ML speakers direct and manage training
negative institutional context		supportive institutional context
little, if any, assessment conducted in ML		assessment conducted wholly in ML
no state funding of provision		state funding of all provision
few, if any, recruitment initiatives		sustained recruitment programmes
no recognition of ML in allocation of places		specified, ring-fenced places on courses for ML
no provision for development of linguistic skills of students		programme(s) for development of linguistic skills of students

A. G. Boyd Robertson, University of Strathclyde April 2004

learn and develop their proficiency compensates for some deficiencies in vocabulary, idiom and intonation. Students who have recently completed immersion courses find it difficult to maintain their linguistic skills in teacher education courses in which they have only minimal exposure to the language. The problem of linguistic deficit is not confined to learners of the language. Fluent and native speakers often have significant gaps in their grasp of grammar and orthography, and, as indicated above, they sometimes lack confidence in their own ability in the language. It is essential, therefore, that programmes of minority-language teacher education afford opportunities for students to develop their linguistic skills and that the use of the minority language as medium of instruction be maximised.

Conclusion

The manner in which the issues discussed above are dealt with will determine the extent and nature of teacher education for a minority language and the adequacy of the training provided. The checklist which follows sets out a continuum of provision ranging from minimal to optimal models. Minority-language communities can apply those criteria to their own situations and assess where their languages are positioned on the scale. An analysis of their current situation will reveal the strengths and weaknesses in the system, and the benchmarks should help pinpoint aspects of provision which need to be addressed and improved.

Mercator-Education: A Support Service

Cor van der Meer

1. Introduction

In recent decades minority languages and cultures have become an increasingly important social issue. Education is one of the key areas in the context of international developments. The creation of some form of bilingual education is in many cases one of the first measures to stimulate a minority language. The situation, circumstances and provision relating to such measures are frequently not well known outside the area where the initiatives are taking place. Often knowledge and experience in developing bilingual education remain in a specific local community. Those experiences could be profitable to other language groups too. Knowledge of problems and prospects regarding the teaching of minority languages is important for all those involved in language planning for minorities.

There are many factors with an influence on the social position and development of language groups, including: use in the family, legal status, the media, and use in cultural life. Other factors are: the development of a written standard, the economic prosperity of the community or its attractiveness for tourism and, last but not least, education in and through the minority language at all school levels.

When there is increasing support at a European level and recognition that education is often one of the first activities undertaken to revive or support minority languages, it seems important to obtain an overview of what is going on in education in the various language communities. That was precisely the topic of the **Voces Diversae** conference and the present volume, and it is also one of the main issues for the Mercator-Education centre.

2. Mercator-Education

The Mercator network is organised as a network of autonomous, specialised Mercator centres. It was set up because of growing interest in various aspects of minority or regional languages. Data about minority or regional languages are generally rather difficult to access, since they are spread throughout language communities. Mercator was initiated by the European Commission in 1987 to improve accessibility and the exchange of information and also to inform the general public and speakers of "majority languages" in a more systematic fashion. The network was named after the famous sixteenth-century cartographer Gerardus Mercator, who was the first to include place names on his maps in the language of the region where they were spoken.

Each of the three Mercator centres has its own thematic programme and specialist role: Mercator-Legislation at the CIEMEN foundation, Barcelona (E), is concerned with language legislation and language in public administration; Mercator-Media at the University of Wales, Aberystwyth (I) deals with the press and media, including new media, while Mercator-Education at the *Fryske Akademy*, Leeuwarden/Ljouwert studies education at all levels.

The Mercator centres maintain close relations with the European Bureau for Lesser Used Languages (EBLUL) in Brussels and Dublin. Of special relevance to

Mercator-Education is the general European education network, Eurydice, maintained by the ministries of education in all member states and also co-ordinated from Brussels by a special office of the European Commission.

Mercator-Education is located on the premises of the *Fryske Akademy* in the province of *Fryslân* ('Friesland') in the Netherlands. This research institute was established in 1938. Its main disciplines are linguistics, history and the social sciences. It investigates the Frisian language and the culture, history and society of the province of *Fryslân* and its inhabitants. It employs about 60 researchers and administrative staff.

Within its programme, Mercator-Education has the following three aims: exchange of information, maintenance of a databank of documentation; and research through comparative analysis. Regarding those three aims, the focus is on all forms and levels of education in regional or minority languages in the European Union. Several activities and projects are undertaken to carry out that threefold objective. That comprises the collection of different types of data about the language groups concerned. Those data are made available for distribution to potential target groups, mainly through the website. In working towards that goal, contacts are maintained with participating regional network centres, organisations and individual experts all over Europe.

In certain cases, the degree to which education can contribute to language maintenance and development depends on background factors and the characteristics of the minority-language group. A national education system built by a state over a lengthy period is not easy to adapt for a minority-language group. Another important role is played by the history of attitudes to language and literacy. Administrative traditions are often persistent and prove a hindrance when trying to improve provision.

Of highest importance are, of course, the final outcomes of teaching the minority language: does it lead to (improved) maintenance, or has it encouraged the transition to the dominant language? Especially in the latter case, a little attention to the minority language in education (a few lessons in primary schools, for example) may work as a stimulus for assimilation to mainstream society rather than as safeguard for the language concerned. Often in such cases the minority language is defined as a "learning deficit" which has to be remedied through education. The "handicap" rests in the parents or child, not in the school or in society. In the case of stronger provision for minority education, the aim is often explicitly to contribute to maintenance. Learning the language is conceived as enrichment. The minority languages are defined as worthy of preservation and promotion. The outcome of such education is a contribution to cultural pluralism. All pupils will become bilingual and biliterate.

Because education is of such prime importance in the revival and development of minority or regional languages, almost all language groups have taken some initiatives. Provision in the field of education varies widely, from barely any attention at all to an almost complete education system parallel to the state system. The concise information, accessible in a more or less standardised form, may be a great help to the target groups of relevance to Mercator, in particular policy-makers and researchers, but also teachers, parents, journalists and "the public at large".

Mercator-Education has carried out several projects in the area of education over the years, for example, on (pre-) primary education, teacher training, learning materials, comparative education and models of bi- and trilingual education.

3. Minority Languages in Europe

The variety of languages in Europe is enormous. In general we can divide the languages into four main groups: state languages such as English, Spanish, German, etc.; immigrant minority languages such as Turkish and Arabic; sign languages, mostly used for deaf people; and regional or minority languages, being discussed here. The regional or minority languages can then be sub-divided. The typology normally used in the European Union for regional or minority languages is the following:

1. **Unique minority languages.** These are minority languages which are not used as a state language elsewhere; they do not have a kin state (see further). We can differentiate between these unique languages: (a) those spoken within one country, such as Welsh, Frisian, Galician and Kashubian; and (b) those spread over more than one country, such as Catalan, spoken in Spain, Italy and France, and Basque, spoken in Spain and France.
2. **Minority languages with a kin state.** These are minority languages which are also used as a state language, mostly of a neighbouring country. In those languages, the following distinction can be made: (a) minority languages with a kin state inside the European Union, such as German (B, Dk, F, I), French (I), Slovene (Au, I), Polish (Lit); and (b) minority languages with a kin state outside the European Union, such as Ukrainian (Sl, Pol), Russian (Est, Lit, Lat).
3. **Special cases.** (a) languages which have the status of state languages but which are currently spoken by a minority of the population. Examples are Irish, Luxemburgish and Maltese; or (b) languages belonging to minorities which are spread across the European Union, such as Romani and Yiddish.

Minority languages are spread widely all over Europe; most are concentrated in the border areas of countries. They show an enormous difference in size, the Cornish language being an example of a small language community, with an estimated 200 to 500 speakers. The Catalan language is an example of a huge language community, with more than 7 million speakers. Most of the other communities are somewhere in between but have rather small numbers of speakers.

Another important organisation for regional or minority languages is the Council of Europe. The Council developed the *European Charter for Regional or Minority languages* (1992) and, somewhat later, the *Framework Convention for National Minorities* (1994). The charter is a convention designed on the one hand to protect and promote regional and minority languages as a threatened aspect of European cultural heritage and on the other hand to enable speakers of a regional or minority language to use it in private and public life. It serves a mainly cultural purpose. The charter intends regional and minority languages to be used in education and the media.

The member states of the Council of Europe can show that they share the interests of the charter by signing and ratifying it. So far, 13 countries have signed the charter not followed by ratification, and 18 countries have done so and subsequently implemented it.

4. Activities of Mercator-Education

To fulfil its objectives, Mercator-Education carries out several activities and projects. Some inventory studies have already been listed. A brief description of some of the current projects and ongoing activities follows.

Regional Dossiers

The current core activity comprises the collection of factual, descriptive data on educational provision for regional or minority languages in the form of so-called "regional dossiers". The activity follows the model of the "national dossiers" of Eurydice. That European body has developed the concept of so-called "national dossiers" to provide an integral overview of the education system of each member state in a structured and unified manner.

With the regional dossiers, Mercator-Education aims to provide concise, descriptive information and basic educational statistics about minority-language education in a specific region of the European Union. Details include features of the education system, recent educational policies, divisions of responsibilities, main actors, legal arrangements, support structures, and qualitative information on a number of schools, teachers, pupils, and financial investments. That information is designed to serve the needs of policy-makers, researchers, teachers, students, and journalists as they assess developments in European minority-language schooling. That information may also serve as a first orientation towards further research (additional readings are suggested and contact information is also provided).

The regional dossiers provide basic information for comparisons between school systems in different communities. With the dossiers it is quite easy to compare the situation in educational provision between areas, for example, in which the language is taught as a subject or is the medium of instruction.

Regional dossiers are updated every five years, something necessary because the situation of a language, especially in education, can change very rapidly, and a dossier would then soon be outdated. Owing to the regular updates of the dossiers, comparisons can be made in time as well, and trends can then be discovered and analysed.

At the moment, more than 30 regional dossiers are published and available, in print as well as downloadable PDF file, from the website of Mercator-Education.

Digibyb: A Digital Library Project

In 2003 the Royal Academy of Arts and Sciences made funds available to carry out a pilot study on the feasibility of a European Digital Library for Minority Languages in the European Union. That resulted in a project called "Digibyb"; the pilot focused on the Frisian language and ran until May 2005. In that pilot project, various techniques and standards were examined and tested to connect several institutes through the Internet and make their collections and information available for central indexing and searching. Even though Digibyb focused mainly on scientific publications of the *Fryske Akademy* and a small number of institutes in the Frisian context, the future project, which has a much larger focus, was always kept in mind.

network of libraries combined with a central library and platform. Language communities will be assisted, if necessary, with tools and state-of-the-art software todevelop a digital library.

The EMILL project will also provide services for all unique minority languages; it will connect the local (digital) library with the central library, which also functions as service portal and platform to exchange information. To ensure participation of as many language communities as possible, it is necessary to use well-known open standards and formats and open-source software. All formats chosen are specially designed to serve in such a complex environment, and although they were developed only recently, they are very popular and are already being used throughout the whole world. The main tool which makes it possible to organise is the Open Archive Initiative (OAI). Based on a simple set of metadata items, it can collect and index information from different sources. After that, all the information can be searched and browsed centrally. The publications and other information offered stay at the local institutes and remain their own responsibility. It need not influence the normal services of the institute.

Network of Schools

The network of schools is an important activity highly valued by visitors and experts in the field. The initiative was taken by Mercator-Education in response to questions that were often received from teachers, students or parents. Teachers may be experiencing problems with bi- or trilingual teaching, parents considering bi- or trilingual education, or the school thinking about starting to use a minority or foreign language as a medium of instruction.

Parents can get nearly all the information that they want on bi- and trilingual education; they can read stories about experiences of other parents with bi- or trilingualism, and they can ask Mercator-Education all kinds of questions regarding bi- or trilingual teaching. Pupils can get in touch with counterparts from other minority-language communities so they are able to ask each other questions and share experiences. Researchers are able to find other research done on bi- and trilingualism, and they are also encouraged to publish their own research on our website. Mercator-Education is keen to hear about other experiences and to include more schools with "good practice" in the network.

The web pages of the network of schools are currently still part of the website of Mercator-Education, but soon it will have its own specialised website. One of the focus points on that new website will be teaching materials. Adequate teaching material has been one of the problem areas for bi- and trilingual schools. For the same reason, we sometimes see beautiful small-scale initiatives, often produced by the teacher. Much can be learnt, especially from those kinds of experiences, even when the language is different and not immediately ready for use. Not all problems can be solved, but it will certainly be helpful if there is the possibility of sharing information and experiences and including the opinions of other experts and researchers. Furthermore, commercial publishers will be asked to share abstracts or descriptions of their professional language-teaching materials on the website of Mercator-Education.

At the moment a little more than 30 schools are members of the network. In total they represent about 11 language communities. The number of schools is expected to

grow in the short term, not only because Mercator-Education puts more effort to the activity and publishes more frequently about the network, but also because there is more information available on the website, meaning that becoming a member is of interest to the schools.
Four times a year, Mercator-Education distributes a special newsletter among the members of the network of schools.

Website (www.mercator-education.org)

The Internet has had an overwhelming influence on the way that we publish and disseminate information, and on the other hand on how we search for information. Those changes all happened in a relatively short period. How we can avoid an information overload for the interested public is currently a major concern. Nevertheless, the Internet is the key medium for distributing our information and documentation on educational provision for minority languages. For years now a website has been maintained, and every year it has showed a growing amount of information and pages accordingly. The website's popularity is also increasing all the time, which can be deduced from the numbers of visitors. On the website one can find not only a great deal of information but also our products, such as regional dossiers, projects, a question-and-answer service, databases and links to the other Mercator centres, links to organisations in the field and many language communities are available as well.

Databases and Bibliographies

Probably the best known database of Mercator-Education is the database of organisations. It contains detailed information about more than 500 organisations in the member states of the European Union, as well as some states outside. Furthermore, there are databases covering experts, the authors of regional dossiers, bibliographies and so on. Some are being updated or will be renewed. The maintenance, updating, extension and enrichment of the available data in the database are time-consuming but of central importance.

Other products of Mercator-Education are a bibliography on bilingualism, bilingual education and the education of regional or minority languages. The library of Mercator-Education contains almost 7,000 titles and is constantly growing.

5. Conclusion

The Mercator project as a whole (education, media and legislation) is financially supported to a substantial degree by the European Union. Within the limited financial possibilities of that framework the Mercator centres play a key role as research and documentation centres. Sharing information and experiences is of crucial importance to the survival of the "old" and often endangered regional and minority languages. It is much easier for the Mercator centres to raise awareness and interest than it is for the language communities individually. The centres have the network and the international platform needed for such. New developments in technology provide new opportunities and challenges to give activities a new impulse. With the digital library project and the network of schools, Mercator-Education has some good examples. Both activities are still at an early stage but will certainly prove of importance and value.

Education in regional and minority languages encounters quite a few problems, mostly in the area of the teachers' language proficiency and the availability of teaching materials. Recent developments such as the Internet and promising new technologies will provide and create new opportunities. Experiences can easily be shared with other language communities, for example, not only about the problem areas, but also about research and other ideas and initiatives in education.

It is clear that much has happened in the last few years in the field of regional languages and bilingual education. It is a dynamic area in which many interesting developments are taking place.

One hopes that it will have become apparent from the above that minority-language education throughout Europe faces many complex linguistic and teaching tasks and that there is a continuing need for the exchange of information and the consideration of problems to enable work on planning European educational policy for the next few years.

References

Breathnach, D. ed. 1998. *Mini-Guide to the Lesser-used Languages of the European Union*. Dublin: European Bureau for Lesser Used Languages.
Beetsma, D. ed. 2002. *Trilingual Primary Education in Europe*. Ljouwert/Leeuwarden: Fryske Akademy / Mercator-Education.
Digibyb project, website 2005. http://www.digibyb.org
Digibyb project group 2005. *Final, Technical and Appendices Report*. Ljouwert/Leeuwarden: Fryske Akademy / Mercator-Education.
EMILL project website 2005. http://www.emill.org
European Council website 2005. http://www.conventions.coe.int
Extra, G. and Gorter D. eds. 2001. *The Other Languages of Europe*. Clevedon, Buffalo, Toronto, Sydney: Multilingual Matters Ltd.
Gorter, D. 1996. 'Information, documentation and research on bilingual education for regional or minority languages in the European Union'. In Helsinki Citizens' Assembly of Moldova. *Language Regulations in Multi-Ethnic Society*. Chişinău. 21–33.
Interarts 2004. Ex-post Evaluation of Activities in the Field of Regional and Minority Languages 1998–2002, Final Report for the European Commission, Directorate-General for Education and Culture.
Mercator-Central, website 2005. http://www.mercator-central.org/
Mercator-Education, website 2005. http://www.mercator-education.org/
Mercator-Legislation, website 2005. http://www.ciemen.org/mercator/
Mercator-Media, website 2005. http://www.aber.ac.uk/~merwww/
Tjeerdsma, R. S. and M. Stuijt 1996. *Bilingualism and Education: A Bibliography on European Regional or Minority Languages*. Ljouwert/Leeuwarden: Fryske Akademy / Mercator Education.

Le défi qui consiste à fournir des livres scolaires et autre matériel pédagogique

Eliane Kerjoant

Je vais vous présenter l'expérience des écoles DIWAN (le germe), créées en Bretagne en 1977 dans le but de redonner un essor et un avenir à la langue bretonne qui périclitait très rapidement en cette seconde partie du 20ème siècle et, surtout, dont la transmission aux jeunes générations dans les familles s'était pratiquement totalement interrompue.

Un groupe de familles, qui avaient fait le choix d'élever leurs enfants en breton, mais avaient conscience de la difficulté dans un environnement désormais très majoritairement en français, ont décidé de créer des écoles associatives qui non seulement feraient du breton le vecteur de l'enseignement, mais qui élargiraient la place de la langue au fonctionnement global de l'école, y compris le temps hors des classes et qui accueilleraient sans distinction tant les enfants dont le breton était la langue première que les enfants élevés dans un milieu entièrement francophone.

Si l'on excepte deux expériences très limitées, l'une dans les années 40 et l'autre dans les années 50, le breton n'avait jamais jusqu'alors été la langue de l'école. Tout était donc à créer et nous avons été rapidement confrontés à la question du matériel pédagogique.

Cette question s'est rapidement révélée être effectivement un véritable défi à plusieurs égards et, malgré les avancées importantes, la mise à disposition des enseignants d'un matériel pédagogique riche, varié, évolutif reste l'une des difficultés que nous avons à surmonter car nous sommes confrontés à plusieurs séries de problèmes, dont certains interfèrent et dont je vais essayer de décrire les plus importants.

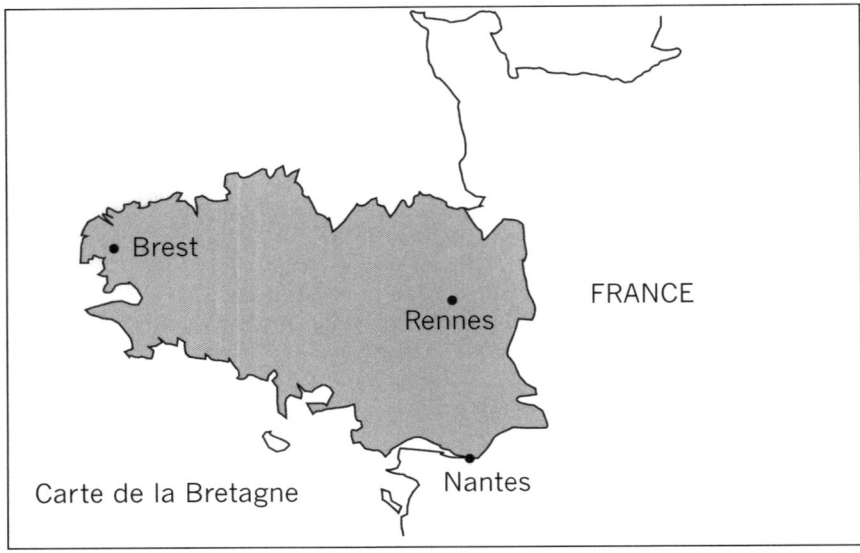

Carte de la Bretagne

1. La situation du breton aujourd'hui.

Le breton a depuis plusieurs décennies une place extrêmement restreinte dans la vie sociale (seuls 12 p.100 de la population bretonne est aujourd'hui capable de parler breton, et surtout ces locuteurs, âgés pour la plupart, n'utilisent la langue que de façon très restreinte, très peu dans les villes, pour leurs relations dans un cercle très limité, et sur des sujets de la vie quotidienne.

Ces locuteurs naturels âgés n'ont la plupart du temps pas élevé leurs propres enfants en breton. Ils ont fait le choix d'une éducation en français, qui leur était proposée comme la seule apte à assurer un avenir florissant à leurs enfants.

Ces locuteurs n'ont donc pour la plupart jamais conversé en breton avec des enfants. Lorsqu'ils sont aujourd'hui mis dans cette situation, d'avoir à parler avec nos élèves, ils ont fréquemment une certaine gêne, l'impression qu'ils ne vont pas être compris, qu'ils ne vont pas comprendre ce que les enfants vont leur dire, sentiment renforcé par le fait que les plus jeunes de nos élèves leur répondront en français ... Donc, difficulté à recréer les conditions d'une transmission intergénérationnelle extra-familiale qui se substituerait à celle non effectuée dans la famille et difficulté à créer le sentiment d'identification à l'adulte locuteur naturel (hors école).

Les familles faisant le choix d'élever leurs enfants en breton sont au contraire citadines pour la plupart, et si leurs origines sont souvent rurales, les parents et aujourd'hui les grands-parents ont le plus souvent été eux-mêmes élevés en ville après la forte migration des populations vers les villes dans les années 5O.

Bien que la culture bretonne (musique, théâtre, ...) soit très vivante, certains de ses aspects ne sont accessibles que par la langue bretonne. En même temps, il y a peu d'activités organisées pour les enfants en langue bretonne en dehors de l'école (problèmes de dispersion géographique, de besoin d'élargir leur groupe de camarades ...) La rupture de la chaîne de transmission intergénérationnelle de la langue a eu comme autre effet une rupture d'une partie de la transmission culturelle.

Effet sur la scolarisation en breton :Pour une très large majorité de nos élèves, pour ne pas dire aujourd'hui une quasi totalité d'entre eux, le breton reste la langue de l'école et seulement la langue de l'école. Nous pouvons bien sûr nous réjouir des compétences qu'ils acquièrent grâce à l'enseignement bilingue immersif, mais l'enseignement que nous leur apportons dans nos écoles ne suffit pas à faire adopter à une majorité d'entre eux le breton comme langue priviliégiée dans leurs relations. .L'école doit être organisée pour apporter le plus possible la langue comme véhicule de relations sociales dans la vie de tous les jours,mais malgré tous nos efforts, l'école reste bien évidemment une école et ne peut compenser à elle seule le manque de statut social du breton.

Or, pour que nos élèves aient envie de communiquer entre eux en breton, au moins partiellement, hors "obligation scolaire", nous devons leur donner une image positive de la langue et le matériel scolaire fait partie (ou devrait faire partie) des éléments participant à la construction de cette image positive et valorisante. Nous devrions pouvoir leur fournir un large éventail de matériel aussi beau, aussi intéressant pour eux, aussi "moderne" que celui dont ils disposent en français (y compris dans nos propres écoles).

Nous devons aussi leur donner une/des raisons de parler breton. Très certainement, l'intérêt pour la culture bretonne est un des moteurs de cette envie d'utiliser la langue. Au-delà de cet aspect, nous avons le souci de voir la langue rester une langue réellement vivante dans laquelle les futures générations continueront à créer et qu'ils continueront à faire évoluer.

Nous devons/nous devrions tenir compte du fait culturel lorsque nous créons ou que nous traduisons des ouvrages pour nos classes.

2. Le contexte du système éducatif français

Nous avons fait le choix d'être des écoles bilingues immersives (donc très différentes des écoles françaises monolingues et différentes aussi des écoles publiques bilingues créées peu après sur un mode de parité horaire entre les deux langues) mais en même temps, le choix d'être aussi des écoles "comme les autres" pour deux raisons principales :

2.1. La décision d'inscrire leurs enfants dans une école Diwan n'est pas une décision facile à prendre pour une bonne partie des familles en raison du contexte que je viens de décrire. Les parents doivent la plupart du temps convaincre leur famille, leurs amis, leurs voisins ... qu'ils ne font pas une folie et qu'ils ne mettent pas l'avenir de leurs enfants en péril. Ils doivent pouvoir expliquer (et nous devons pouvoir nous-mêmes le leur assurer) que leurs enfants auront aussi les compétences nécessaires en français (malgré leur scolarité effectuée par le biais du breton pour la majeure partie) pour poursuivre leurs études, pour trouver du travail, pour ne pas avoir une vie sociale "tronquée". Nous devons nous-mêmes prendre en considération le fait que, dans l'état actuel, certaines filières d'études secondaires (toutes les filières techniques) et l'ensemble des études supérieures seront poursuivies exclusivement en français. De même, les diplômes importants qui jalonnent la scolarité (le baccalauréat en particulier, qui ouvre la porte des études supérieures) n'ont pas de déclinaison en langue minoritaire. Nos élèves étudient les mathématiques, la physique, la philosophie, etc. ... en breton mais ils doivent justifier de leurs acquis en passant des épreuves en français. Cet élément d'ailleurs a un côté positif, puisque les bons résultats de nos lycéens au baccalauréat ont permis de prouver qu'ils sont réellement bilingues, que leur avenir socio-professionnel n'était pas compromis et cet élément a un impact évident sur l'opinion publique à notre égard.

2.2. Nous devons aussi nous situer dans ce contexte éducatif français sans aucune équivoque pour pouvoir bénéficier des contrats d'association avec l'Etat qui nous permettent de faire prendre en charge le salaire de nos enseignants (ou du moins de certains d'entre eux car d'autres critères sont pris en considération) par l'Etat et bénéficier de certaines subventions locales auxquelles nos écoles non contractualisées n'ont pas accès. Nous devons donc rendre compte à l'Education Nationale du fonctionnement pédagogique de nos écoles et en particulier de l'application des programmes (horaires, matières et programmes pour ces matières). Or, en même temps, nous ne fonctionnons pas comme les autres écoles.

Effet sur la scolarisation en Breton: Nous avons à résoudre la difficulté de faire fonctionner un système pédagogique différent dans un cadre qu'on peut considérer comme relativement rigide et non prévu pour ce système d'immersion linguistique. Nous devons donc réorganiser les horaires officiels prévus pour faire une place à l'enseignement du breton (pour compléter les compétences acquises par l'enseignement en breton) tout en gardant une place suffisante à l'enseignement du et en français pour que les compétences nécessaires soient acquises. Or, l'enseignement en breton, et du breton pour élèves bilingues, étant notre spécificité, aucun programme officiel et aucun matériel pédagogique adapté n'existe. Nous devons nous organiser nous-mêmes. De même, il n'existait pas sur le marché de matériel pédagogique d'enseignement des matières en breton. Et même, malgré la quantité, la variété et la qualité des ouvrages existant pour l'enseignement du français, ces ouvrages ne sont pas adaptés à notre enseignement puisque les concepts généraux sont découverts par nos élèves en breton d'abord et sont revus en français à l'occasion d'exercices d'application, mettant en le français en situation de vecteur d'enseignement en même temps que sujet d'étude.

Enfin, les programmes officiels d'enseignement ne prévoient pas de transmission de la culture bretonne (ou tout au moins de façon incomplète, ponctuelle et non obligatoire). Or, nous devons pouvoir proposer à nos élèves un enseignement de l'histoire de Bretagne, de sa géographie, sa littérature ... Mais nous devons aussi penser à donner un environnement breton aux problèmes de mathématiques par exemple (noms de lieux dans un problème sur le calcul des distances, prénoms des personnages dont ils doivent, par exemple, calculer ce qu'ils ont dépensé au marché ... Ainsi les "simples" traductions d'ouvrages en français ne suffisent pas toujours car elles ne sont pas toujours adaptées.

3. Les compétences disponibles

L'un de nos soucis est le manque de personnels suffisamment formés (enseignants mais aussi traducteurs, concepteurs ...) à la fois en breton et dans les disciplines concernées.
- D'une part, l'enseignement de matières en breton à l'université n'existe pas dans le programme de licence des différentes matières. L'université ne crée donc pas directement de spécialistes bretonnants dans les matières enseignées en école primaire ou dans le secondaire.
- D'autre part, l'enseignement du breton dans les collèges et lycées français ne présente pas une cohérence suffisante (nombre d'heures, conditions d'enseignement, permanence de l'enseignement tout au long du cursus ...) et seul un petit nombre de lycéens parvient à une bonne compétence en breton. Les étudiants qui choisissent d'étudier le breton à l'université sont donc pour la majorité d'entre eux des débutants. Le nombre réduit d'heures d'enseignement à l'université ne permet pas non plus à la totalité d'entre eux de maîtriser parfaitement le breton en trois années d'étude.

Nos jeunes enseignants d'écoles primaires, malgré leur bonne volonté et le complément de formation en breton que nous leur apportons pendant leur première année d'études dans notre centre de formation (un tiers du temps d'enseignement consacré à la langue et la plupart de l'enseignement effectué en immersion) ne peuvent avoir encore acquis les compétences nécessaires à la création de matériel pédagogique fiable. Sur ce point, on peut dire (en schématisant, bien entendu) que la tendance s'est inversée depuis la création de Diwan : les premiers enseignants de Diwan avaient globalement une meilleure connaissance du breton, et surtout une meilleure connaissance de la culture bretonne. Ils connaissaient des chansons, ils savaient danser des danses bretonnes, ils possédaient des romans en breton ... Si leur formation pédagogique n'était pas aussi poussée (car en ce domaine aussi nous avons dû faire preuve d'imagination), ils avaient ensemble suffisamment de compétences dans chacune des matières enseignées en primaire et la grande majorité d'entre eux pouvait au moins concevoir une programmation d'enseignement du breton, traduire des ouvrages existant en français et créer du matériel pour l'étude du breton et de la littérature bretonne, au moins pour les écoles primaires.

Pour le secondaire, le problème se pose également, tout au moins pour faire évoluer le matériel existant. En prévision de la création du premier établissement secondaire (1988), et conscients de la quantité et de la qualité de travail nécessaires à la création des livres dans l'ensemble des matières, Diwan a fait appel aux compétences de ses sympathisants spécialistes (professeurs, médecins, ingénieurs, ...) et compétents en breton. Ils ont créé les premiers outils pour les collégiens en se réunissant en commissions distinctes selon les matières. Les professeurs du secondaire disposent encore de ce matériel de base, mais bien entendu il ne correspond plus toujours aux besoins actuels dans sa forme, et parfois dans son contenu en raison de l'évolution des programme. Or, il est extrêmement difficile de faire perdurer pendant plusieurs décennies un fort investissement bénévole.

4. L'évolution de la langue

4.1. La terminologie

Le breton n'ayant jamais été vecteur d'enseignement auparavant, et son utilisation sociale ayant très fortement reculé dans les décennies où l'évolution des sciences et des techniques étaient considérables, se posait (et se pose encore parfois) le problème de la terminologie. Dès le début de la création de matériel pour le secondaire, la réflexion a été menée dans les groupes de travail de Diwan et une commission de terminologie a été créée. Non sans problèmes, et même parfois avec de véritables désaccords sur les orientations prises, le choix a été, pour ceux des termes dont aucun vocable attesté correspondant n'existait en breton, de créer en s'appuyant sur les racines dites "internationales" (et donc pas systématiquement d'origine celtique) et de les adapter au breton en utilisant le système très riche de préfixes et de suffixes qui lui est propre. L'autre élément déterminant dans la création des termes scientifiques est aussi la validation du terme par les scientifiques eux-mêmes et non simplement par les linguistes. Des lexiques par matières ont donc été établis pour permettre l'élaboration ou la traduction d'ouvrages pédagogiques.

4.2. La normalisation linguistique

S'il existe désormais une langue dite "unifiée", les différences dialectales d'une région à l'autre de Basse-Bretagne sont encore bien vivantes fort heureusement car elles constituent une bonne part de la richesse linguistique. Pour l'édition de matériel pédagogique, une langue unifiée s'impose car il est impossible d'éditer le même ouvrage en plusieurs déclinaisons où seraient introduites des particularités linguistiques. On peut d'ailleurs se demander jusqu'à quel point un tel choix serait justifié. Il n'en reste pas moins que, pour certains dialectes, celui parlé dans le pays de Vannes en particulier (dans le sud de la Bretagne), la quantité de mots lus par les élèves mais jamais utilisés peut parfois être suffisamment importante pour de jeunes enfants. Les derniers ouvrages édités par TES, dont je vais parler dans quelques instants, (manuels de mathématiques) ont tenté de résoudre ce problème en introduisant systématiquement des vocables vannetais dans la langue "unifiée". Cette décision a été majoritairement approuvée par les enseignants, vannetais ou non.

5. Le financement

Créer du matériel pédagogique coûte extrêmement cher, tant pour la création du matériel elle-même que pour son édition. Or, le marché, même s'il s'est élargi et qu'il peut parfois intéresser aussi les adultes nouveaux apprenants, n'est pas suffisant pour qu'une maison d'édition de matériel pédagogique puisse vivre. Les premiers ouvrages créés (et nombre de ceux encore créés aujourd'hui) sont donc très artisanaux : collage de traduction, photocopies de plus ou moins bonne qualité, dessins et photos en noir et blanc ... En 1994, en réponse aux demandes de l'ensemble des écoles bilingues (DIWAN et autres réseaux), et grâce au financement obtenu des pouvoirs régionaux, l'Education Nationale a accepté de créer un département d'édition de matériel pédagogique pour les écoles bilingues bretonnes. Cet établissement, Ti Embann ar Skolioù (la maison d'édition des écoles) a permis à nos écoles de bénéficier gratuitement d'ouvrages de qualité, et surtout dont la qualité de présentation égale à celle des ouvrages en français. Malheureusement, il est impossible à T.E.S. de répondre à l'ensemble des besoins: ils n'ont pas suffisamment de personnel; ils ne créent pas le matériel (qui continue donc à être créé bénévolement par les enseignants); et ils éditent des ouvrages qui doivent pouvoir convenir à l'ensemble des écoles bilingues alors qu'elles ne fonctionnent pas toutes sur le même modèle d'enseignement bilingue. Nous devons donc poursuivre le travail artisanal ...

6. Les types de matériels

Utiliser les techniques modernes: Il serait bon que nos élèves puissent utiliser des CD-roms et autres DVD pour conforter l'image qu'ils ont du breton, d'une part, mais aussi pour leur permettre de travailler en autonomie et accentuer ainsi la permanence de leur exposition à la langue à l'école et même à la maison. Malheureusement, ces types de matériels demandent un investissement beaucoup trop important pour nous. Il s'agit là à mon sens d'un des très nombreux domaines où une collaboration entre nos langues serait très profitable.

L'une des solutions, dans le même esprit mais moins onéreuse, auxquelles nous réfléchissons pour multiplier les ouvrages est la création d'un site internet d'échanges de matériels. Cette solution permettrait à chacun de modifier tel exercice pour correspondre aux besoins de ses élèves, d'adapter tel matériel aux besoins dialectaux. Surtout, ne serait édité sur papier que ce qui aurait été vraiment éprouvé en classe et approuvé par une majorité d'enseignants. Mais, pour créer ce site interne se pose le problème des compétences en informatique et de l'équipement informatique de nos enseignants ...

Enfin, la nécessaire entente globale des enseignants sur les méthodes didactiques et pédagogiques pour une entente globale sur le type de matériel dont ils souhaitent disposer, car pour l'instant il est impensable de multiplier les modes de présentation (certains veulent surtout des fiches pour les enseignants, d'autres des fiches pour les élèves ...).

Je pense avoir évoqué les problèmes principaux liés à la création de matériel pédagogique pour les écoles Diwan et pour terminer je dirai que nous consacrons désormais une bonne part de notre effort à l'élaboration de documents de base pour les enseignants (dossiers sur l'apprentissage de la lecture, programmes d'enseignement du breton et du français en primaire ...). En effet, l'entente implicite de tous les enseignants qui ont participé à l'élaboration de notre système d'enseignement dans ces presque trente dernières années, ne peut plus suffire. Nous espérons aussi donner aux jeunes enseignants les éléments de base devant leur permettre de créer plus aisément leur propre matériel. L'accroissement important du nombre d'élèves par classe, la diminution de la proportion d'enfants parlant breton en-dehors de l'école et la persistance de classes à plusieurs niveaux pour la presque totalité d'entre elles, nous imposent en effet d'être plus efficaces plus rapidement.

Notre autre axe de travail est, pour ces mêmes raisons, la nécessaire intensification des échanges entre écoles pour permettre d'élargir le champ des relations en breton (par exemple, nous organisons une action que nous appelons 'Lenn ha Dudi", Lecture et loisir/plaisir qui est une sorte de prix littéraire des écoles Diwan pour la littérature enfantine en breton. Dans le même esprit, nous organisons des rencontres sportives, etc. ...

Voilà ainsi résumé notre travail et nos façons de résoudre les difficultés d'enseigner dans une langue largement minoritaire.

Linguistic Diversity In University Education: Are Traditional University Structures Sufficient?

Wallace Ewart

The title of this paper could have been "Virtual University Education". It is not, however, about information technology or e-learning; it is about exploring the type of university institution or model that can deliver education where the medium of teaching is a lesser-used language. That issue must, I suggest, be explored, since it is apparent that, while there is significant support for such linguistic diversity in university education, the traditional university model has not provided it, is not providing it, and perhaps cannot do so – certainly not in a sustainable way. We must, therefore, explore alternative models. Let me accept that the case has been made for university education through the medium of a lesser-used language (see *University Education in Irish: Challenges and Perspectives*, 2003) and recognise that the population which fluently and frequently uses such a lesser-used language is now comparatively small and perhaps not concentrated in one area; there would normally be clusters of intensity, which are typically geographically dispersed.

It is helpful, in considering such issues, to separate them into two stages:

1. **What are we trying to achieve**? What are the student learning objectives and the research, socio-economic and cultural objectives;
2. **How can it be provided**? How can we achieve those objectives regarding space, governance, finance and meaningful community impact?

Let me give an example of what I mean by referring to the Springvale Educational Village project, with which I was involved.

The Springvale Educational Village project proposed the development of an educational campus strategically located across the peace line in West Belfast, an area where there was evidence of long-standing underdevelopment and which had a profile of poor educational attainment (but no evidence of poor educational ability) and high unemployment. The project had three parallel aims: to enhance the quality and accessibility of education and training in West Belfast; to give added thrust to economic regeneration; and to contribute to improving the social and cultural condition of people in that area of Belfast and farther afield by opening the door to new opportunity for all.

To meet those aims, two autonomous institutions of higher education, the University of Ulster and the Belfast Institute of Further and Higher Education, proposed the joint development and management of a new campus providing for 3,000 full-time-equivalent students; a community outreach centre to provide a bridge between divided communities where people of all ages would be able to come together to study, explore social and economic issues of mutual concern, and develop joint initiatives in community regeneration; and an applied research centre, which would provide a research base for local industry and incubator facilities for new companies, spin-offs from campus research. Developing an academic plan for a campus housing two separate institutions and trying to accommodate intense community interest was not a straightforward undertaking, but it was achievable, provided appropriate decision-making structures were put in place. It could be achieved without compromising the statutes, ordinances and regulations of the two autonomous institutions. However, it very rapidly became clear that the issue of developing the campus, maintaining its fabric, managing and owning it, would not fit neatly into the well-developed methodologies that existed in each institution. The solution was to create a separate company, owned jointly by the two institutions, with a board of directors (and an independent chairperson) consisting of nominated representatives from each of the two institutions. That company, legally incorporated, would build, maintain, and manage the campus and charge each of the two institutions for use of it. Each institution would teach, carry out research and support the social and economic development of the local communities; it would be responsible for ensuring that the needs of its own students were provided for to at least the same level as they were on its main campus. However, to achieve that, each institution would use the shared teaching space, library, catering and recreational space provided by the newly formed company. Note the separation of "what" and "how"; the latter was enshrined in quite complex and necessary legal documentation.

I shall briefly summarise the key objectives of a lesser-used-language university (Ó Cinnéide 2004). Many commentators have used the terminology that it must be a "proper university". At its core is the development of the individual through adding to his or her knowledge and understanding and creating an environment that encourages independent and critical thought. It cannot, therefore, only be about the provision of courses through the medium of a different language. Of equal importance is a research and scholarship culture which provides the foundation for teaching and which enables the university to contribute to and lead economic, social and cultural development, particularly that which is related, but not necessarily exclusively, to the specific development needs of the community that it serves. Without that research culture as part of the foundation of a university education programme, it is unlikely that an inquiring mind or the ability to conduct systematic scientific investigation can be fostered in students (Skilbeck 2001). In other words, the quality of the educational output, in all its manifestations, must be as good as that provided by the traditional universities; and the public must be in no doubt regarding its merits.

Let us now turn to the "how" and reflect on the structures needed to allow that lesser-used-language university to be provided and to be a sustainable organisation. A key determinant is student numbers. Given where we are, the lesser-used-language student population is likely to be fewer than 5,000 full-time-equivalent students, probably fewer than 3,000, and perhaps even smaller in the initial years. In other words, it will be providing for a much smaller number of students than the traditional university. Where the numbers are greater, perhaps the terminology "lesser-used language" does not apply. This paper focuses on the lesser-used-language scenario.

The answer to the question "how" is related mainly to five issues: space (and location), student and staff numbers, meaningful partnerships with the specific community that it serves, finance, and governance.

There are three main models regarding space that we should consider (and there will be variants of these): traditional physical space; e-university or electronic space; and new distributed model (or multi-campus physical space). Let us explore each with a 3,000 student population in mind. However, let us also assume that, typically, the 3,000 student population will come primarily from a number (say eight) of major lesser-used-language clusters of population distributed across the country.

Traditional Physical Space

The increase in physical university space over the past two decades is testament to the durability, acceptability and flexibility of that model. It is, however, a model based primarily on the concept of the full-time student, one who is "in residence", or relatively adjacent to the campus in travel time. Part-time students, that is, those who are in full-time employment, normally travel to the campus in the evening. As the number of full-time students undertaking significant part-time employment continues to grow, patterns of teaching and learning must change to reflect that trend.

More traditional universities will increasingly use electronic space, both to teach students at a distance and to provide complementary learning opportunities on campus. Indeed, several universities have announced an e-campus to reach out to such distant students, but for most the use of e-learning on campus means providing very efficient and effective learning facilities. As the technology and our understanding of how best to exploit it in the learning environment develops, I believe that we may be able – we have not yet – to define qualities of electronic space which match, although they may in some ways be different from, those qualities of physical space that over the years we have come to accept as defining the optimal higher education learning environment.

The characteristics of a new 3,000-student campus in capital costs, start-up costs and annual running costs, while they will vary from country to country, will typically be of the order of £60 million to £70 million for capital, £10 million to £12 million for start-up costs and £15 million to £20 million for recurrent costs. It will employ some 450 to 500 full-time-equivalent staff, of whom 150 or so will be academic staff, and all of those staff will be bilingual and fluent in the lesser-used language of the university. It will, being a single-campus institution, aim strongly to support the local language community throughout the country and contribute strongly to national and international research initiatives. However, being a single-campus institution, it will inevitably more strongly support those language clusters geographically adjacent to the campus.

The E-university or Electronic Space Model

A key characteristic of e-university institutions is the level of investment required and, therefore, the number of potential students needed to justify it. Given the parameters described for the typical lesser-used-language university, such numbers fall significantly below that required to justify an e-university model.

The Distributed Model

Over the past two decades, universities have forged relationships and alliances with other universities and colleges to a degree that would have been considered quite remarkable in the 1960s and 1970s. Terminology such as "franchised courses" and "associated colleges" is now widely accepted, to the extent that the website of the Higher Education Funding Council for England (http://www.hefce.ac.uk) provides templates outlining legal agreement between a university and such collaborating institutions, wherever they may be located.

The distributed model recognises two important issues: that there are lesser-used-language communities distributed geographically across the country; and that those communities all hope to – and, indeed, must – be able to benefit economically, socially and culturally from the university's influence. There are **three broad options**:

1. a university consisting of a main (small) campus and a set of smaller campuses or centres distributed across the country;
2. a university consisting essentially of an administrative headquarters with a set of smaller campuses or centres distributed across the country and located on existing college campuses (colleges of further and higher education);
3. a university consisting essentially of an administrative headquarters with a set of smaller campuses or centres distributed across the country and located on existing university campuses.

Option 1 might therefore consist of eight smaller campuses, each providing for between 300 and 500 students. The whole operation is managed from a main campus that contains the core administrative and management functions. Such a multi-campus structure of small traditional campuses is inevitably more expensive than a single campus, and, regarding the broader student experience, it provides narrower and more isolated opportunities. It would, however, provide stronger support for the language cluster areas in which each campus was situated.

Option 2 might also consist of eight centres or smaller campuses located on existing college campuses, purchasing their use of existing physical facilities as well as augmenting library and IT resources. This is the UHI Millennium Institute model, whereby the new institution of higher education has a central headquarters from where it manages students, courses, staff and resources located at each of a number of colleges, all of which are bound together by an academic partnership agreement (UHI Academic Partnership Agreement 1998). The new institution expects to be granted university status within a few years. Note that in the case of the UHI Millennium Institute the impetus for the structure is not a lesser-used language but a thinly spread population of students separated by large distances. It is interesting to note that two of its colleges are all-Gaelic institutions, in which all teaching, assessment and administration are conducted through the medium of Gaelic. This model is clearly cost-efficient regarding capital and start-up costs. However, it also builds on the established location of the colleges and, in partnership with them, is in a key position strongly to support the area and communities in which they are situated, in economic, social and cultural terms.

Option 3 is similar to option 2, with the colleges being replaced by universities. Thus, for example, the island of Ireland might have a University of the Island of Ireland, with up to nine or ten traditional universities, each "renting" campus space and facilities to the Irish-language university. They would not just be sharing physical space and campus amenities with the Irish-language students, but also the wider university collegiate atmosphere within which the minority student group can create, develop and foster a unique Irish-language environment. Many universities on the island in any case aspire to nurture and support such an environment on their campuses.

The Irish-language university would admit its own students and have its own statutes and ordinances, regulations and structure of governance; it would rent physical facilities, add to existing library resources and communications technology;

and it would hire its own staff and, by agreement, purchase staff time from the host university.

The programmes offered by the new university would identify areas of need in the local language community as well as nationally, and would take cognisance of existing expertise on the campus. Students wishing to study modules available at other campuses would be accommodated through the use of electronic communications and e-learning.

I have used Ireland as an example of such a distributed university; it can be applied elsewhere, and in European terms it can be applied in transnational situations where the lesser-used languages cross national boundaries. I have outlined three distributed options, the second and third of which offer significant added value, and, while perhaps the most difficult to deliver, the third may offer the greater opportunity. Many variations could be explored within the context of wanting to make the concept of a lesser-used-language university a reality. Of course, there is a great deal of negotiation to be undertaken to define legal frameworks, finance structures and quality issues. In the final analysis, an economic appraisal would need to be undertaken. All those issues can be resolved, provided we want to find and deliver a solution. Collaboration between autonomous institutions is not easy and cannot be taken for granted (Littlejohn 2000). However, if we wish to provide university education through the medium of a lesser-used language, the distributed approach offers an alternative and probably a more effective model.

My final point is that the impetus for such models is not only lesser-used languages; in the case of the UHI Millennium Institute it was a sparse population separated by large distances. It is a solution that might also be applied in other situations where minority circumstances prevail that we want to preserve. We must develop innovative structures to enable us to meet the new challenges facing higher education, but we must be equally innovative to preserve its enduring values where they are under attack. If we do so, our students will have cause to thank us for preserving those values for future generations.

References

Littlejohn, J. 2000. "Inter- and Intra-University Collaboration in a Time of Competition". Downloadable from http://www.bath.ac.uk/learning-support/webb/d53.htm

Ó Cinnéide, M. 2004. "University Education in Irish with Particular Emphasis on the Requirements of the Gaeltacht". In *University Education in Irish: Challenges and Perspectives*. ed. C. Nic Pháidin. Dublin: Fiontar, Dublin City University. 107-123. [Proceedings of a Conference originally held on 7-8 February, 2003.]

Skilbeck, M. 2001. *The University Challenged: a Review of International Trends with Particular Reference to Ireland*. Dublin: Higher Education Authority.

UHI Academic Partnership Agreement, 1998. Downloadable from http://www.uhi.ac.uk/ceandsec/APA.htm

Websites

http://www.hefce.ac.uk
http://www.uhi.ac.uk

Na Féidearthachtaí atá ann do Líonráil agus do Roinnt Eolais

Liam Ó Dochartaigh

Réamhrá

Léachtóir le Gaeilge ab ea mé féin ar feadh na mblianta fada, in Ollscoil Uladh, Cúil Raithin, ar dtús, agus ina dhiaidh sin i gColáiste Oideachais Thuamhumhan, Luimneach, agus in Ollscoil Luimnigh. Sa chomhthéacs sin, bhí mé i measc na buíne a bhunaigh an líonra do na teangacha neamhfhorleathana sa bhliain 1994 sílim, mar a dúras cheana, ar chuireadh ó Tomeu Quetgles in Ollscoil na nOileán Bailéaracha, Mallorca. Reachtáladh sraith de chruinnithe pleanála agus de dhianchúrsaí seachtaine faoi choimirce an líonra seo. Chomh fada le mo bharúil, bhain na páirtithe acadúla agus na mic léinn a glac páirt an-taitneamh as clár gníomhaíochtaí an líonra seo fad a mhair sé. Naoi n-institiúid a bhí páirteach ar dtús as An Chatalóin, an Ghailís, Tír na mBascach, Friuili, an Fhreaslainn, an Bhriotáin, an Bhreatain Bheag, Alba agus Éire. Cuireadh Sáimigh na hIorua agus Ocsatánaigh leis an ngrúpa le himeacht aimsire. Bhí fear ón Iodáil againn freisin ag an gcéad dá chruinniú, cainteoir Laidínise as Bozen/Bolzano, ach ní raibh sé ceangailte le haon institiúid tríú leibhéil. Fadhb ab ea í seo don Laidín agus don Ocsatáinis – nárbh fhéidir iad a aithint, ná maoiniú a éileamh ar a son, laistigh den chlár Erasmus ag an am. Ina theannta sin, cé gurbh iad na teangacha neamhfhorleathana a thug le chéile sinn, agus a b'ábhar suime comónta eadrainn, bhí orainn ceannteidil eile a aimsiú laistigh de threoirlínte oifigiúla an Choimisiúin Eorpaigh le cur síos ar ár gclár oibre, mar shampla, léann na réigiún, oiliúint mhúinteoirí agus mar sin de. Is fiú a rá anois gur tháinig an Béarla chun cinn go tapaidh mar *lingua franca* inár gcuid cumarsáide le chéile agus inár gcuid oibre. Beidh tuilleadh le rá agam faoi leathadh an Bhéarla san ardoideachas san Aontas Eorpach ar ball.

Bhíomar-na a bhí páirteach sa líonra Erasmus seo do na mionteangacha (1994, 1995, 1996) an-sásta lenar baineadh amach, agus go háirithe leis na dianchláracha bliantúla seachtaine, ceann i Luimneach, ceann i Palma Mallorca, agus ceann i Ljouwert/Leeuwarden sa bhFreaslainn. B'iontach an deis líonrála iad agus do mhalartú eolais don líon beag mac léinn ó na hinstitiúidí rannpháirteacha a d'fhreastail; cuireadh iachall orthu machnamh a dhéanamh ar chás a dteangacha féin agus páipéir a chur i láthair, rud a d'fhág bunábhar do staidéar comparáideach acu faoi dheireadh na seachtaine. B'iontach an deis chomh maith na cruinnithe rialta pleanála don bhfoireann acadúil ós na hinstitiúidí éagsúla le heolas a roinnt agus le bun a chur faoi staidéar comhpháirteach scolártha ar dhála na dteangacha neamhfhorleathana (e.g. firící bunúsacha, stádas, cúrsaí oideachais, na meáin, etc.) i gceist sa líonra áirithe Erasmus seo. Bhí díomá orainn nuair nár deineadh athnuachan ar mhaoiniú don líonra seo tar éis 1996; bhraitheamar nach raibh bá ag an gCoimisiún linn ná tuiscint ar ár gcúinsí logánta. Bheadh fiúntas fós le líonra den chineál seo mar dheis do roinnt eolais agus don staidéar comparáideach; féach a bhfuil de dhul chun cinn déanta i gcás na Gaeilge féin san idirlinn (TG4, foras trasteorann don Ghaeilge (An Bord Teanga), *Acht na dTeangacha Oifigiúla*, an feachtas ar son stádas mar theanga oifigiúil san Aontas Eorpach a bhaint amach don Ghaeilge, etc.), dul chin cinn a mbeadh suim ag idir mhic léinn agus chomhghleacaithe acadúla i réigiúin na mion-teangacha ann. Ní hé amháin sin, ach tá an deis roinnt eolais agus líonrála á cheilt ar na 'glúnta' mac léinn, ar lucht labhartha teangacha neamhfhorleathana iad, ó shin i leith.

Le trí bliana anuas, tarlaíonn gur mé atá freagrach as gnóthaí a bhaineann le mic léinn ón iasacht a thagann go Ollscoil Luimnigh agus as ár gcuid mac léinn féin a théann thar lear ar scéimeanna malartaithe. Mar sin, cé nach mé a bhíonn ag deighleáil ó lá go lá leis na cúraimí seo, is mé go bunúsach atá freagrach as feidhmiú an chláir Socrates in Ollscoil Luimnigh. Athraíonn cúrsaí ó bhliain go bliain, ach anuraidh (bliain acadúil 2002–03) bhí 177 páirtí ag Ollscoil Luimnigh i 22 tír san Aontas Eorpach agus sna Ballstáit nua. I gcomhnard le líon na mac léinn againn, deirtear linn go bhfuil an clár Erasmus is mó in Éirinn againn in Ollscoil Luimnigh. Chuaigh 216 mac léinn dár gcuidne 'amach' as Luimneach anuraidh agus tháinig 390 mac léinn 'isteach' chugainn. Beidh a thuilleadh le rá faoi seo agam go gairid.

Caithfear a rá gur mo an taithí atá agam féin anois i ngluaiseacht mac léinn faoin gclár Erasmus, agus is ag tarraingt as an taithí sin a bheidh mé d'fhormhór ábhar na cainte seo.

Erasmus

Tá dúshláin faoi leith le sárú ag lucht labhartha na dteangacha is lú a labhraítear san Eoraip (cuma cé acu an teangacha oibre iad, teanga chonartha, nó teangacha neamh-aitheanta nó neamhfhorleathna). Mar gheall ar thraidisiúin mhúineadh teangacha i dtíortha na hEorpa, tá – agus beidh – forlámhas ag an mBéarla, an Fhraincis, an Ghearmáinis agus an Spáinnis sna córais oideachais. Seo iad na teangacha a bhfuil an svae leo, agus is mó a mhúintear sna hollscoileanna. Dá réir sin, is iad is mó a ndéanann mic léinn a théann thar lear staidéar orthu, agus is iad is mó freisin a úsáidtear mar mheán teagaisc. Sa tslí sin, níl an oiread sin difríochta idir cás lucht labhartha na Gréigise, na Seicise, na Catalóinise, ná na Gaeilge dá ndéarfainn é. Ina gcás siúd go léir agus i gcás na mac léinn a labhraíonn na teangacha seo, is le barr slachta a chur ar a gcumas i gceann de na mórtheangacha eile a luas, a théann a bhformhór mór ag déanamh léinn thar lear, agus is trí mheán cheann de na mórtheangacha seo a dhéantar an léann chomh maith céanna.

Níl sé furasta cláracha oibre a leagan amach do lucht labhartha na dteangacha is lú a labhraítear san Aontas Eorpach laistigh de chláracha reatha oideachais an Aontais, go háirithe sa mhéid a bhaineann le gluaiseacht mac léinn. Glac an cás againn féin: i gcás na mac léinn sin i Luimneach a bhfuil an Ghaeilge agus ceann de mhórtheangacha na mór-roinne mar ábhair léinn acu, agus ar mhaith leo tamall a chaitheamh ag staidéar sa Bhriotáin, mar shampla, nó i gceann de réigiúin na Spáinne, go praiticiúil, beidh mar chéad aidhm acu feabhas a chur ar a gcumas sa Fhraincis nó sa Spáinnis. Sin í an aidhm freisin a bheidh ag a gcuid ollúna agus a gcuid léachtóirí sna teangacha sin. Rud tánaisteach a bheidh i bhfoghlaim na Briotáinise, na Catal-óinise, na Bascaise nó na Gailísise. Bíonn gnó taidhleoireachta le déanamh ag foireann na Gaeilge le cur ina luí ar a gcomhghleacaithe sna mórtheangacha gur aidhm dhlisteanach oideachais í staidéar a dhéanamh ar na teangacha neamh-fhorleathana chomh maith. Is minic lucht múinte na mórtheangacha seo neamhbháúil le teangacha eile a thagann, dar leo, idir a gcuid mac léinn agus príomhaidhm na tréimhse staidéir thar lear. An fhadhb seo is cúis le deacrachtaí le cuid de na socruithe malartaithe idir Ollscoil Luimnigh agus páirtithe sna 'réigiúin'.

B'fhéidir go mbítear ag súil le barraíocht ó na mic léinn, ag éileamh go gcuirfeadh siad feabhas ar an bpríomhtheanga léinn, agus go bhfoghlaimeodh siad cuid éigin de theanga eile ar fad ag an am céanna. Mic léinn eisceachtúla amháin a thabharfadh faoina leithéid seo, mar lena gcumas teangacha nua a fhoghlaim, mar lena bhféinspreagadh agus a bhfiosracht i leith na dteangacha neamhghnácha, agus mar lena bhféinmhuinín ina gcuid teagmhálacha le foirne acadúla agus riaracháin sa bhaile agus i gcéin. Éan fánach, corr!

Nílim róchinnte go dtuigeann Coimisiún na hEorpa na dúshláin speisialta a bhíonn le sárú ag lucht labhartha na dteangacha is lú a labhraítear, agus go háirithe na teangacha sin a bhí faoi thrácht i rith na comhdhála seo. É sin ráite, is léir go bhfuil iarracht éigin de bhuairt ar an gCoimisiún. Féach leat *Cinneadh Uimh. 253/2000EC Pharlaimint na hEorpa agus na Comhairle, dar dáta 24 Eanáir 2000,* ina gcruthaítear an dara céim de chlár gníomhaíochta an Chomhphobail san oideachas, SOCRATES, don tréimhse 2000 go 2006. I measc Aidhmeanna an Chláir seo a leagtar síos in Airteagal 2, tá:

> (b) to promote a quantitative and qualitative improvement of the knowledge of the languages of the European Union, in particular those languages which are less widely used and less widely taught, so as to lead to greater understanding and solidarity between the peoples of the European Union and promote the intercultural dimension of education.

Ní mé céard go sonrach atá molta ná curtha i gcrích ag an gCoimisiún leis an aidhm áirithe seo a bhaint amach. Tá aighneachtaí seolta againn féin chuig an gCoimisiún agus chuig an Údarás um Ard-Oideachas, 'gníomhaireacht náisiúnta' SOCRATES in Éirinn ar an gceist seo, chomh maith le ceisteanna eile, ach ní léir dom aon tionscadal faoi leith dírithe ar an éagsúlacht teanga a bheith á bheartú.

'Fadhb' an Bhéarla

Sa bhliain 2000, sílim, foilsíodh tuarascáil do Choimisiún na hEorpa dar teideal *SOCRATES 2000 Evaluation Study – Executive Summary* (conradh Uimh. 1999 – 0979/001 – 001 SOC 335BEV). I measc na n-ábhar ar deineadh staidéar orthu, bhí an éagsúlacht teanga i gcláracha SOCRATES. I gcás chlár Erasmus, rinneadh comparáid idir fheidhmiú an chláir seo sa bhliain 1999/2000 agus tús na nóchaidí, go háirithe sa mhéid a bhain le gluaiseacht agus malartú mac léinn. Tá na pointí spéisiúla seo leanas sa tuairisc faoi thrí chomhthéacs múinte teanga.

LINGUA A:
- four languages predominated as the most common target languages; English, French, German and Spanish
- in 40% of the projects surveyed at least one of the less widely used and less taught languages was targeted

LINGUA D
- there was a broad variety of target languages, the most common being Italian, English, German, French and Spanish
- the less widely used and less taught languages (LWULT) were clearly present, as almost two-thirds of the projects surveyed had at least one LWULT among its target languages

LINGUA B
- The less widely used and less taught languages were not significantly covered by LINGUA B grants which largely funded participation in courses for teaching English, French and German, since these are the main languages taught in secondary schools.

Mar conchlúid, mheas lucht scríofa na tuarascála seo "the use of different European languages did not decline substantially amidst *lingua franca* pressures."

Thug An tÚdarás um Ard-Oideachas againn féin mórán an claonadh céanna seo faoi deara. I dtuarascáil ar chláracha Eorpacha sa bhliain 2002 *(Report on European Programmes 2002*, HEA 2003) dúradh:

> Language of teaching: 85.6% of Irish students are taught in the host language, which is a slight increase of 2.8% over 2000-2001. Only 7% of Erasmus outgoing students from Ireland studying in France were not taught in the host language, 5.8% in Germany and 2.5% in Spain. (lch. 14)

Ach tugadh claonadh eile faoi deara mar thoradh ar rannpháirtíocht thíortha Oirthear agus Lár na hEorpa sa chlár Erasmus:

> However, 92.9% of outgoing Irish Erasmus students studying in the Czech Republic, 81.8% in Finland and 77.7% in Denmark, were taught in English.

Creidim féin go bhfuil an claonadh i dtreo an Bhéarla ag treisiú le blianta beag anuas. Sa chás againn féin in Ollscoil Luimnigh, sa bhliain 2002/2003, rinne 74 as 216 mac léinn dar gcuidne a chuaigh thar lear a gcuid staidéir trí mheán an Bhéarla; i mbliana tá 66 as 207 ag staidéar trí Bhéarla. Is iad na tíortha atá i gceist i mbliana: An Danmhairg, an Fhionlainn, An tSualainn, an Iorua, An Ísiltír, An Ghréig, Malta, An Ríocht Aontaithe, Poblacht na Seice, An Bhulgáir, An Ghearmáin, An Ostair, agus den chéad uair, an Fhrainc agus an Spáinn. Is fíor go bhfuil réimse leathan ábhar léinn i gceist (Teicneolaíocht Adhmaid; An Stair, An Pholaitíocht agus an tSocheolaíocht; Staidéar Gnó agus Árachais; An Riarachán Poiblí; Léann an Chultúir; Spórt; agus Dlí), agus nach gnách teanga iasachta a bheith mar chuid den siollabas i roinnt de na cúrsaí, ar a laghad, ach tá an claonadh i dtreo an Bhéarla le sonrú. Tá cuid de mhíniú an scéil sna cúrsaí nua céime atá á dtabhairt isteach ag an Ollscoil, cúrsaí gan teanga iasachta mar chuid díobh, ach mar sin féin le riachtanas tréimhse a chaitheamh ag staidéar thar lear.

Is ceart a rá ag an bpointe seo go bhfuil an-éileamh ar ollscoileanna na hÉireann mar pháirtithe sa chlár Erasmus. Faightear fiosruithe rialta ó ollscoileanna ar fud na hEorpa ag lorg comhpháirtíochta. Mar a tharlaíonn sé, glacann Ollscoil Luimnigh le i bhfad níos mó mic léinn ón iasacht ná mar a sheolann muid féin thar lear. Éire féin a mheallann iad cinnte, ach is é an deis feabhas a chur ar a gcumas sa Bhéarla an tarraingt is mó, cheapfainn.

Creidim gurb é nádúr na cumarsáide i gcomhthéacs ilteangach, dála staid reatha an Aontais Eorpaigh, go dtiocfaidh *lingua franca* amháin, nó níos mó b'fhéidir, chun cinn luath nó mall. Tá cuma ar an scéal go bhfuil an Béarla chun tosaigh sa bhfeiniméin seo, is é sin an ghluaiseacht i dtreo úsáid teanga amháin mar phríomh-*lingua franca*. Braithim go bhfuil sé seo tarlaithe cheana féin i réimsí áirithe léinn agus go dtreiseofar ar an gclaonadh seo le páirtíocht na ndeich mBallstát nua san Aontas ón 1 Bealtaine 2004 ar aghaidh.

Ní hionann an dearcadh i leith an Bhéarla sna tíortha Ceilteacha agus i dtíortha eile an Aontais. Is é an Béarla atá ag cur crua ar na teangacha Ceilteacha, cés moite den Bhriotáinis. Dearcadh eile ar fad atá ag daoine as tíortha eile: san Eoraip agus i Meiriceá Thuaidh, sa Rúis agus i gCónaidhm na Stát Neamhspleácha (CIS), agus i gcuid mhaith de thíortha na hÁise, is é an Béarla an mhórtheanga idirnáisiúnta, teanga an chultúir chomónta domhanda, an phopcheoil agus na scannán, teanga na teicneolaíochta agus na méan nua, teanga an idirlín. Teanga riachtanach í don saol comhaimseartha. Tá an t-ádh linn in Éirinn go bhfuil sí againn le hoidhreacht na staire, ach sna tíortha Ceilteacha, in Éirinn in Albain agus sa Bhreatain Bheag, mar a deirim, is namhaid é don éagsúlacht teanga.

Féidearthachtaí

Cá bhfágann seo na teangacha is lú a mhúintear, gan trácht ar na teangacha neamhfhorleathana, i gclár Erasmus? Cáipéis eile a tháinig ón Eoraip chugainn, Feabhra 2003, ab ea ceann a d'éiligh tuairimíocht agus moltaí faoi chláir éagsúla oideachais an Aontais Eorpaigh tar éis na bliana 2006 (*Public Consultation on Future Development of the Socrates, Leonardo da Vinci, Tempus and Youth Programmes* [after 2006]).

Seo sliocht as aighneacht Ollscoil Luimnigh dar dáta 28 Feabhra 2003, ina ndéantar talamh slán de cheannas an Bhéarla, ach ina moltar chomh maith scéim le mic léinn a mhealladh le tabhairt faoi theangacha eile a fhoghlaim. D'fhéadfaí a rá gur suimiú é seo ar a raibh i gceist agam in ábhar mo chuid cainte ar maidin.

> The few opportunities for Irish students to gain competence in lesser-taught languages such as Danish, Dutch, Finnish, Greek, Italian, Portuguese, and Swedish, not to mention lesser-used (or non-official) languages such as Catalan, or Welsh, resulted in the early years of Socrates/Erasmus, in Irish students not being in a position to avail of opportunities for study abroad in countries other than those in which French, German or Spanish are spoken, the languages taught at third level in the University of Limerick. In recent years, an increasing number of bilateral agreements involving instruction through English are being signed by the University of Limerick to meet the demands of our own faculty and students for English-medium provision. This phenomenon is also already manifest in agreements with partners in the candidate and other non-EU European countries, and will be exacerbated with the accession of the applicant countries. There seems to be little prospect of reversing the movement towards English-medium instruction in partner institutions on the continent of Europe.
>
> In consequence, the European Union will need to adopt radical proposals to encourage even minimal levels of language learning aside from the EU languages dominant in second and third level education (French, German, Spanish and English). Perhaps after 2006, institutions receiving English-speaking students from Ireland and the UK under Socrates agreements, should be required to implement measures to assist such students acquire basic competence in the local language, not only through the provision of preparatory (pre-sessional) language courses (as happens currently), but also

through the provision of concurrent ab initio and intermediate language courses during the duration of the Socrates placement (perhaps 20% of the total course load, or 50% of the cultural component). While the provision of courses by institutions might be mandatory, the taking of such courses by visiting students might be optional; but perhaps the EU could institute a significant reward system for students opting to learn a lesser-taught or lesser-used language during their Socrates placement. This might also include the learning of Irish, or Welsh, or Scottish Gaelic, in the case of students coming to Ireland and the UK.

Tuigim go maith nach bhfuil na féidearthachtaí do lionráil agus do roinnt eolais i réimse na héagsúlachta teanga pléite go mion agam sa chaint seo, ach theastaigh uaim cuid den chomhthéacs a phlé – cláracha an Aontais, agus gluaiseacht mac léinn laistigh de chlár Erasmus go háirithe. Deirtear go mbíonn an t-ádh le duine má bhíonn fiú mórshmaoineamh fiúntach amháin aige i gcaitheamh a shaoil. Sin é mo cheannsa thuas le deiseanna a chruthú agus a chothú le gur féidir lenár gcuid mac léinn cuid éigin de na teangacha is lú a mhúintear agus a labhraítear ar fud an Aontais, a fhoghlaim. Is mó mo shuim féin inniu i mórchláracha oideachais an Aontais Eorpaigh agus i moladh Dhónaill Uí Riagáin blianta ó shin i dtaca le 'mainstreaming' – is é sin, ár dteangacha a thabhairt isteach i gcroílár na hEorpa agus i bpríomhchláracha oideachais an Aontais. Tá an deis seo á soláthar do mhic léinn idirnáisiúnta in Ollscoil Luimnigh ón mbliain 1991 anall, cúrsaí *ab initio* Gaeilge gach seimeastar agus cúrsa leanúnach sa dara seimeastar do mhic léinn a fhanann linn ar feadh bliana. Bíonn éileamh seasta ar na cúrsaí seo agus creidim gur cheart do gach institiúid cúrsaí dá leithéid a sholáthar do mhic léinn iasachta faoi ghné na gluaiseachta de chlár Erasmus.

The Possibilities for Networking and Information-Sharing

Liam Ó Dochartaigh

Introduction

I was a lecturer in Irish for many years, first at the University of Ulster, Coleraine, later at Thomond College of Education, Limerick, and also at the University of Limerick. In that context, I was among the group who founded the Erasmus network for lesser-used languages in 1994 at the invitation of Tomeu Quetgles of the University of the Balearic Islands, Mallorca. A series of planning meetings and intensive programmes was organised under the auspices of this network. In my view, the academics and students who took part greatly enjoyed the activities programme of this network while it lasted. Nine institutions were involved at the outset – from Catalonia, Galicia, the Basque Country, Friuli, Friesland, Brittany, Wales, Scotland and Ireland. Sámis from Norway and Occitanians were added to the group in due course. We also had a representative from Italy at the first two meetings, a speaker of Ladin from Bozen/Bolzano, but he was not affiliated with any third-level institution. This was a problem for Ladin and Occitan – it was not possible to recognise them, or to seek funding on their behalf, within the Erasmus programme at the time. Even though the lesser-used languages brought us together, and were a common interest to us, we had to look for headings within the official guidelines of the European Commission into which we could fit our working programme – for example, regional studies, teacher training, and so on. It's worth saying at this stage that English came quickly to the fore as the lingua franca in our communications with each other and in our work. I will have more to say about the spread of English in higher education in the European Union later.

Those of us who took part in this Erasmus network for the lesser-used languages (1994, 1995, 1996) were very pleased with what was achieved, particularly with the annual intensive programmes, one in Limerick, one in Palma, Mallorca, and one in Ljouwert/Leeuwarden, Friesland. They provided an excellent networking and information-exchange opportunity for the small number of students from each participating institution who attended; they were made to reflect on the case of their own languages and to present papers, which provided them with the raw material for a comparative study by the end of the week. The regular planning meetings were also a wonderful opportunity for the academic team from the various institutions to share information and to lay the foundations for scholarly partnership study on the circumstances of the lesser-used languages (e.g. basic facts, status, education matters, the media, etc.) in this particular Erasmus network. We were disappointed when funding for this network was not renewed after 1996; we felt that the Commission was neither sympathetic to us nor understanding of our local issues. A network of this sort would still be worthwhile as an opportunity for information-sharing and comparative study. Look at progress made in the case of Irish itself in the meantime (TG4, a cross-border body for Irish (An Bord Teanga), the *Official Languages Act*, the campaign to achieve status as a working language in the European Union, etc), progress which would be of interest to both students and academic colleagues in the sphere of lesser-used languages. Not only that, but the opportunity for information-sharing and networking has been denied to 'generations' of students, who are speakers of lesser-used languages, since then.

For the past three years it happens that I have been responsible for matters relating to international students who come to the University of Limerick, and our own students who go abroad on exchange programmes. Therefore, although I do not deal with these matters on a day-to-day basis, I am ultimately responsible for the operation of the SOCRATES programme in the University of Limerick. Things change from year to year but, in the academic year 2002-03, the University of Limerick had 177 partner institutions in 22 countries in the European Union, the applicant and other European countries. In relation to our own student population at University of Limerick, we are told that we have the largest Erasmus programme in Ireland pro rata in the University of Limerick. 216 of our students went 'out' of Limerick in 2002–03 and 390 students came 'in' to us. I will have more to say about this shortly.

It must be said that I personally now have more experience of student mobility under the Erasmus programme than other EU programme in education, and I will be drawing on that experience for most of this talk.

The Erasmus Programme

There are particular challenges to be overcome by speakers of the lesser-spoken languages in Europe (be they working languages, a treaty language, non-official or lesser-spoken languages). Because of the language-teaching tradition in European countries, the upper hand is – and will be – with English, French, German and Spanish in the education systems. These are the languages which hold sway, and which are mainly taught in the universities. Accordingly, it is mainly these which are studied by students who go abroad, and it is also these which are used as teaching mediums. In that regard, there is not that much difference between the case of speakers of Greek, Czech, Catalan and, if I may say so, Irish. In all these cases, and in the case of the students who speak these languages, it is to improve their competence in one of the other major languages just mentioned that the vast majority study abroad, and it is through one of these major languages that study is also conducted.

It is not easy to set out work study programmes for speakers of the lesser-spoken languages in the European Union inside the Union's current education programmes, particularly those involving student mobility. Look at our own situation: in the case of those students in Limerick who study Irish and one of the major continental languages, and who would like to spend a time studying in Brittany, for example, or in one of the Spanish regions, practically speaking, their primary aim will be to improve their competence in French or in Spanish. That will also be the aim of their professors and lecturers in those languages. Learning Breton, Catalan, Basque or Galician will be a secondary matter. The Irish language faculty has to use diplomacy to impress upon their peers in the major languages that it is a legitimate educational aim also to study lesser-used languages. Frequently, those who teach the major languages are unsympathetic towards other languages which come – they reckon – between their students and the primary aim of the foreign study period. This problem explains difficulties with some of the exchange arrangements between the University of Limerick and partner institutions in the 'regions'.

Perhaps too much is expected from the students – demanding that they should improve their main language of study and that they should learn something of another language altogether at the same time. Only exceptional students would attempt this, with their ability to learn new languages, their self-motivation and curiosity about lesser-used languages, and their self-confidence in their dealings with academic and administrative staff at home and abroad.

I am not overly certain that the European Commission understands the particular challenges which have to be overcome by speakers of the lesser-spoken languages, especially those languages which have been under consideration during this conference. That said, it is clear that the Commission has shown some concern. See Decision No. 253/2000EC Parliament of Europe and the Council, dated 24 January 2000, in relation to the second stage of the action programme of the Community in Education, 'SOCRATES', for the period 2000 to 2006. Among the Aims of the Programme set out in Article 2 is:

(b) to promote a quantitative and qualitative improvement of the knowledge of the languages of the European Union, in particular those languages which are less widely used and less widely taught, so as to lead to greater understanding and solidarity between the peoples of the European Union and promote the intercultural dimension of education.

I am not clear what has been recommended specifically or actioned by the Commission to achieve this particular aim. We have ourselves made representations to the Commission and to the Higher Education Authority, the 'national agency' for SOCRATES in Ireland, about this question, as well as other matters, but I am not aware of any particular project being planned geared towards linguistic diversity.

The Anglophone 'Problem'

In 2000, a report for the European Commission, *SOCRATES 2000 Evaluation Study: Executive Summary* (contract No. 1999 – 0979/001 – 001 SOC 335BEV)' was published. The report investigated linguistic diversity in SOCRATES programmes. In the case of the Erasmus programme, comparison was made between the operation of this programme in the year 1999-2000 and the start of the 1990s, particularly in relation to student mobility and exchange. The report made the following interesting points about three scenarios:

LINGUA A
- four languages predominated as the most common target languages: English, French, German and Spanish
- in 40% of the projects surveyed at least one of the less widely-used and less-taught languages (LWULT) was targeted

LINGUA D
- there was a broad variety of target languages, the most common being Italian, English, German, French and Spanish
- the LWULT were clearly present, as almost two-thirds of the projects surveyed had at least one LWULT among its target languages

LINGUA B
- The LWULT were not significantly covered by LINGUA B grants, which largely funded participation in courses for teaching English, French and

German, since these are the main languages taught in secondary schools.

In conclusion, the writers of this report reckoned that "the use of different European languages did not decline substantially amidst lingua-franca pressures."

The Irish Higher Education Authority noted much of this same tendency. A report on European programmes in the year 2002 (*Report on European Programmes 2002*, HEA 2003) stated:

> Language of teaching: 85.6% of Irish students are taught in the host language, which is a slight increase of 2.8% over 2000-2001. Only 7% of Erasmus outgoing students from Ireland studying in France were not taught in the host language, 5.8% in Germany and 2.5% in Spain. (p. 14)

But another tendency was noted as a result of the participation of Northern and Central European countries in the Erasmus programme:

> However, 92.9% of outgoing Irish Erasmus students studying in the Czech Republic, 81.8% in Finland and 77.7% in Denmark, were taught in English.

I, myself, believe that the tendency towards English has been increasing in recent years. In our own case in the University of Limerick, in the year 2002-03, 74 of our 216 students who went abroad studied through English; in 2003-04, 66 out of 207 are studying through English. The countries in question in 2003-04 are: Denmark, Finland, Sweden, Norway, The Netherlands, Greece, Malta, the United Kingdom, the Czech Republic, Bulgaria, Germany, Austria and, for the first time, France and Spain. It is true that a wide range of subjects is being studied (Wood Technology; History; Politics and Sociology; Business and Insurance Studies; Public Administration; Cultural Studies; Sport; and Law), and it is not usual for a foreign language to be part of the syllabus in some of these courses, at least, but the tendency towards English is to be noted. Part of the explanation lies with the new degree courses which are being introduced by UL, courses without a foreign language component, but nevertheless with a compulsory period of study abroad.

It should be said at this point that there is a large demand for Irish universities as partners in the Erasmus programme. Enquires are received regularly from universities all over Europe seeking partnership agreements. As it happens, the University of Limerick accepts many more European students than we ourselves send abroad. Ireland itself attracts them certainly, but it is the opportunity to improve their ability in English that is the biggest attraction, I would think.

I believe that it is the nature of communication in a multi-lingual context, a condition of the current state of the European Union, that one lingua franca, or more perhaps, will come to the fore sooner or later. It appears that English is in pole position in the movement ('convergence') towards the usage of just one language as primary-lingua franca. I feel that this has happened already in particular disciplines, and that this tendency will be strengthened with the participation of the 10 new Member States in the European Union from 1 May 2004 onwards.

The view of the English language in the Celtic countries is not the same as in other Union countries. With the exception of Breton, English continues to threaten the Celtic languages. People in other countries do not perceive English in the same way: in Europe and North America, Russia and the Confederation of Independent

States (CIS), and in many Asian countries, English is the primary international language, the language of global popular culture, pop music and films, the language of technology and the new media, the language of the internet. It is an essential language for contemporary life. We are fortunate in Ireland that we have English through the inheritance of history, but in the Celtic countries, in Ireland, in Scotland and in Wales, the English language is also in fact intolerant of linguistic diversity.

Possibilities

Where does this leave the lesser-taught languages, not to mention the lesser-used languages, in the Erasmus programme? Another document which came to us from Europe in February 2003, sought opinions and recommendations about various educational programmes of the European Union after the year 2006 (*Public Consultation on Future Development of the Socrates, Leonardo da Vinci, Tempus and Youth Programmes* [after 2006]). The following is an excerpt from the submission by the University of Limerick, dated 28 February 2003, in which the dominant role of English is assumed, but in which a scheme to encourage students to learn other languages is also recommended. It could be said that this is a summary of my presentation.

> The few opportunities for Irish students to gain competence in lesser-taught languages such as Danish, Dutch, Finnish, Greek, Italian, Portuguese, and Swedish, not to mention lesser-used (or non-official) languages such as Catalan, or Welsh, resulted in the early years of Socrates/Erasmus, in Irish students not being in a position to avail of opportunities for study abroad in countries other than those in which French, German or Spanish are spoken, the languages taught at third level in the University of Limerick. In recent years, an increasing number of bilateral agreements involving instruction through English are being signed by the University of Limerick to meet the demands of our own faculty and students for English-medium provision. This phenomenon is also already manifest in agreements with partners in the candidate and other non-EU European countries, and will be exacerbated with the accession of the applicant countries. There seems to be little prospect of reversing the movement towards English-medium instruction in partner institutions on the continent of Europe.
> In consequence, the European Union will need to adopt radical proposals to encourage even minimal levels of language learning aside from the EU languages dominant in second and third level education (French, German, Spanish and English). Perhaps after 2006, institutions receiving English-speaking students from Ireland and the UK under Socrates agreements, should be required to implement measures to assist such students acquire basic competence in the local language, not only through the provision of preparatory (pre-sessional) language courses (as happens currently), but also through the provision of concurrent ab initio and intermediate language courses during the duration of the Socrates placement (perhaps 20% of the total course load, or 50% of the cultural component). While the provision of courses by institutions might be mandatory, the taking of such courses by visiting students might be optional; but perhaps the EU could institute a

significant reward system for students opting to learn a lesser-taught or lesser-used language during their Socrates placement. This might also include the learning of Irish, or Welsh, or Scottish Gaelic, in the case of students coming to Ireland and the UK.

I well understand that I have not discussed the possibilities for networking and for information-sharing in depth in this talk, but I wanted to discuss part of the context – European Union programmes, and student mobility within the Erasmus programme in particular. It is said that a person is fortunate if he or she has even one good idea during their lifetime. That is mine – to create and foster opportunities so that our students can learn something of the lesser-taught and lesser-spoken languages throughout the Union. Today, I have a greater interest in the major educational programmes of the European Union, and in the recommendation of Dónall Ó Riagáin some years ago for 'mainstreaming' – that is, bringing our languages to the heart of Europe and into the main educational programmes of the Union. This opportunity has been provided for international students in the University of Limerick since 1991, ab initio Irish courses every semester, and a continuation course in the second semester for students who stay with us for a year. There is a continuing demand for these courses, and I believe that every institution should provide similar language courses for visiting students within Erasmus student mobility programmes.

The European Network of Language Planning Boards

Meirion Prys Jones

> The Founding Fathers of the European Community had a very ambitious vision ... they wanted to create – for the first time in history – an economic and political space in which no single culture or language would dominate. Rather they wanted Europe to be a place where a multiplicity of languages and cultures could flourish in a climate of mutual respect. (Commissioner Viviane Reding, former Commissioner for Culture, Education and Sport)

On 1 May 2004, the European Union became the most diverse entity in the world, as an additional 12 countries became the newest members of the European club. That resulted in a population of 380 million people speaking more than 60 languages. Europe's strength lies in its diversity, and, as Commissioner Reding emphasised, that is a founding principle underpinning the very existence of the EU.

First, here are some linguistic facts to put Europe's diversity in context. Since 1 May 2004 the EU has had 20 official working languages, which constitute on the whole the main languages of the member states. However, while Irish is the official state language of Ireland, it does not have working status in the EU. There is a high-profile campaign being waged by the Irish Government to make Irish an official working language of the EU. The Spanish Government has followed suit in respect of Basque, Catalan and Galician. English is unsurprisingly the most "widely" spoken language in the EU, despite being the mother tongue of only 16% of the European population.

The customary definition of regional and minority languages is laid out in the *European Charter for Regional and Minority Languages*, 1998, which is currently ratified by 17 member states. The Charter is an international treaty supervised by the Council of Europe. The definition specifies that regional and minority languages are languages traditionally used by part of the population of a state that are not dialects of official languages of the states, languages of migrants or artificially created languages. That definition of course covers a wide variety of languages, as well as a wide variety of social and political situations: from Catalan, which is spoken by approximately 7 million people in Spain, France and Sardinia, to Saami, which is a family of languages spoken by indigenous people across northern Finland, Sweden, Norway and the Kola peninsula of Russia, of which some members have only a few hundred speakers and are in imminent danger of extinction.

Although the social, linguistic, economic and political situations of those communities vary enormously, there are many factors which unite them as communities in the effort to ensure the survival and continued development of their languages.

The Welsh Language Board is a statutory organisation, funded by public money. It was established in December 1993 under the terms of the *Welsh Language Act*. Its main function is to promote and facilitate the use of the Welsh language. Put simply, the Board's main aim is to make it easier for everyone to use Welsh in all walks of life, to increase people's confidence in their ability to use the language, to encourage more people to speak, read or write it in new situations, and to pass on the language to their children. The Board seeks to work in partnership with public-sector bodies, private businesses and voluntary organisations, offering advice and resources to help service-providers in Wales to provide a natural choice of language to their customers. The Board agreed four main challenges noted in its *Strategy for the Welsh Language* (1996): changing habits of language use and encouraging people to take advantage of opportunities provided; providing opportunities to use the language; increasing the number of people able to speak Welsh; and strengthening Welsh as a community language.

Following a wide-ranging public review of the Welsh language, the Welsh Assembly Government published its action plan for the language in 2003: *Iaith Pawb*. It sets out several targets for the language by 2011. The key targets in *Iaith Pawb* for the language are: the percentage of people in Wales able to speak Welsh to increase by 5% from the 2001 census; the decline in the number of communities where Welsh is spoken by over 70% of the population to be arrested; the percentage of children receiving Welsh-medium pre-school education to increase; the percentage of families where Welsh is the principle language of conversation between adults and children at home to increase; and more services, by public, private and voluntary organisations, able to be delivered through the medium of Welsh.

During the past 20 years, many European regional democratic institutions have established similar language boards or organisations with a statutory role to promote regional and minority languages. It became apparent at the beginning of the twenty-first century that there would be considerable benefits if those organisations were to work together. The Network of European Language Boards was set up in October 2001 to fill the vacuum that existed for those language planning agencies on a European level. It was a joint venture by the Welsh Language Board, Foras na Gaeilge of Ireland and the language planning department of the regional government of the Basque Country.

At the first meeting of the network, a list of main objectives was drawn up whereby the network would strive to strengthen the co-operation between official agencies with a legislative basis that promote minority languages; to agree priorities for co-operating on future projects; to explore the opportunities arising from the expansion of the EU; and to develop a co-ordinated voice for minority languages on a European level.

The criterion for membership of the network is that the language concerned has a legislative basis. The membership of the network includes the following regional institutions, which all have a linguistic legislative basis (similar to the *Welsh Language Act* 1993): the Welsh Language Board, Wales, Bord na Gàidhlig, Scotland, Foras na Gaeilge, Ireland, the Regional Government of the Basque Country, the Regional Government of Galicia, the Regional Government of Catalonia, Berie foar it Frysk, Friesland, and Svenska Finlands folkting, Finland

In December 2003, the network was successful in gaining funding from the European Commission's action plan for language learning and linguistic diversity call for proposals to extend its work further. The grant funding has allowed the network to focus on a list of priority issues that affect regional and minority languages across Europe, while identifying and supporting best practice in language planning.

The following four issues were chosen by all members of the network as those upon which they wanted to concentrate their work: language transmission, information technology and communication, immersion and trilingual education and marketing.

Language Transmission

This is the cornerstone of the promotion of bilingualism in a minority or regional language context, and a necessary prerequisite for the survival of small languages the world over. The network is collating and exchanging best practice in the field to counteract language shift and negative trends.

The family is the building block of language transmission. Above all, it is in the family that a deep bond with language and language activities is fostered, shared and fashioned into personal and social as well as cultural and linguistic identity. Without mother-tongue transmission, language maintenance is well nigh impossible. In many instances, speakers of a minority language may decide to give up their language, even though they may be favourably disposed to it, by not reproducing it in their children.

In the *Encyclopaedia of Bilingualism and Bilingual Education*, it is stated that Joshua A. Fishman, "sees the intergenerational transmission of a language as crucial to its survival. Once a language ceases to be reproduced within the family, it is very difficult to reverse its decline. Thus the dwindling of bilingualism within families mirrors the attitudes of society to the minority language and the fate of bilinguals in the wider community".[1] Language production was one of the main focuses of the EU-commissioned report *Euromosaic* (1996), which noted that many of the regional languages of Europe were not being transmitted from parent to child.

Information Technology and Communication

The network is gathering experience from wider language communities in the fields of machine translation and translation memory software, terminology management, multilingual document management and workflow systems, speech synthesis and recognition, localisation processes, integration of legacy translations into translation memory systems, and standardisation of technology.

It is especially looking at ways in which ITC can be used to provide minority language-learning opportunities and help to create new speakers. The network is also drawing on *Information Technology and the Welsh Language: a Strategy Document*, prepared by the Welsh Language Board, which went out to public consultation at the beginning of 2005, intertwining with the work done in distance learning and e-learning in other areas and by other organisations in the partner regions. The network is examining how new technologies can help adult learners acquire the language, thereby feeding into language production processes through the creation of new speakers.

Immersion and Trilingual Education

The school system is often heavily depended upon to create new speakers of regional and minority languages, but, more often than not, the only entry point to that immersion system is at a very early age, typically three or five years old. The project

---

[1] *Encyclopaedia of Bilingualism and Bilingual Education*. eds. Colin Baker and Sylvia Prys Jones. Clevedon: Multilingual Matters, 1998. p. 30.

will gather experiences of multiple entry points to immersion education (for example, 7 and 11 years old) and disseminate relevant good practice.

Marketing

Partners must learn from each other to operate in the most effective and efficient manner possible. That important principle should be applied to the diverse expertise and materials developed by the individual language planning boards in marketing. Extensive research has been undertaken in the field of marketing and language-behaviour-changing strategies, and it must be disseminated to all partner organisations. Likewise, work done on social psychology in a regional or minority language context also needs a wider audience and translation for the lay reader. Social psychology is another cornerstone of language survival, and partner organisations must be aware of the latest developments to target their activities best.

Four websites will be set up during the lifetime of the project, corresponding to each of the above four priority areas. They will contain information, expertise, case studies, and resources collated during the project. The websites will serve to strengthen contacts within the language planning community and will be regularly updated with new information as the network matures. They will also serve as a useful reference tool for other regional and minority language communities across the world. A conference will take place in Cardiff in November 2005 to present the findings of the project and discuss and disseminate relevant information.

The Board is currently working closely with the network, the European Commission, and the Wales European Centre (WEC) in Brussels to improve links with the new member states of the European Union. The opportunities afforded by the expansion of the EU to the east will provide a different perspective to our view of language planning in the 'older' member states. The challenges facing European regional and minority languages are numerous. In light of the current trend in world communication of using only a few languages, it is vitally important that regional and minority languages be safeguarded, thus ensuring the continuity of the cultural richness of the European Union.